MODERN TOURISM: ISSUES AND CHALLENGES

MODERN TOURISM: ISSUES AND CHALLENGES

Anurag Fadia

CYBER TECH PUBLICATIONS
4264/3, Ansari Road, Daryaganj, New Delhi-110002 (India)
Ph.: 011-23244078, 011-43559448 Fax: 011-23280028
E-Mail: cyberpublicationsdelhi@yahoo.com
Website: www.cybertechpublications.com

MODERN TOURISM: ISSUES AND CHALLENGES

Anurag Fadia

First Edition 2010

Asian Offset Printers

Published by :

G.S. Rawat for **Cyber Tech Publications**
4264/3, Ansari Road, Daryaganj, New Delhi-110002 (India)
Ph.: 011-23244078, 011-43559448 Fax: 011-23280028
E-Mail: cyberpublicationsdelhi@yahoo.com
Website: www.cybertechpublications.com

Preface

Tourism is one of the fastest growing sector of the global economy, which account for about 11 percent of the gross Global Domestic Product (GDP) and employ about 200 million people worldwide. There are about 700 million international travellers per year. Tourism and travel related sectors have become dynamic sources of income and a major strategic sector for development in many countries. Tourism businesses operate globally and many have opted for a competitive advantage of internationalisation. Technology, information and reduction of boundaries have created new forms of service companies, not only the large multinational corporations, but also small niche specialists. The growing importance of strategic alliances in creating networks of business relationships has become a trend also in tourism.

The book examines the current trends in international tourism markets along with emerging opportunities and challenges in the field. It provides a set of tools for monitoring tourism management, policy implementation, promoting sites in a changing global environment. It also reviews roles of government organisations, international organisations and private sector. The book will be highly useful for tour operators, policy makers, administrators and general readers interested in tourism.

The main objectives of the book are to show the complexity of tourism development and conservation in the Bay Islands. The use of political ecology to the environmental- and human-related problems gives the reader a deep sense of the multifaceted issues involved in tourism planning and development. While not all issues in the Bay Islands are applicable to all destinations, there are many that are and that can be valuable lessons for planners in other locations.

— *Author*

CONTENTS

1

BACKGROUND

Tourism is the act of travel for predominantly recreational or leisure purposes, and also refers to the provision of services in support of this act. According to the World Tourism Organization, tourists are people who "travel to and stay in places outside their usual environment for not more than one consecutive year for leisure, business and other purposes not related to the exercise of an activity remunerated from within the place visited".

Tourism, however long its incident duration, has become an extremely popular, global activity. In 2004, there were over 763 million international tourist arrivals.

As a service industry, tourism has numerous tangible and intangible elements. Major tangible elements include transportation, accommodation, and other components of a hospitality industry. Major intangible elements relate to the purpose or motivation for becoming a tourist, such as rest, relaxation, the opportunity to meet new people and experience other cultures, or simply to do something different and have an adventure.

Tourism is vital for many countries, due to the income generated by the consumption of goods and services by tourists, the taxes levied on businesses in the tourism industry, and the opportunity for employment and economic advancement by working in the industry. For these reasons NGOs and government agencies may sometimes promote a specific region as a tourist destination, and support the development of a tourism industry in that area. The contemporary phenomenon of mass tourism may sometimes result in overdevelopment, however alternative forms of tourism such as eco-tourism seek to avoid such outcomes by pursuing tourism in a sustainable way.

The terms tourism and travel are sometimes used interchangeably. In this context travel has a similar definition to tourism, but implies a more purposeful journey. The terms tourism and tourist are sometimes used pejoratively to imply a shallow interest in the cultures or locations visited by tourists.

Definition and Classification

One of the earliest definitions of tourism was provided by the Austrian economist Hermann Von Schullard in 1910, who defined it as, "sum total of operators, mainly of an economic nature, which directly relate to the entry, stay and movement of foreigners inside and outside a certain country, city or a region."

Hunziker and Krapf, in 1941, defined tourism as "the sum of the phenomena and relationships arising from the travel and stay of non-residents, in so far as they do not lead to permanent residence and are not connected with any earning activity."

In 1976 Tourism Society of England defined it as "Tourism is the temporary, short-term movement of people to destination outside the places where they normally live and work and their activities during the stay at each destination. It includes movements for all purposes." In 1981 International Association of Scientific Experts in Tourism defined Tourism in terms of particular activities selected by choice and undertaken outside the home environment. United Nations classified 3 forms of tourism in 1994 in its Recommendations on Tourism Statistics as follows:

1. Domestic tourism, involving residents of the given country traveling only within this country;
2. Inbound tourism, involving non-residents traveling in the given country;
3. Outbound tourism, involving residents traveling in another country.

UN also derived different categories of tourism by combining the 3 basic forms of tourism:

1. Internal tourism, which comprises domestic tourism and inbound tourism;
2. National tourism, which comprises domestic tourism and outbound tourism;
3. International tourism, which consists of inbound tourism and outbound tourism.

Modern View

Intrabound tourism is a new academic terminology coined by the Korea tourism organization and widely accepted in Korea. Intrabound tourism differs from 'domestic tourism' in that the former is more dynamic and comprehensive, encompassing policy-making and implementation of national tourism policies in consideration of the tourism ecosystem consisting of inbound, outbound and intrabound tourism.

Entering into 21st century, the tourism industry has undergone a paradigm shift form the promotion of inbound tourism to the promotion of intrabound tourism since many countries are experiencing a tough competition for inbound tourists. Also realizing that it is impossible to advance the inbound tourism in the absence of active intrabound tourism, national policy makers have shifted their policy priority onto the promotion of intrabound tourism such as the promotion of local tourism to contribute to the local economy.

Examples of such policies are "See America," "Getting Going Canada," and "See Korea Campaign". Taking a Korean case as an example, Korea Tourism Organization has recently launched a nationwide campaign to promote introbound tourism, named "Guseok Guseok, literally meaning corner to corner.

The Prerequisites

Before people are able to experience tourism they usually need at least:

1. disposable income, i.e. money to spend on non-essentials
2. leisure time

3. tourism infrastructure, such as transport and accommodation

Individually, sufficient health is also a condition, and of course the inclination to travel. Furthermore, in some countries there are legal restrictions on travelling, especially abroad. Certain states with strong governmental control over the lives of citizens (notably established Communist states) may restrict foreign travel only to trustworthy citizens. The United States prohibits its citizens from traveling to some countries, for example, Cuba.

Historical Perspective

Wealthy people have always travelled to distant parts of the world to see great buildings or other works of art, to learn new languages, to experience new cultures, or to taste new cuisine. As long ago as the time of the Roman Republic places such as Baiae were popular coastal resorts for the rich.

The terms tourist and tourism were first used as official terms in 1937 by the League of Nations. Tourism was defined as people travelling abroad for periods of over 24 hours.

Health Tourism and Leisure Travel

The history of European tourism can perhaps be said to originate with the medieval pilgrimage. Although undertaken primarily for religious reasons, the pilgrims in the Canterbury Tales quite clearly saw the experience as a kind of holiday (the term itself being derived from the 'holy day' and its associated leisure activities).

Pilgrimages created a variety of tourist aspects that still exist-bringing back souvenirs, obtaining credit with foreign banks (in medieval times utilising international networks established by Jews and Lombards), and making use of space available on existing forms of transport (such as the use of medieval English wine ships bound for Vigo by pilgrims to Santiago De Compostela). Pilgrimages are still important in modern tourism-such as to Lourdes or Knock in Ireland. But there are modern equivalents-Graceland and the grave of Jim Morrison in Père Lachaise Cemetery.

During the seventeenth century, it became fashionable in England to undertake a Grand Tour. The sons of the nobility and gentry were sent upon an extended tour of Europe as an educational experience. The eighteenth century was the golden age of the Grand Tour, and many of the fashionable visitors were painted at Rome by Pompeo Batoni. A modern equivalent of the Grand Tour is the phenomenon of the backpacker, although cultural holidays, such as those offered by Swann-Hellenic, are also important.

Health tourism has always existed, but it was not until the eighteenth century that it became important. In England, it was associated with spas, places with supposedly health-giving mineral waters, treating diseases from gout to liver disorders and bronchitis. Bath was the most fashionable resort, but Buxton, Harrogate, and Tunbridge Wells, amongst others, also flourished. Of course, people visited these places for the balls and other entertainments, just as much as 'the waters'. Continental Spas such as Karlsbad attracted many fashionable travellers by the nineteenth century.

It could be argued that Britain was the home of the seaside holiday. In travelling to the coast, the population was following in the steps of Royalty. King George III made regular visits to Weymouth when in poor health. At the time, a number of doctors argued the benefits of bathing in sea water, and sea bathing as a widespread practice was popularised by the Prince Regent (later George IV), who frequented Brighton for this purpose.

Leisure travel was associated with the industrialization of United Kingdom-the first European country to promote leisure time to the increasing industrial population. Initially, this applied to the owners of the machinery of production, the economic oligarchy, the factory owners, and the traders. These comprised the new middle class. Cox & Kings were the first official travel company to be formed in 1758. Later, the working class could take advantage of leisure time.

The British origin of this new industry is reflected in many place names. At Nice, one of the first and best-established holiday resorts on the French Riviera, the long esplanade along the seafront is known to this day as the Promenade des Anglais; in many other historic resorts in continental Europe, old well-established palace hotels have names like the Hotel Bristol, the Hotel Carlton or the Hotel Majestic-reflecting the dominance of English customers.

Winter Tourism

Winter sports were largely invented by the British leisured classes, initially at the Swiss village of Zermatt (Valais), and St Moritz in 1864. The first packaged winter sports holidays took place in 1902 at Adelboden, Switzerland. Winter sports were a natural answer for a leisured class looking for amusement during the coldest season. Organized sport was well established in Britain before it reached other countries. The vocabulary of sport bears witness to this: rugby, football, and boxing all originated in Britain, and even tennis, originally a French sport, was formalized and codified by the British, who hosted the first national championship in the nineteenth century, at Wimbledon.

The Fun Ski & Snow Festival, which has been organized annually by Korea tourism organization since 1998 and participated by about 10,000 tourists from Asia, is one of the most successful winter tourism products in Asia. The festival provides a variety of events such as ski and sled competitions, ski and snow board lessons, performances and recreational activities. Majority of the event participants are foreign visitors who come from countries with a warm climate that have no snow. The event offers them opportunities to enjoy winter and winter sports in Korea. In addition, southern South American countries making up the Patagonia region in Chile and Argentina attract thousands of tourists every year. Skiing is extremely popular in the mountanous areas.

MASS TRAVEL AND ITS ASPECTS

Mass travel could only develop with two crucial features:

1. improvements in technology allowed the transport of large numbers of people in a short space of time to places of leisure interest, and

2. greater numbers of people began to enjoy the benefits of leisure time.

The pioneer of modern mass tourism was Thomas Cook who, on 5 July 1841, organized the first package tour in history. He arranged for the rail company to charge one shilling per person for a group of 570 temperance campaigners from Leicester to a rally in Loughborough, eleven miles away. Cook was paid a share of the fares actually charged to the passengers, as the railway tickets, being legal contracts between company and passenger, could not have been issued at his own price. There had been railway excursions before, but this one included entrance to an entertainment held in private grounds, rail tickets and food for the train journey. Cook immediately saw the potential of a convenient 'off the peg' holiday product in which everything was included in one cost. He organised packages inclusive of accommodation for the Great Exhibition, and afterwards pioneered package holidays in both Britain (particularly in Scotland) and on the European continent (where Paris and the Alps were the most popular destinations).

He was soon followed by others (the Polytechnic Touring Association, Dean and Dawson etc.), with the result that the tourist industry developed rapidly in late Victorian Britain. Initially it was supported by the growing middle classes, who had time off from their work, and who could afford the luxury of travel and possibly even staying for periods of time in boarding houses.

The Bank Holidays Act 1871 introduced a statutory right for workers to take holidays, even if they were not paid at the time. By the last quarter of the nineteenth century, the tradition of the working class holiday had become firmly established in Britain. These were largely focussed upon the seaside resorts.

The spread of the railway network in the nineteenth century resulted in the growth of Britain's seaside towns by bringing them within easy distance of Britain's urban centres. Blackpool was created by the construction of a line to Fleetwood, and some resorts were promoted by the railway companies themselves-Morecambe by the Midland Railway and Cleethorpes by the Great Central Railway. Other resorts included

Scarborough in Yorkshire, servicing Leeds and Bradford; Weston-super-Mare in Somerset, catering for the inhabitants of Bristol; and Skegness, patronised by the residents of the industrial East Midlands.

The cockneys of London flocked to Southend-on-Sea, mainly by Thames Steamer, and the South Coast resorts such as Broadstairs, Brighton, and Eastbourne were only a train ride away, with others further afield such as Bournemouth, Bognor Regis and Weymouth.

For a century, domestic tourism was the norm, with foreign travel being reserved for the rich or the culturally curious. A number of inland destinations, such as the English Lake District, and Snowdonia appealed to those who liked the countryside and fine scenery.

The holiday camp began to appear in the 1930s, but this phenomenon really expanded in the postwar period. Butlins and Pontins set this trend, but their popularity waned with the rise of overseas package tours and the increasing comforts to which visitors became accustomed at home. Towards the end of the 20th century this market has been revived by the upmarket inland resorts of Dutch company Center Parcs.

Cox & Co, the forebear of Cox & Kings were in existence from 1758 largely entwined with the travel arrangements for the British Army serving around the Empire. While acting as 'agents' for various regiments, they organised the payment, provision, clothing and travel arrangements for members of the armed forces. In the 19th century their network of offices contained a banking and also travel department. The company became heavily involved with affairs in India and its Shipping Agency had offices in France and the Middle East.

Other phenomena that helped develop the travel industry were paid holidays:

* 1.5 million manual workers in Britain had paid holidays by 1925
* 11 million by 1939 (30% of the population in families with paid holidays)

INTERNATIONAL MASS TOURISM

Increasing speed on railways meant that the tourist industry could develop internationally.

To this may be added the development of sea travel. By 1901, the number of people crossing the English Channel from England to France or Belgium had passed 0.5 million per year. Shipping companies were anxious to fill cabin space that was under utilised. For example, P&O found that the majority of their passengers for India and the Far East joined the ship at Marseilles. Consequently, they marketed holidays based upon sea trips from London to Lisbon and Gibraltar. Other companies diverted their older ships to operate cruises in the summer months.

However, the real age of international mass travel began with the growth of air travel after World War Two. In the immediate postwar period, there was a surplus of transport aircraft, such as the popular and reliable Douglas Dakota, and a number of ex military pilots ready to fly them. They were available for charter flights, and tour operators began to use them for European destinations, such as Paris and Ostend.

Vladimir Raitz pioneered modern package tourism when on 20 May 1950 his recently founded company, Horizon, provided arrangements for a two-week holiday in Corsica. For an all inclusive price of £32.10s.-, holiday makers could sleep under canvas, sample local wines and eat a meal containing meat twice a day-this was especially attractive due to the continuing austerity measures in postwar United Kingdom. Within ten years, his company had started mass tourism to Palma (1952), Lourdes (1953), Costa Brava (1954), Sardinia (1954), Minorca (1955), Porto (1956), Costa Blanca (1957) and Costa del Sol (1959).

However it was with cheap air travel in combination with the package tour that international mass tourism developed. The postwar introduction of an international system of airline regulation was another important factor. The bilateral agreements at the heart of the system fixed seat prices, and airlines could not fill blocks of empty seats on underused flights by discounting. But if they were purchased by a tour operator and hidden within the price of an inclusive holiday package, it would be difficult to prove that discounting had taken place-even though it was obvious that it had! This was the origin of the modern mass package tour.

These developments coincided with a significant increase in the standard of living in Britain. At the end of the 1950s, Harold Macmillan could say "you've never had it so good."

Another significant development also happened at the end of this decade. The devaluation of the Spanish peseta made Spain appear a particularly attractive destination. The cheapness of the cost of living attracted increasing numbers of visitors. Mass package tourism has at times been an exploitative process, in which tour operators in a country with a high standard of living make use of development opportunities and low operating costs in a country with a lower standard of living. However, as witness the development of many tourist areas in previously poor parts of the world, and the concomitant rise in standards of living, when there is equality of bargaining power, both parties can gain economic benefits from this arrangement.

Spain and the Balearic Islands became major tourist destinations, and development probably peaked in the 1980s. At the same time, British tour operators developed the Algarve in Portugal. The continuing search for new, cheaper, destinations spread mass tourism to the Greek Islands, Italy, Tunisia, Morocco, parts of the coast of Turkey, and more recently Croatia.

For the worker living in greater London, Venice today is almost as accessible as Brighton was 100 years ago. Consequently, the British seaside resort experienced a marked decline from the 1970s onwards. Some, such as New Brighton, Merseyside have disappeared. Others have reinvented themselves, and now cater to daytrippers and the weekend break market.

RECENT DEVELOPMENTS

There has been a discernible upmarket trend in tourism over the last few decades, especially in Europe where international travel for short breaks is commonplace. Tourists have higher levels of disposable income and greater leisure time. They are also better educated and have more sophisticated tastes. There is now a demand for a better quality product in many quarters. This has resulted in the following trends:-

* The old 'sun, sea, and sand' mass market has fragmented. People want more specialised versions of it, such as 'Club 18-30', quieter resorts with select hotels, self-catering, etc.
* People are taking second holidays in the form of short breaks/city breaks, ranging from British and European cities to country hotels.
* There has been a growth in niche markets catering for special interests or activities, including growth of destination hotels.

The developments in technology and transport infrastructure (particularly the advent of jumbo jets) have placed some types of holiday in the affordable mainstream:-

* The development of a mass cruise holiday market.
* The advent of affordable holidays to long-haul destinations such as Thailand or Kenya.
* The phenomenon of the low budget airline, utilising a new generation of small regional airports.

There have also been changes in lifestyle, which may call into question the current definitions of tourism. Some people (particularly the 45+ and retired) may be adopting a tourism lifestyle, living as a tourist all the year round-eating out several times a week, going to the theatre, daytripping, and indulging in short breaks several times a year.

Much of this results in impulse purchasing. This is facilitated by internet purchasing of tourism products. Some sites have now started to offer dynamic packaging, in which an inclusive price is quoted for a tailor-made package requested by the customer upon impulse.

There have been a few setbacks in tourism, such as the September 11, 2001 attacks and terrorist threats to tourist destinations such as Bali and European cities. Some of the tourist destinations, including the Costa del Sol, the Baleares and Cancún have lost popularity due to shifting tastes. In this context, the excessive building and environmental destruction often associated with traditional "sun and beach" tourism may contribute to a destination's saturation and subsequent decline. This appears to be the case with Spain's Costa Brava, a byword for this kind of tourism in the 1960s and 1970s. With only 11% of the Costa Brava now unblemished by low-quality development, the destination now faces a crisis in its tourist industry.

Sustainable tourism is becoming more popular as people start to realize the devastating effects tourism can have on communities. Receptive tourism is now growing at a very rapid rate in many developing countries, where it is often the most important economic activity in local GDP.

In recent years, second holidays or vacations have become more popular as people's discretionary income increases. Typical combinations are a package to the typical mass tourist resort, with a winter skiing holiday or weekend break to a city or national park. On December 26, 2004 a tsunami, caused by the 2004 Indian Ocean earthquake hit Asian countries bordering the Indian Ocean, and also the Maldives. Tens of thousands of lives were lost, and many tourists died. This, together with the vast clean-up operation in place, has stopped or severely hampered tourism to the area.

FORMS OF TOURISM

For the past few decades other forms of tourism, also known as niche tourism, have been becoming more popular, particularly:

* Adventure tourism involving travel in rugged regions, or adventurous sports such as mountaineering and hiking (tramping).
* Agritourism farm based tourism, helping to support the local agricultural economy.
* Ancestry tourism (also known as genealogy tourism) is the travel with the aim of tracing one's ancestry, visiting

the birth places of these ancestors and sometimes getting to know distant family.

* Armchair tourism and virtual tourism not travelling physically, but exploring the world through internet, books, TV, etc.
* Audio tourism includes audio walking tours and other audio guided forms of tourism including museum audio guides and audio travel books.
* Bookstore Tourism is a grassroots effort to support independent bookstores by promoting them as a travel destination.
* Creative Tourism is a new form of tourism that allows visitors to develop their creative potential, and get closer to local people, through informal participation in hands-on workshops that draw on the culture of their holiday destinations.
* Cultural tourism includes urban tourism, visiting historical or interesting cities, and experiencing their cultural heritages. This type of tourism may also include specialized cultural experiences, such as art museum tourism where the tourist visits many art museums during the tour, or opera tourism where the tourist sees many operas or concerts during the tour.
* Coastal Tourism involves tourist products located along Coastal Environments-due to the limited extent of coastal environments they often are amongst the first places to experience coastal tourist congestion for a region.
* Dark tourism is the travel to sites associated with death and suffering. The first tourist agency to specialise in this kind of tourism started with trips to Lakehurst, New Jersey, the scene of the Hindenburg airship disaster.
* Disaster tourism travelling to a disaster scene not primarily for helping, but because it is interesting to see. It can be a problem if it hinders rescue, relief and repair work.

* Drug tourism travel to a country to obtain or consume drugs, either legally or illegally.
* Eco-tourism sustainable tourism which has minimal impact on the environment, such as safaris (Kenya), Rainforests (Belize) and hiking (Lapland), or national parks.
* Educational tourism may involve travelling to an education institution, a wooded retreat or some other destination in order to take personal-interest classes, such as cooking classes with a famous chef or crafts classes.
* Extreme tourism associated with high risk.
* Free Independent Traveler a sector of the market and philosophy of constructing a vacation by sourcing one's own components eg accommodation, transport.
* Gambling tourism, e.g. to Atlantic City, Las Vegas, Palm Springs, California, Macau or Monte Carlo for the purpose of gambling at the casinos there.
* Garden tourism visiting botanical gardens famous places in the history of gardening, such as Versailles and the Taj Mahal.
* Heritage tourism visiting historical (Rome, Athens, Cracow) or industrial sites, such as old canals, railways, battlegrounds, etc.
* Health tourism usually to escape from cities or relieve stress, perhaps for some 'fun in the sun', etc. Often to Sanatoriums or "health spas".
* Hobby tourism alone or with groups to participate in hobby interests, to meet others with similar interests, or to experience something pertinent to the hobby. Examples might be garden tours, amateur radio expeditions, or square dance cruises.
* Inclusive tourism marketed to those with functional limits or disabilities. Referred to as "Tourism for All" in some regions. Destinations often employ Universal Design and Universal Destination Development principles.

* Mass Tourism is an eco-tourism policy to minimise the footprint of tourists by concentrating them into a small area. Mass tourism also maximises the ultisation of tourist infrastructure.
* Medical tourism, e.g.:
  - o for what is illegal in one's own country, such as abortion or euthanasia
  - o for advanced care that is not available in one's own country
  - o in the case that there are long waiting lists in one's own country
  - o for use of free or cheap health care organisations
* Mystical tourism for people that believe feel energy and travel to places to meditate, yoga, special events, ceremonies, mystical rituals.
* Pop-culture tourism by those that visit a particular location after reading about it or seeing it in a film.
* Perpetual tourism individuals always on vacation; some of them, for tax purposes, to avoid being resident in any country.
* Pilgrimage Tourism pilgrimages to ancient holy places (Rome and Santiago de Compostela for Catholics, temples and stupas of Nepal for the Hindus and Buddhist, Mount Athos or Painted churches of northern Moldavia for the Orthodox), religious sites such as mosques, shrines, etc.
* Sex tourism travelling solely for the purpose of sexual activity, usually with prostitutes
* Shopping tourism promoting shopping festivals as tourist drawcards such as the Dubai, Singapore, Hong Kong and the Gold Coast.
* Solo Travel travelling alone
* Sport travel skiing, golf and scuba diving are popular ways to spend a vacation. This could also include travelling to a major international sporting event such

as the FIFA World Cup or following a tour such as the Ashes or British and Irish Lions.

* Space tourism traveling in outer space or on spaceships.
* Vacilando is a special kind of wanderer for whom the process of travelling is more important than the destination.
* Wine tourism, the visiting of growing regions, vineyards, wineries, tasting rooms, wine festivals, and similar places or events for the purpose of consuming or purchasing wine.

RECENT TRENDS

The World Tourism Organization (UNWTO) forecasts that international tourism will continue growing at the average annual rate of 4 %. By 2020 Europe will remain the most popular destination, but its share will drop from 60 % in 1995 to 46 %. Long-haul will grow slightly faster than intraregional travel and by 2020 its share will increase from 18 % in 1995 to 24 %.

With the advent of e-commerce, tourism products have become one of the most traded items on the internet. Tourism products and services have been made available through intermediaries, although tourism providers (hotels, airlines, etc.) can sell their services directly. This has put pressure on intermediaries from both on-line and traditional shops.

Space tourism is expected to "take off" in the first quarter of the 21st century, although compared with traditional destinations the number of tourists in orbit will remain low until technologies such as a space elevator make space travel cheap. Technological improvement is likely to make possible air-ship hotels, based either on solar-powered airplanes or large dirigibles. Underwater hotels, such as Hydropolis, expected to open in Dubai in 2006, will be built. On the ocean tourists will be welcomed by ever larger cruise ships and perhaps floating cities.

Some futurists expect that movable hotel "pods" will be created that could be temporarily erected anywhere on the planet, where building a permanent resort would be unacceptable politically, economically or environmentally.

BACKPACKING

Backpacking is a term used to denote a form of low-cost independent international travel, differentiating it from other forms of tourism notably by the following typical attributes: minimal budget use, longer duration traveling, use of public transport and multipliable destinations/countries. The origin of the name comes from the backpacks that budget travelers generally carry in the interests of mobility and flexibility.

Many commentators see backpacking as descriptive, not only of low-cost travel, but of the culture and philosophy often associated with it, especially anti or trans-nationalism as well as a romanticization of wanderlust and a desire for "authentic" contact with local culture.

History

The term backpacking is said to have originated in the early 1970s with the advent of low-cost jet airplane fares. During this era it became common for young Westerners, to follow the hippie trail into India and Southeast Asia. This period also gave birth to the first budget guidebooks and began to change the way that many people looked at the possibilities and opportunities of travel.

More recently, backpacking has become something of a rite of passage in the popular culture of some countries, most notably Australia, Israel and New Zealand where after finishing high school, university or a period in the army they take several months to two year's break in Europe (some of whom work in this region), Asia or the Americas.

This can be put down to the light population and geographic isolation of these two countries from much of the world's population and history, the fact that Australia and New Zealand are both affluent English-speaking countries where the majority of their citizens can afford overseas travel, and that both countries have a tradition of students attending university in the home city rather than moving away for college.

A substantial amount of young adults from Israel also undertake long-term backpacking trips, particularly after they finish their mandatory military service. Travel of a backpacking nature is also extremely popular with Northern Europeans, particularly the Dutch and British and with small sections of North Americans and Japaneses.

Culture

Low-cost options are popular: such as sharing lifts, budget flights, rail/bus passes (or if the backpacking trip is circumglobal, a relatively cheap round-the-world air ticket which permits numerous stops), youth hostels, free hospitality services and buying food at local stores abroad instead of going to restaurants.

Hostels and other budget accommodations in the 'developed' world tend to be communal to some degree, and thus backpacker culture is often highly social and emphasizes the camaraderie of communal life, such as the shared kitchens common in many hostels. When backpackers stay in one place for a while, they often seek a house-share with numerous other backpackers and are likely to share a room to keep the costs down. In the 'developing' world accommodation is normally found in cheap hotels, pensions or guesthouses.

The common language of backpackers is overwhelmingly English in varying levels of fluency while German is arguably the second most common language encountered due to the large presence of backpackers from Germany or Switzerland. (However, German-speakers will usually only speak German informally amongst one another, and will otherwise speak English in most other situations). Britons, Australians, Canadians and Germans typically form among the most common backpacker nationalities in the world, in addition to Israelis, Americans, New Zealanders and numerous other Western European nations such as Switzerland or The Netherlands. Backpackers from Spain are very common in Latin America, where there is little or no language barriers and the cost of travel and living expenses is often very favorable for the Spanish. The same is true of French in West Africa. Per head of population, Australia is thought to have the highest representation of backpackers, although there is no data available to demonstrate this empirically.

Backpacker culture is perhaps typified by the Lonely Planet (Australian) series of guidebooks, which caters to budget travelers both in its regular guides as well as, more specifically, the "On a Shoestring" regional compilations. The Rough Guide (UK) and Let's Go (USA) series of guidebooks are also popular. In France, the traditional backpacker's guidebook is the Guide du routard.

Traditionally, backpackers do not travel with expensive electronic equipment such as laptop computers and PDAs due to concerns about theft, damage, and additional luggage weight. However, the desire to stay connected coupled with trends in lightweight electronics have given rise to the flashpacking trend.

Some backpackers take a high resolution digital camera and/or high capacity MP3 Player with them on their travels. Blogging from various Internet cafes around the world is also a growing phenomenon, offering a more convenient way to relay information to interested friends and family at home.

AGE OF BACKPACKERS

Backpackers can be of any age to theoretically be part of the backpacker scene and subculture; however, the vast majority of budget travelers are clearly in their 20s. Patrons at most youth hostels are rarely under 18 (some even mandate a minimum age of 18) while guests over 30 constitute a minority. The 'stereotypical' backpacker is often envisioned as a senior college student or recent college graduate about 20 to 25 years of age with no dependents (spouse, children, etc.), therefore making it relatively easy to put typical daily responsibilities on temporary hiatus to go traveling for up to many months at a time. Depending on the part of the world people backpack through, the median age can vary slightly.

Philosophy

Rolf Potts writes in his book Vagabonding about what he sees as the myths that surround conventional travel: Of all the outrageous throwaway lines one hears in movies, there is one that stands out for me. It doesn't come from a madcap comedy, an esoteric science-fiction flick, or a special-effects-laden action thriller. It comes from Oliver Stone's Wall Street, when the Charlie Sheen character-a promising big shot in the stock market-is telling his girlfriend about his dreams.

"I think if I can make a bundle of cash before I'm thirty and get out of this racket," he says, "I'll be able to ride my motorcycle across China."

When I first saw this scene on video a few years ago, I nearly fell out of my seat in astonishment. After all, Charlie Sheen or anyone else could work for eight months as a toilet cleaner and have enough money to ride a motorcycle across China. Even if they didn't yet have their own motorcycle, another couple months of scrubbing toilets would earn them enough to buy one when they got to China.

For many, this sums up the allure of backpacking, promising an "exotic" or "adventurous" experience that is also deemed "authentic," that is, an experience that, because it is self-planned and directed, does not fit within the typical Western-style vacation or travel industry.

This desire to experience "authentic" travel may be a reaction to the commercialization of the travel industry. Many backpackers express disdain towards "packaged" travel experiences including cruise ships and guided or bus tours which typically consist of a large number of tourists led by a guide. In contrast, backpacker philosophy encourages self-reliance and individuality, like overcoming the language barrier without the help of a translator or making all of one's own travel arrangements (to present two examples). John Gregory sums up this philosophy as:

Those spending big bucks for guided travel get peace-of-mind in return. They are guaranteed no worries, no hassles, an experience as close as possible to being home, without being home. They get an hour and fifteen minutes for the guaranteed-open museum, then a two-hour sightseeing ride that catches all the picture-postcard highlights. They break for lunch at a "recommended" restaurant, where the food is reasonable and ordering is easy. And as the next bus pulls in they re-board theirs to repeat the routine, ending with an easy check-in at a reasonable hotel, populated with plenty of other tourists, pretty much like themselves. While all travel is good for the human spirit, budget backpacking is unparalleled for meeting people and experiencing worlds on their own intimate terms. There are many travelers who have the resources for pampered-class but choose to strap on a backpack and see the world via the seat-of-their-pants, because they know it's the best way to experience cultures and interact with local people

In the United States among many other Western countries, this backlash against the large-scale commercial travel industry as expressed in the philosophy of backpacking has made some inroads into mainstream culture, such as in the popular travel guide writer Rick Steves who, like Tony and Maureen Wheeler of Lonely Planet, spun his experiences as a backpacker in the 1970s into a successful guidebook series.

In addition to notions of authenticity, some backpackers value the sense of freedom and independence in this mode of travel. Especially on extended trips, there is often only a rough itinerary, which can be changed at will. If a backpacker does not like a place, she can move on. If she likes it, she is free to stay and kick back for a while. Travel directions may change when a backpacker meets other independent travelers and learns about destinations she had not considered before or joins up with new friends. The semblance of "gypsy" life has its own romantic allure.

Of course, while backpack travel is carefree in this respect, it is more complicated in that backpackers have to plan everything and deal with all adversities themselves. There is no cruise director taking care of them. However, some backpackers also view this as a positive: It is a challenge and adventure, and the sometimes intense problem-solving in unfamiliar surroundings helps to hone their life skills.

WORKING NATURE

Many backpackers gain temporary work (usually low-paid, unskilled, casual, and sometimes in violation of local labor laws) in the countries they visit. For instance, London's pubs are well known for the number of Australian bartenders working in them; "Irish pubs" around the world hire Irish backpackers. In Australia, fruit picking is a popular job among backpackers, although it can be physically demanding. Although while staying in one place for a long duration, say while working and living in semi-permanent accommodation it could be questioned whether you are still backpacking in the form of the adjective.

Backpackers are also commonly employed by hostels, where English-language proficiency and familiarity with hostel operations are considered assets. Hostels around the world are increasing their revenue by inaugurating work and travel programs, where hostelers can work for accommodation by performing basic hostel upkeep and operational duties.

Criticisms

Backpacker philosophy is sometimes criticized for being hypocritical. Some travelers have been known to forego finding "authentic" contact with a culture, and instead congregate only with other travelers in international hostels or guesthouses.

In addition, backpackers are sometimes blamed for the commercialization of the destinations they travel to. By definition, any "undiscovered paradise" cannot remain pristine under the demand of thousands of visitors. This can often lead to the overuse of certain natural and cultural resources, a vice backpacking shares with other forms of tourism. A notable example of this phenomenon is Byron Bay in Australia, which was a largely quiet backpacker town in the 1970s and is now considered one of the most popular destinations in the 2000s with a bias for yuppies.

This is sometimes said to actually pervert the backpacking culture itself: while backpackers seek genuineness and "authentic" cultural interactions, thus often looking for places with as few other foreigners as possible, they very often tend to meet in so-called "backpacker paradises"-places where all backpackers meet and that, eventually, end-up being modern-day "hippie-resorts". Examples include San Pedro de Atacama, a formerly isolated village in Chile and now a town dependent on tourism. This phenomenon is perhaps not unlike the phenomenon of gentrification that happens in urban ecologies.

A third layer of criticism is economic. Backpackers' pursuit of "cheap" travel destinations is only possible through the imbalance of living costs between Western and developing nations. Thus, backpacking can be seen as an inherently exploitative activity that benefits from the poverty of destination countries. Bolivia and Cambodia are notable examples of very inexpensive countries which backpackers visit and have the ability to stay comfortably for months even on a relatively small budget, all the while contributing little to the local have-nots. A more recent example includes the collapse of the peso currency in Argentina in the early 2000s, which quickly made that country a very attractive destination for budget backpackers. However, backpackers, involved as they are in an inherently pragmatic project, rarely give this concern any more thought than it deserves. The idea that the passing of money from the more affluent to the less affluent is "exploitative" is not as compelling as it may have been in decades past. A more plausible economic criticism, from the point of view of the local economy, is that backpackers do not spend as much money as packaged or luxury tourists.

Advantages

In their defense, some backpackers say that budget travel pumps money into the economies of Third World countries, increasing their standard of living and creating jobs, and doing this in a way that is inherently more egalitarian than mainstream tour companies, who often operate with minimal contact with third party vendors or average citizens. Backpacking in comparison, frequently makes use of local food vendors, merchants and accommodations, and thus does more to benefit the local economy. The lower cost to the budget-conscious young Western tourist and the increased patronage to local merchants actually makes the economics of backpacking a win-win situation in many cases.

Backpackers are accused of traveling to exotic places only to associate with other backpackers. That perception is probably correct but requires some explanation. Generally backpackers are from developed countries, speak fluent English (even if from a non-English speaking country). When these backpackers arrive in developing countries they congregate at the hostels and guesthouses in the center of town where they tend to not blend in. In these areas the best English speakers among the locals tend to be touts who will prey upon the backpackers to visit the factories that they "own", to buy jewels to smuggle back and resell in their home countries, to purchase their services as a "guide" and to undertake illegal activities such as gambling, prostitution and drug use.

Most backpackers would like to interact with locals, but have a hard time fending off the touts, as bargaining and negotiating hassle are key factors of backpacking in parts of the world. Locals with the intent of approaching a backpacker are generally not as aggressive as the touts. Backpackers would consider it obtrusive to approach a local in English and ask to join the local in their home for dinner for instance. The inability to travel beyond the areas covered by public transportation further strain the situation.

WORLD DESTINATIONS

It is worth noting that there is a notable difference between backpacking travel in the developed world, typically Australia, New Zealand, North America and Europe where hostel are commonly used, than in the developing world, typically South and South-East Asia, Africa and Latin America. In such developing nations travel is cheaper, but often harder. Equally where backpacking is popular, whole industries have established to tend to the needs of backpackers offering services to make their lives easier (laundry, visa applications, train tickets) and goods from 'home' countries not commonly available such as Falafel for Israelis, Marmite/vegemite for British/Australian.

Plus bars/restaurants showing sporting events from 'back home' and bootleg copies of movies. Well know examples of such places would be the Khaosan Road in Bangkok, Anjuna in Goa and Antigua in Guatemala. In backpacker hot-spots, many bars and restaurants are set up primary for backpackers with few locals patronizing them-this again fosters the social aspect of backpacking travel.

Favorite

Classically, Western Europe is a very common backpacker destination because of the availability of public transport and the large number of hostels and other budget accommodations. However, since the fall of the Berlin Wall and the dissolution of the Soviet states, Eastern Europe has become a rapidly growing destination for budget travelers. Originally this meant cities such as Prague and Budapest, but more recently Croatia, Slovenia, the Balkans, and the Baltic Republics have become a popular stops on the backpacking circuit

Long-term backpacker destinations are places in the developing world with low costs of living such as Goa (India), Essaouira (Morocco), or Thailand. Australia's East Coast is also a very popular destination for many backpackers. Latin America is quickly becoming a hot-spot for backpackers, who are drawn to the continent by the often favorable exchange rates and unique culture and beauty. Machu Picchu, Patagonia, the Triple Frontier and the cities of Buenos Aires, Rio de Janeiro, La Paz and Cusco are often the highlights for travelers to this continent and see the most 'traffic'.

As mentioned above, certain destinations are so popular on the backpacking circuit that some cities house "backpacker ghettos," whole districts where large numbers of travellers congregate to find cheap accommodation, street food, and share travel information. The most famous of these is the Khaosan Road area of downtown Bangkok.

It is true to say that most backpacking follows established routes with terms such as the 'gringo trail' in Latin America and the 'Banana Pancake' or trail' in Southeast Asia used. These routes and popular countries generally focus on three factors. One reputation, what is the current hot destination? Two popular sights that everyone seems to want to see: Machu Picchu, the Sydney Opera House, Prague, etc.

And finally round the world air travel routing and airline hubs. It is easy to argue that Thailand's huge popularity is in no small measure a result of (it's ease of travel and natural beauty aside) the fact it is an obvious stop-off between Europe and Australia.

Consider the Philippines which has no overland connections, is not a major stop-off and holds similar attributes to Thailand is far less popular. The same is true of Eastern Europe's and Central America's proximity to affluent Western Europe and North America. Africa and notably, West Africa see relativity few backpackers since including them in a round-the-world ticket is difficult and expensive.

What to Avoid

While largely a matter of nationality, personal taste and the current political situation, some generalizations can be made about the destinations many backpackers avoid. For example, a fair number of backpackers, like many other tourists, avoid countries where there is a perceived danger of terrorism, food poisoning or hassle in the way of getting a visa or repeatedly being accosted to purchase goods/services. Some countries, wising up to what's good for their travel economy, have tried to address these issues.

Morocco, which at some point had one of the worst reputations in this regard, is reported to have clamped down on hustling and touting aimed at foreign travelers. In Asia and Eastern Europe visa regulations are being greatly relaxed encourage more travelers. In Egypt, Turkey and Pakistan huge efforts are made to safe-guard travelers from terrorism and countries such as Syria and Iran, while holding terrible reputations abroad are welcoming of backpackers (once issued with a visa).

High Cost Regions

Regions with a high cost of living, such as Scandinavia for example, are avoided by many long-term backpackers because of the expense. Other destinations have high costs for transportation, such as Polynesia, and are also avoided by the majority of backpackers. This rule applies to a lesser degree to many destinations in Western Europe, where costs are generally high enough to discourage extensive (three months and longer) budget travel. Travel to popular but extremely expensive cities such as New York City or London is generally limited to just several days, and backpackers tend to try and fit as much daily sight-seeing as possible in such locations.

Infrastructure

While not an absolute, countries without developed infrastructure, especially in the form of public transportation, are more difficult for backpackers to travel in because of the serious limits on mobility. This includes many African countries and the greater part of Central Asia.

Some travellers also avoid the United States of America for similar reasons, because of the general lack of public transport, the expense of renting a car and the lack of hostels in many destinations, which are largely relegated only to the most major cities, the California Coast, parts of New England, and parts of Florida.

Hostels in the United States are also generally expensive in comparison to many other countries, often between $US20-30 per night. This has given the United States a reputation for being relatively 'unfriendly' towards backpacking culture even though it is a highly desirable, varied, and generally safe country to be explored for foreign backpackers.

The prevalence of motel chains, catering primarily to private motorists, may contribute to the relatively small number of backpacker hostels in the USA. These same problems are also present to an extent in parts of Canada, where the centrally-located provinces generally have few options for backpackers.

People who wish to travel the United States extensively and as cheaply as possible often decide to purchase an economical van with improvised bedding within the vehicle. Even this option is becoming increasingly expensive however, as oil prices in the 2000s remain stubbornly high. This lifestyle also may discourage many solo backpackers, as they must pay many bills entirely by themselves and establish few social connections.

Instability

While the desire to travel at low cost and the desire to travel with convenience and security are often at odds, some countries are generally avoided by backpackers because of the general political instability.

In the most extreme cases, such as Iraq, Somalia or North Korea opportunities for travel may be severely curtailed or an outright impossibility. Other areas are avoided by many backpackers because of the perceived general hostility of the political climate, including some parts of the Middle East and Central Asia, Myanmar and parts of Central Africa.

These are generalizations made by the majority of the community and are disputed by many others (Myanmar being a recent example of debate), especially travelers drawn to "dangerous" destinations.

RISKS AND DANGERS

Some countries are largely avoided by backpackers due to a substantially increased risk of being kidnapped or mugged of their possessions, to the point where the benefits of travel may not compensate for their dangers. Colombia in South America is a notable example, which has the unfortunate reputation of having one of the highest number of kidnappings per capita in the world.

Many other South American cities, such as Rio de Janeiro, São Paulo and Lima, also have high crime rates. Moreover, African cities such as Johannesburg or Nairobi are also discouraged on the backpacker circuit due to their high crime rates and perceived danger of visiting.

Generally a backpacker will keep his main funds and important documents in the hostel or guesthouse room or safe to minimize damage if robbed or lost during the day. Backpackers are thus most vulnerable when traveling between locations when they are carrying all their belongings and items most often go missing on public transport or at bus/train stations. Traveling by day will always minimize this risk as does being careful and/or in a group.

It seems backpackers universally trust other backpackers based on the logic that someone wouldn't come all the way from [Stockholm, Berlin, Sydney, etc.] just to steal from other tourists (Although the wisdom of this logic is drawn into question due to the desperate financial woes often encountered by poorly planned backpackers). On the whole dangers while backpacking, when put in perspective and if using common sense are not overly great (certainly lower than that of the dangers of road traffic accidents, in many parts of the world), but unfortunately some travelers are either over confident, don't exercise common sense or (the minority) unlucky and fall victim to some annoyance. Health is another issue of concern for backpackers with sometimes poor health facilities away from urban hubs and prevalence of diseases such as in some regions, malaria. More common, however are minor ailments like sun burn, diarrhea or food poisoning, which seems to be an unfortunate caveat of third world travel.

Many backpackers try to avoid crowds of other (ordinary) tourists. The first rule is to avoid traditional package holiday destinations such as Benidorm or Cancún because it goes against the backpacker's image. Such places may also be undesirable because of high costs, inauthentic culture, limited sightseeing options and exclusively prebooked accommodation.

Lingual Hurdels

While a matter of personal taste, willingness to learn foreign languages, and other stipulations, countries where the English language is not widely understood or holds little sway in everyday life can or cannot be seen as a hinderence for independent travel.

This may include a significant part of Latin America, many parts of Africa, Central Asia, and more rural areas of East Asia. However, this can also be seen as challenging, so it can just as well draw many backpackers to these regions.

THE HOTELS AND RESORTS

A hotel is an establishment that provides paid lodging, usually on a short-term basis. Hotels often provide a number of additional guest services such as a restaurant, a swimming pool or childcare. Some hotels have conference services and meeting rooms and encourage groups to hold conventions and meetings at their location.

Hotels differ from motels in that most motels have drive-up, exterior entrances to the rooms, while hotels tend to have interior entrances to the rooms, which may increase guests' safety and present a more upmarket image.

In Australia, a hotel may also be an establishment that serves alcoholic drinks, and usually meals in a casual setting but which does not necessarily provide accommodation. This type of establishment would more usually be called a pub or bar in other countries. In general use in Australia the terms "'hotel" and pub are usually taken to be synonymous.

In India, the word may also refer to a restaurant since the best restaurants were always situated next to a good hotel.

Origin

The word hotel derives from the French hotel, which referred to a French version of a townhouse, not a place offering accommodation (in contemporary usage, hotel has the meaning of "hotel", and hotel particulier is used for the old meaning). The French spelling (with the circumflex) was once also used in English, but is now rare. The circumflex replaces the 's' once preceding the 't' in the earlier hostel spelling, which over time received a new, but closely related meaning.

Services and Facilities

Basic accommodation of a room with only a bed, a cupboard, a small table and a washstand has largely been replaced by rooms with en-suite bathrooms and, more commonly in the United States than elsewhere, climate control. Other features found may be a telephone, an alarm clock, a TV, and broadband Internet connectivity. Food and drink may be supplied by a mini-bar (which often includes a small refrigerator) containing snacks and drinks (to be paid for on departure), and tea and coffee making facilities (cups, spoons, an electric kettle and sachets containing instant coffee, tea bags, sugar, and creamer or milk). In the United Kingdom a hotel is required by law to serve food and drinks to all comers within certain stated hours; to avoid this requirement it is not uncommon to come across "private hotels" which are not subject to this requirement.

However, in Japan the capsule hotel supplies minimal facilities and room space.

Classification of The Hotels

The cost and quality of hotels are usually indicative of the range and type of services available. Due to the enormous increase in tourism worldwide during the last decades of the 20th century, standards, especially those of smaller establishments, have improved considerably. For the sake of greater comparability, rating systems have been introduced, with the one to five stars classification being most common.

Boutique Hotels

"Boutique Hotel" is a term originating in North America to describe intimate, usually luxurious or quirky hotel environments. Boutique hotels differentiate themselves from larger chain or branded hotels by providing an exceptional and personalized level of accommodation, services and facilities.

Boutique hotels are furnished in a themed, stylish and/or aspirational manner.

Although usually considerably smaller than a mainstream hotel (ranging from 3 to 100 guest rooms) boutique hotels are generally fitted with telephone and wi-fi Internet connections, honesty bars and often cable/pay TV. Guest services are attended to by 24 hour hotel staff. Many boutique hotels have on site dining facilities, and the majority offer bars and lounges which may also be open to the general public.

Of the total travel market a small percentage are discerning travelers, who place a high importance on privacy, luxury and service delivery. As this market is typically corporate travelers, the market segment is non-seasonal, high-yielding and repeat, and therefore one which boutique hotel operators target as their primary source of income.

Famous Hotels

Some hotels have gained their renown through tradition, by hosting significant events or persons, such as Schloss Cecilienhof in Potsdam, Germany, which derives its fame from the so-called Potsdam Conference of the World War II allies Winston Churchill, Harry Truman and Joseph Stalin in 1945. Other establishments have given name to a particular meal or beverage, as is the case with the Waldorf Astoria in New York City, USA, known for its Waldorf Salad or the Raffles Hotel in Singapore, where the drink Singapore Sling was invented. Another example is the Hotel Sacher in Vienna Austria, home of the Sachertorte. There are also hotels which became much more popular through films like the Grand Hotel Europe in Saint Petersburg, Russia when James Bond stayed there in the Blockbuster, Goldeneye. Cannes hotels such as the Carlton or the Martinez become the center of the world during Cannes Film Festival (France).

A number of hotels have entered the public consciousness through popular culture, such as the Ritz Hotel in London, UK ('Putting on The Ritz') and Hotel Chelsea in New York City, subject of a number of songs and also the scene of the alleged stabbing of Nancy Spungen by her boyfriend Sid Vicious. Hotels that enter folklore like these two are also often frequented by celebrities, as is the case both with the Ritz and the Chelsea. Other famous hotels include the Beverly Hills Hotel, the Hotel Bel-Air and the Chateau Marmont, in California, Watergate complex in Washington DC, the Hotel Astoria in Saint Petersburg, Russia, the Hotel George V and Hotel Ritz in Paris, Palazzo Versace hotel on the Gold Coast, Queensland, Australia, Hotel Hermitage and Hotel de Paris in Monaco (in the French Riviera), Peninsula Hotel in Hong Kong and Hotel Leningradskaya in Moscow.

Many hotels can be considered destinations in themselves, by dint of unusual features of the lodging and/or its immediate environment: Some hotels, such as the Costa Rica Tree House in the Gandoca-Manzanillo Wildlife Refuge, Costa Rica, or Treetops Hotel in Aberdare National Park, Kenya, are built with living trees as structural elements, making them treehouses. The Ariau Towers near Manaus, Brazil is in the middle of the Amazon, on the Rio Negro. Bill Gates even invested and had a suite built there with satellite internet/ phone.

Another hotel with treehouse units is Bayram's Tree Houses in Olympos, Turkey.

Desert Cave Hotels: Desert Cave Hotel in Coober Pedy, South Australia and the Cuevas Pedro Antonio de Alarcón (named after the author) in Guadix, Spain, as well as several hotels in Cappadocia, Turkey, are notable for being built into natural cave formations, some with rooms underground.

Capsule Hotels: Capsule hotels are a type of economical hotels that are quite common in Japan.

Ice Hotels: Ice hotels, such as the Ice Hotel in Jukkasjärvi, Sweden, melt every spring and are rebuilt out of ice and snow each winter.

Snow Hotels: The Mammut Snow Hotel in Finland is located within the walls of the Kemi snow castle, which is the biggest in the world. It includes The Mammut Snow Hotel, The Castle Courtyard, The Snow Restaurant and a chapel for weddings, etc. Its furnishings and its decorations, such as sculptures, are made of snow and ice.

There is snow accommodation also in Lainio Snow Hotel in Lapland (near Ylläs), Finland.

Garden Hotels: Garden hotels, famous for their gardens before they became hotels, includes Gravetye Manor, the home of William Robinson and Cliveden, designed by Charles Barry with a rose garden by Geoffrey Jellicoe.

Underwater Hotels: As of 2005, the only hotel with an underwater room that can be reached without Scuba diving is Utter Inn in Lake Mälaren, Sweden. It only has one room, however, and Jules' Undersea Lodge in Key Largo, Florida, which requires scuba diving, is not much bigger.

Hydropolis is an ambitious project to build a luxury hotel in Dubai, UAE, with 220 suites, all on the bottom of the Persian Gulf, 20 meters (66 feet) below the surface. Its architecture will feature two domes that break the surface and an underwater train tunnel, all made of transparent materials such as glass and acrylic.

OTHER TYPE OF HOTELS

The Library Hotel in New York City is unique in that its ten floors are arranged according to the Dewey Decimal System.

The Rogers Centre, formerly Sky Dome, in Toronto, Canada is the only stadium to have a hotel connected to it, with 70 rooms overlooking the field.

The Burj al-Arab hotel in Dubai, United Arab Emirates, built on an artificial island, is structured in the shape of a sail of a boat.

The RMS Queen Mary in Long Beach, California is the only 1930s ocean liner still in existence. Its elegant first-class staterooms are now used as a hotel.

The Oriental Pearl Tower in Shanghai houses an extremely expensive hotel with only 20 rooms.

WORLD-RECORD OF THE HOTELS

Tallest: The tallest hotel in the world is the Burj al-Arab in Dubai, United Arab Emirates, at 321 metres, which however will soon be surpassed by the nearby Rose Rotana Suites at 333 meters (1,091 feet). The Ryugyong Hotel in Pyongyang was intended to reach 330 meters (1,083 feet), but is unlikely to be completed; it has been under construction since 1987 and was abandoned in 1992. The highest hotel rooms are in the Grand Hyatt in the Jin Mao Building in Shanghai, the highest floor being at around 350 m.

Largest: The largest hotel in the world is the MGM Grand Las Vegas in Las Vegas, Nevada, USA with a total of 6,276 rooms as of December 20, 2006. On December 18, 2006 Guinness World Records listed the First World Hotel in Genting Highlands, Malaysia as the worlds largest hotel. It has a total of 6,118 rooms and is part of the Genting Highlands Resort and Casino. The First World Plaza which is joined to the two hotel towers boasts 500,000 square feet of indoor theme park, shopping centres, casino gaming areas, and eateries. Previously, Guinness had listed the MGM Grand Las Vegas in Las Vegas, Nevada, USA with 5,005 rooms as the largest hotel in the world.

Oldest: According to the Guinness Book of World Records, the oldest hotel still in operation is the Hoshi Ryokan, in Awazu, Japan. It opened in 717, and features hot springs.

Hotel Staff

The owner, chairman, or CEO of a hotel or hotel group is known as a hotelier.

The American billionaire Howard Hughes lived much of his life in hotels. He moved with his entourage from hotel to hotel and from Beverly Hills to Boston before deciding to move to Las Vegas and become a casino baron. Less than a month after his November 27, 1966 arrival, Hughes made a public offer to buy the Desert Inn.

The hotel's 8th floor became the nerve center of his empire and the 9th floor penthouse became Hughes's personal residence. Hughes moved to the Bahamas, Vancouver, London and several other locations-always taking up residence in the top floor penthouse of the hotel. Between 1966 and 1968, he also purchased several other hotel-casinos from the Mafia: Castaways, New Frontier, The Landmark Hotel and Casino, Sands and Silver Slipper.

Coco Chanel made the Hotel Ritz in Paris her home for more than thirty years, until the day of her death, at 87, in a suite now named "Coco Chanel Suite".

King Peter II of Yugoslavia spent much of the Second World War at Claridge's, a hotel in London. His son, Aleksandar Karadordevic, was born in the hotel.

Prince Felix Yusupov lived in the Hotel Vendome in Paris.

Alois Brunner, Austrian Nazi war criminal, is believed to have lived in the Meridian Hotel in Damascus, Syria, under the name Georg Fischer.

Sultan Said Bin Taimur of Muscat lived at Dorchester Hotel in London after he was deposed by Qaboos of Oman in

1970, He died in the hotel in 1972. Eleftherios Venizelos, Greek statesman and diplomat, lived in the Hotel Ritz Paris while he was in exile in France from 1935-1936.

MYTHS ABOUT HOTELS

Hotels have been chosen by authors as settings for crime fiction, farce and mystery works. A hotel is perfect as a mysterious, anonymous setting where various characters may gather. Hotels also feature in films, television series, songs and even theme park rides.

RESORTS: DEFINATION AND MEANING

A resort is a place used for relaxation or recreation, attracting visitors for holidays or vacations. Resorts are places, towns such as Newport, Rhode Island or St. Moritz, Switzerland, or larger regions, like the Adirondack Mountains or the Jersey Shore. A resort is not merely a commercial establishment operated by a single company, although in the late twentieth century this sort of faciltiy became more common. Such a self-contained resort attempts to provide for all or most of a vacationer's wants while remaining on the premises, such as food, drink, lodging, sports, entertainment, and shopping. The term "resort" sometimes is misused to identify a hotel that does not provide the other amenities required of a full resort. However, a hotel is frequently a central feature of a resort, such as the Grand Hotel at Mackinac Island, Michigan. Towns that contain resorts-or where tourism or vacationing is a major part of the local activity-are often called resort towns.

The Walt Disney World Resort is a prominent example of a modern, self-contained commercial resort. Resorts exist throughout the world, increasingly attracting visitors from around the globe. Thailand, for instance, has become a popular destination. Resorts are especially prevalent in Central America and the Caribbean.

Closely related to resorts are convention and large meeting sites. Generally these occur in cities where special meeting halls, together with ample accommodations as well as varied dining and entertainment are provided.

CLASSIFICATION OF RESORTS

Resort at a Destination: A commercial establishment at a resort destinaton such as a recreational area, a scenic or historic site, a theme park, a gaming facility or other tourist attraction competes with other businesses at that destination.. Examples would be hotels in and around Disney World, resorts in St. Martin in the Caribbean, and establishments at Aspen, Colorado in the USA.

Destination Resort: A destination resort is a resort that contains, in and of itself, the necessary guest attraction capabilities-that is to say that a destination resort does not need to be near a destination (town, historic site, theme park, or other) to attract its public. Consequently, another characteristic of a destination resort is that is offers food, drink, lodging, sports, entertainment, and shopping within the facility so that guests have no need to leave the facility throughout their stay. Commonly these facilities are of higher quality than would be expected if one were to stay at a hotel or eat in a town's restaurants. Some examples are Atlantis in the Bahamas, Costa do Sauípe in the Northeastern Brazil, Laguna Phuket in Thailand and Sun City near Johannesburg in South Africa.

All-inclusive Resort: An all-inclusive resort is a resort that, besides providing all of the common amenities of a resort, charges a fixed price that includes most or all items. At a minimum, most inclusive resorts include lodging, unlimited food, drink, sports activities, and entertainment for the fixed price.

Historical Resorts: A famous resort of the ancient world was Baiae, Italy, popular over 2,000 years ago. Capri, an island near Naples, Italy, has attracted visitors since Roman times.

Resorts/Hotels

The carrying capacity studies of the region revealed that the six sites acquired for the Baikal Project can accommodate up to 500 units. The resorts will be Star / Deluxe category Resorts. Ayurveda health holidays centres, theme parks, heritage homes, crafts/arts resorts or (other theme resorts), gardens etc can also be developed, provided there is a feasible proposal plan for each. At present there are no major Ayurveda centres in the region and hence new centres have plenty of scope for development. The land for infrastructure and common facilities includes public beach, water sports facilities etc.

Location and Parameters for the Resorts

- o Only Deluxe/3 star and above Resorts
- o Considering the specific nature of resort development and the relative tariff range, proximity to a beach will be ideal.
- o The resorts will be self-contained and hence proximity to any existing settlement isn't essential.
- o These resorts will not induce much change in the surrounding verdant landscapes, except in the case of build access roads.
- o Proximity to existing settlements and good road networks is important such that development costs can be shared.
- o Use of existing commercial facilities as far as possible in order to reduce land use.
- o Closeness to nearby prime tourist attractions such as public beach.

COMMON TOURIST DESTINATIONS

The Republic of India, commonly known as India, is a country in South Asia. It is the seventh-largest country by geographical area, the second most populous country, and the most populous liberal democracy in the world. India has a coastline of over seven thousand kilometres, bounded by the Indian Ocean on the south, the Arabian Sea on the west, and the Bay of Bengal on the east. India borders Pakistan to the west; People's Republic of China, Nepal and Bhutan to the northeast; and Bangladesh and Myanmar to the east.

Home to the Indus Valley Civilization and a region of historic trade routes and vast empires, the Indian subcontinent was identified with its commercial and cultural wealth for much of its long history.

Four major world religions, Hinduism, Buddhism, Jainism and Sikhism originated here, while Islam, Christianity, Judaism and Zoroastrianism, arrived in the first millennium CE and shaped India's variegated culture. Gradually annexed by the British East India Company from the early 18th century and colonised by Great Britain starting the mid-19th century, India became a modern nation-state in 1947 after a struggle for independence marked by widespread use of nonviolent resistance as a means of social protest.

With the world's fourth largest economy in purchasing power and the second fastest growing large economy, India has made rapid progress in the last decade, especially in information technology. Although India's standard of living is projected to rise sharply in the next half-century, it currently battles high levels of poverty, persistent malnutrition, and environmental degradation. A multi-lingual, multi-ethnic society, India is also home to a diversity of wildlife in a variety of protected habitats. India is one of the popular tourist destinations in Asia. Bounded by the Himalayan ranges in the north, and surrounded on three sides by water (the Arabian Sea, Bay of Bengal, and the Indian Ocean), with a long history and diverse culture, India offers a wide array of places to see and things to do. In 2004, foreign tourists visiting India spent 15.4 billion USD-the ninth highest in the world. India is also ranked among the top 3 adventure tourism destinations.

Taj Mahal

Perhaps India's best-known site is the Taj Mahal, one of the world's greatest architectural achievements. It was built between 1631 and 1653 by Emperor Shah Jahan in honor of his wife, Arjumand Banu, more popularly known as Mumtaz Mahal. The Taj Mahal serves as her tomb. Taj Mahal is a 3 hour drive from Delhi.

The Golden Triangle

One of the popular tourist circuits is called the Golden Triangle: the cities Delhi; Agra (site of the Taj Mahal); and Jaipur. Delhi is approximately 200 kilometers away from Agra, and 250 kilometers from Jaipur.

WILDLIFE SANCTUARIES

India also has a large variety of protected wildlife. The country's protected wilderness consists of 75 National parks of India and 421 Sanctuaries, of which 19 fall under the purview of Project Tiger. Its climatic and geographic diversity makes it the home of over 350 mammals and 1200 bird species, many of which are unique to the subcontinent. Some well known national wildlife sanctuaries include Corbett, Kanha, Sariska, Periyar, Ranthambore, and Bharatpur.

Andhra Pradesh

Andhra Pradesh is very good place for tourism. Andhra Pradesh is India's fifth largest state. AP is also known as the "Rice Granary of India". The main languages spoken in Andhra Pradesh are Telugu, Hindi, Urdu and English. The weather is mostly tropical. June to September are the monsoon months and travel is not advised during this time. November to January are the best time to visit. Andhra Pradesh has a rich cultural heritage. Andhra Pradesh has a variety of attractions including beaches, hills, wildlife, forests and temples.

People coming to Andhra Pradesh visit:

* Hyderabad
* Tirupati
* Vizag
* Nagarjuna sagar
* Vijaywada
* Warangal

Delhi

The capital of the vast, mystic subcontinent that is India. A fine blend of old and new, ancient and modern in every stream of life is the soul of Delhi. A melting pot of cultures and traditions, religions and castes Delhi is true to its democratic nature. Delhi has ruled... always from the mythological days to the present, the Aravali ridges and the Yamuna river stand a mute witness to it. The rulers left behind their trade marks in the architecture. Tughlakabad fort and the Qutab Minar, the

Jama Masjid and the Lotus temple, The Humayun's tomb and the Red Fort, and India Gate and the Magnificent President's house. Delhi is famous for its wide roads and crisp winters. One of the few places in India where colours of nature changes with the seasons. From Kerala to Kashmir and from Gujarat to Assam all the mouth watering delicacies and shopping goods are found in Delhi. The cosmopolitan nature of the city has only added to the beauty and glory of it. Big gardens, wide roads, ancient structures, and power of politics is what Delhi is all about.

Goa

Goa is a tiny emerald land on the west coast of India situated between the borders of Maharashtra and Karnataka and is better known to the world as the former Portuguese enclave on Indian soil. With the rule of the Portuguese for over 450 years and the consequential influence of the Latin culture, Goa presents a somewhat different picture to the foreign visitor than any other part of the country. Not only is the proportion of Christians (almost all of whom are Catholics) in the total population of Goa much higher than that obtaining in most of the other States; the general way of living is also markedly different. Western influence is evident in the dress and food habits, and the general life of the people is quiet and peaceful. A striking feature of Goa is the harmonious relationship between the two principal religious communities, the Hindus and the Catholics, who have lived together peacefully for generations. The Bom Jesus cathedral is another famous attraction in Goa.

Jammu and Kashmir

Tourist destinations in Jammu and Kashmir include:

* Srinagar
* Jammu
* Leh
* Amarnath
* Vaishno Devi
* Dull Lake

Other cities of interest in Northern India include Gwalior, Khajuraho, Varanasi, Mathura, and Haridwar. Moving south, many places are a mix of ancient historic sites as well as industrial/technological hubs. Some of these are listed below.

Karnataka

The southern state of Karnataka offers:

* Bangalore, the IT capital of India, is also significant for its history
* Mysore, about 140 km from Bangalore, has palaces, KRS Dam, several temples, a Hindu temple atop Chamundi Hills, Chamundeswari Temple.
* Srirangapatna, where nearby fortresses can be found (Tipu's)
* Hampi the city of ruins (1500s when the Muslim kings destroyed the prosperous Vijayanagar empire)
* The Belur and Halebidu temples are famed for their sculptural beauty.
* Sravanabelagola has a Jain temple dedicated to king Bahubali. The statue is massive and a Maha Masthaka Abhishekham performed one every year, attracts a huge number of pilgrims
* Sringeri, located in the western ghats, has a wonderful temple dedicated to Sarada devi.
* The Western Ghats offer many other places of exceptional beauty like Agumbe, Horanadu etc.
* Madikeri, Kodagu, Talakaveri, Kemmanagundi all places of immense natural beauty.

Kerala

Kerala is an evergreen lush state, tucked away in the southern corner of India. It is one of the most haunted visits of tourists in India. The state has its own tourism brand name- "God's Own Country", which has super-brand status. The state was nicked as one of the "10 paradises of the world" by the National Geographic traveller, the only other Indian place listed being the Taj Mahal. Kerala is famous for its backwaters and lagoons. There are also several beautiful beaches along the coastline of Kerala. There are also hill stations and tropical rainforests with exquisite flora and fauna including endangared animals like elephant, tiger, nilgiri thar and lion-tailed macaque. Recently, a new brand of tourism was introduced called Monsoon Tourism, aimed at beckoning tourists to enjoy the beauty of the state's hauntigly beautiful rainy season extending from June to September. Kerala is also known for its Ayurveda, the ancient medicinal system of India. The government of Kerala offers tourism packages related to Ayurvedaand promotes health tourism since treatment charges are low in Kerala. On the cultural front, the several unique and colourful festivals of Kerala like Onam, Thrissur Pooram, the snake boat races etc. provide great attraction to tourists. The classical artforms Kathakali, Mohiniyattam etc. are also a delight. The martial artform Kalaripayattu is the parent form of all famous martial arts like karate and kungfu. The Kerala Cuisine is also world famous. Also Kerala's rich history of maritime trade from ancient times has left a number of interesting historical monuments.

The major attractions in Kerala include:

* Kumarakom, Kuttanad, Kumbalanghi and other backwater locations.
* Vembanad Lake and the housboats of Alappuzha
* Beaches like Kovalam, Marari etc.
* Hill stations at Thekkady and Munnar
* The city of Kochi with its Chinese fishing nets, Bolgatty Palace, Mattanchery Jewish Synagogue, Jew Street, Fort Kochi etc.
* Enchanting waterfalls at Athirappilly and Vazhachal
* Periyar Tiger Reserve, Iravikulam National Park, Thattekad Bird Sanctuary and other forests
* Its historical monuments like Bakel Fort, Edakal cave of Wayanad
* Kerala Kalamandalam, deemed university teaching classical artforms

* Kalady, birthplace of Adi Sankaracharya, Sabarimala Temple, Guruvayur Temple, Malayatoor Church and other pilgirimage centres

Orissa

Orissa has been a preferred destination from ancient days for people having interest in spirituality, religion, culture, art and beauty of the nature. Ancient and medieval architecture, pristine sea beaches, nature at her beautiful best, the classical and ethnic dance forms and a variety of festivals, all in combine attract tourists from far off places to explore this state to a have a divine exposure of love and hospitality. Orissa has kept alive Buddhism and the Buddha in its ancient womb. The spirit of Buddhism still haunts the very air of Orissa. Rock-edicts that have challenged time stand huge and over-powering by the banks of the river Daya. The silent stones sing out songs of peace and non-violence. The torch of Buddhism is still ablaze in the sublime triangle at Udayagiri, Lalitgiri & Ratanagiri, on the banks of river Birupa. The surrounding hills of Langudi and Kayama stand as mute witness to the quirks and twists of history. Precious fragments of a glorious past come alive in the shape of stupas, rock-cut caves, rock-edicts, excavated monastries, viharas, chaityas and sacred relics in caskets. Rock-edicts of Ashoka are a bonus for your eyes. Orissa is the home for various tribal communities who have contributed uniquely to the multicultural and multilingual character of the state. Their handicrafts, different dance forms, jungle products and their unique life style blended with their healing practices have got world wide attention.

Pondicherry

* Aurobindo Ashram
* Auroville

Rajasthan

Rajasthan has a rich history and culture making it one of the most popular tourist destinations in India. Shown here is the Hawa Mahal in Jaipur, Rajasthan. Rajasthan, the "Land of the Kings", is one of the most attractive tourist destinations in Northern India. The vast sand dunes of the Thar Desert attract millions of tourists from around the globe every year. Major visitor attractions in Rajasthan include:

* Jaipur-The capital of Rajasthan, famous for its rich history and royal architecture
* Jodhpur-fortress-city at the edge of the Thar Desert, famous for its blue homes and architecture
* Jaisalmer-famous for its golden fortress
* Barmer-Barmer and surrounding areas offer perfect picture of typical Rajasthani villages.
* Bikaner-famous for its medieval history as a trade route outpost
* Mount Abu
* Pushkar-It has the only Brahma temple in the world

Sikkim

Originally know as Suk-Hem, which in the local language means "peaceful home", Sikkim was an independent kingdom till the year 1974, when it became a part of the Republic Of India. The capital of Sikkim is Gangtok, located approximately 185 kilometres from New Jalpaiguri, the nearest railway station to Sikkim. Although an airport is under construction at Dekiling in East Sikkim, the nearest airport to Sikkim would be Bagdogra.

Sikkim is the land of Orchids and mystic culture and colourful tradition. Sikkim is well know among trekkers and adventure lovers, as West Sikkim has a lot to give them. Some must-visit places within Sikkim include:

1. NIT (National Institute Of Tibetology)
2. Hanuman and Ganesh Tok
3. Nathula pass
4. Baba Harbajan Mandir
5. Seven View Points
6. Rumtek Monastery
7. Lachen and Lachung
8. Pelling

9. Pemayantzy
10. Uttaray
11. Dzongri
12. Chewa-bhanjang
13. Barsay
14. Legship-Hot water spring
15. Khorong Hotwater spring 16.Samdrupsey at Namchi

Places near Sikkim include Darjeeling also know as the Queen of hills and Kalimpong. Darjeeling, other than its world famous "Darjeeling tea" is also famous for its refined "Prep schools" founded during the British Raj. A few of the top Schools in the District are:

1. St.Paul's School-Known as Eton of the East. It is 190 years old, thus one of the oldest schools in India.
2. Mt.Hermon School.
3. St.Joseph's School-where the H.M of Bhutan and the Late H.M of Nepal did their schooling.
4. Loreto Convent-where Late Mother Teresa served for many years.
5. Dr.Graham's Homes.
6. St.Joseph's Convent.
7. St.Augustine's School. Kalimpong is famous for its Flora cultivation and is home to many internationally known Nurseries.

National Policy on Tourism Development

The National Policy for Tourism development in India is based on a broad action plan including:

- o Preservation of natural heritage
- o Socio-economic development of the tourism destinations
- o Increasing employment opportunities
- o Development of domestic tourism
- o Development of international tourism and optimisation of foreign exchange earnings
- o Diversification of tourism products

All of which together will increase India 's share in world tourism. In the 1990's, World Tourism Organization projections indicated that global international tourist arrivals would increase at around 4.8% p.a. from around 500 millions in 1993 to 661 millions by the year 2000, and then by 3.6% p.a. to 937 million by the year 2010. The South Asia region, within which India is located, received 3.2 million international arrivals, i.e. 0.7% of global tourist arrivals in the 90's. After analysing this scenario, the Government of India concluded that more destinations should be identified for integrated resort development. This was implemented by the 'Special Tourism Area' programme aimed at development and popularisation of 'Beach Tourism' in the country. 'Special Tourism Area' scheme to attract investment in hitherto unknown destinations, which held immense beach tourism potential.

BAIKAL: A SPECIAL TOURISM AREA

In 1992, the Government of India declared Baikal as a Special Tourism Area. Extremely scenic landscape, extensive beaches, numerous estuaries and backwaters and unspoilt environs qualified Baikal as a potential site for an international standard beach destination. Baikal is unarguably one of the best potential beach resort destinations in South Asia. India has a very few comparable locations that offer the diversity of attractions to be found in Baikal. Yet, unlike most other existing resort destinations which are close to a major urban centre, and thus already over developed, the Baikal area is still virgin and pristine, offering the opportunity to set up a new planned resort destination. The basic thrust of the project is sustainable tourism and is considered in terms of the socio-economic and environmental sustainability.

Baikal Project: India 's First Planned Beach Destination

Historical Perspective

Government of India in an effort to develop potential beach locations, which could be developed as international standard beach destinations had the western cost, surveyed in 1990. The survey identified Baikal the village in Kasaragod district in northern most part of Kerala as potential locale for the development of beach resort destination. In 1992 the Government of India declared Baikal as "Special Tourism Area" for integrated resort development. Thereafter Government of Kerala entrusted a multidisciplinary team consisting of planners, landscape architects, urban and transport specialists, structural consultants and tourism leisure industry experts with the preparation of project of project blue print for the development of Baikal. In 1995 Baikal Resort Development Corporation was formed for the implementation of Baikal Tourism Project. The Baikal Project envisages setting up of an integrated beach destination at Baikal, with the objective of developing including social infrastructure in the region. BRDC conducted systematic surveys of the region through CESS (Centre for Earth Science Studies) and has developed 76 hectares (189 acres) of land that is ideal for setting up resorts.

Techno-economic Feasibility Studies

It is prepared by experts in the concerned areas. The following broad issues were examined during the studies, in order to sustain the destination:

- o Environmental issues-an appraisal of the environment, natural forces and ecology of the region and assessment of the impact of tourism on these.
- o Infrastructure-Reconnaissance, inventory preparation and assessment of the existing infrastructure.
- o Socio-cultural issues-Appraisal of cultural background and lifestyle, economic status, possibility of local participation, their relocation implications, measure to sustain socio-economic development.
- o Market potential and cost benefit-Assessment of market potential of the region, possible economic benefits to the region, development costs, fund sourcing and preparation of viable investment plan.

The findings have been translated into a physical plan in which tourism plays a major role in the overall development of the region.

Broad Essentials

- o Minimize shift in Agricultural land use-Minimize loss of existing agricultural land and to strengthen the resource base for traditional sectors like fishing and agriculture
- o Provide employment to the locals.
- o Resorts and protect the bio-diversity of the area, and safeguard the interests of fishermen and farmers
- o Keep a check on the commercialization of cultural values and art forms

PROJECT FEATURES

Land Development

Necessary development works have been carried out on the land. These include fencing, approach road construction, provision of HT lines. Water supply lines are being provided.

Landscape Policy

The landscape policy for Baikal aims at:-

- o Conserving and strengthening the existing natural systems
- o Enhancing the scenic properties of the region

Areas of concern include landform/topography and hydrogeology. Modification of terrain should be in tune with the natural drainage patterns. Topsoil conservation through protection of existing vegetation and provision of new vegetative cover on fallow land. Protection of watersheds and catchments areas to maintain the ecological balance. Storm water drainage systems should minimise erosion and maximise both percolation and ground water recharge.

BASIC INFRASTRUCTURE

The basic infrastructure of the land includes power, water supply, communication, road networks, street lighting, public amenities and tourist attraction facilities. Some of the work completed include:

- o Roads, with the participation of the concerned Panchayats

- o Access roads to resort sites
- o Road junction improvements
- o Studies and surveys like master plan etc
- o Extension of HT Electric Line to Resorts
- o 7 mld water supply scheme which is nearing completion

Further infrastructure developments taken up and proposed include:

- o Development and improvement of further roads and junctions
- o Sanitation facilities
- o Public wayside amenities
- o Street lighting

FACILITIES TO TOURISTS

To offer varied experience to tourists within a short distance and time, attractive tourist spots have been developed nearby. Facilities include:

- o Thanal Vishrama Kendram (tourist facility near Baikal Fort)
- o Beautification of the surrounding areas of the Baikal Fort
- o Seaside pathway along the Baikal Fort
- o Erection of display and signboards in Kasargod district
- o Public beach at Pallikkara near Baikal Fort
- o Aqua Park and Chandragiri Boat Club
- o House boating cruise in Tejaswini backwaters in Valiyaparamba
- o Backwater Tourism-Houseboat
- o Children's parks at Baikal Fort and Thanal Vishrama Kendram
- o Trekking and adventure tourism

PLAN FOR FUTURE ACTIVITIES

- o Heritage tourism projects for conservation and development of 8 Forts around Baikal.

- o Development of Valiyaoaramba as a Backwater destination of north Kerala.
- o Development of Baikal Fort Beach
- o Setting up of Eco lodges and other tourism products.
- o International standard water sports centre
- o Theme Parks
- o Augmenting facilities for tourists visiting Baikal

Baikal Fort

Over three and a half centuries old, Baikal Fort looms large against the backdrop of the Arabian Sea, rising dramatically from amidst the tall grass. Easily one of the best-preserved forts in the State, Baikal shows little signs of the many aeons that have passed by. And standing on a 35-acre headland, 130 feet above sea level, the fort is the largest in the State. Soaring observation towers, once cannon emplacements, lend Baikal Fort a majesty quite becoming of its former role as a military station. These will be your vantage points to take in the splendours of the sea that spread to the north, south and west and the rich naturescapes to the east. A water reservoir with a long flight of steps and a magazine for storing ammunition add to the mystery of the place. Folklore has it that there are several secret underground passages here, once used for military purposes. With two of them now open to the public, you can as well take a walk down the corridors of time. Baikal is the most famous of the forts of Kasaragod, renowned as the land of forts; the others being Kumbala, Kasaragod, Kundankuzhi, Bandadukka and Povval.

Chandragiri Fort

Six km away, perched beside the Chandragiri River, is the Chandragiri Fort. Built during the 17th century by Sivappa Naik of Bedanore, who is said to have built the Baikal Fort too, Chandragiri's western rampart is an ideal place to watch sunsets.

Hosdurg Fort

Further down, 15 km away from Baikal is the Hosdurg Fort-a chain of forts built by Somasekhara Nayak of the Ikkeri dynasty. Today Hosdurg's historic aura has a spiritual touch to it, thanks to the Nityanand Ashram located there.

UNTOUCHED PICTURES OF SERENITY

Valiyaparamba

Perhaps the most beautiful backwater stretch of Kerala, Valiyaparamba is 19 km from Baikal. Four rivers give shape to this network of waterways that lazily snake through the land, between palm groves and paddy fields. Hire a Kettuvallam-the traditional houseboat of Kerala-for an unmatched experience of the backwaters. Nothing lets you take in the rustic beauty of Kasaragod; the refreshing glimpses of life around the waterways, as does a houseboat cruise. What makes this goods carrier turned leisure boat much sought after by tourists are the luxuries on offer-one /two bedrooms, an attached toilet / bath, a kitchenette plus a crew comprising a cook, oarsmen and guide. And, as you glide past little thatched houses, past the clusters of green; past fleets of ducks you'll finally discover that serenity has a name. A visit to the turtle hatchery centre nearby will provide the perfect finale.

Chandragiri

Unveil more frames of tranquility at Chandragiri River. Flowing beside the famous fort by the same name, boat trips are available from here to nearby islands and palm groves.

UNTAINTED PORTRAITS OF BEAUTY (BEACHES)

Baikal Beach

An unmatched experience of the sun, sea and the sand is this shallow beach, that offers, apart from the charm of unexplored nature, spectacular views of the Baikal Fort nearby. Adding more charm to the spectacular landscape are the swaying palm trees that border the beach.

Kappil Beach

Five km away is Kappil Beach. Vast, remote and secluded, it is refreshingly different from popular beach destinations in its inspiring settings and ambience. Nearby is the Kodi Cliff that looks as if it sprang straight out of the sea. Take in one of the most panoramic views of the sea from here.

Kanwatheertha Beach

Located 3 km from Manjeswaram, what makes this beach special is a large swimming-pool like formation of the sea on the vast beach.

Azhithala Beach

Serene, secluded and punctuated with casuarinas trees, Azhithala Beach, located 25 km to the south of Baikal, is the ideal setting for long walks and out-of-this-world moments.

UNEXPLORED AREAS

Ranipuram

Shola woods, monsoon forests and grasslands ..... Ranipuram, 58 km from Baikal is a stunning landscape in every shade of green. Situated at a cool 750 m above sea level, it is popular not just as a natural haven, but also as an adventure hotspot. For hidden beneath the evergreen canopy are delightful trekking trails that nature enthusiasts are slowly discovering. Formerly known as Madathumala, Ranipuram's extensive forests merge with those of the nearby State of Karnataka.

While the varied vegetation will make this place a favourite with nature lovers, the wild elephants that wander the mountains will offer the experience of a lifetime for wildlife enthusiasts.

Kottancherry

Visitors can have more of adventure at Kottancherry which resembles the famous hill station of Kodaikanal in its scenic beauty. The rainforests near Konnakkad present excellent options for trekking.

Possadigumpe

Ideal for an enchanting one-day tour is Possadigumpe, located on a hillock 323 m above sea level and 18 km east of

Mangalpady in Dharmathadka. The delightfully cool environs of this place make it just the right place for a picnic.

ARTISTIC FORMS

Perhaps the most enduring image of Kasaragod is the Theyyam, the oldest ritualistic temple art form of India and one of the most spectacular in artistry and symbolism. Watch a grand display of this unique ritual art at the numerous Kaliyattoms held here from October to May every year. Two other art forms that are performed in Kasaragod are Kalaripayattu, the martial art form of Kerala and Yakshagana, the art form that has its roots in Karnataka.

PLACES OF WORSHIP

Kasaragod has the rare distinction of housing some of the historically and religiously important places of worship in India. Foremost among them is the Malik Dinar Juma Masjid-believed to have been built by Malik Ibn Dinar-at Thalankara.

Equally significant is the 9th century Ananthapuram Lake Temple, said to be the original abode of Ananthapadmanabha, the presiding deity of Kerala's most famous place of worship, Sree Padmanabhaswamy Temple. Situated 30 km from Baikal, this is the only lake temple in Kerala.

Other prominent pilgrim centres include Madiyankulam Durge Temple at Kanhangad, famous for the Bhutha dance held during the annual festival, the Sree Mahalingeswara Temple at Adoor on the banks of River Payaswini, the Madhur Temple with its rich architecture and copper plate roofing and Manjeswaram, home to 15 mosques and two Jain temples.

Anandashram is an internationally renowned spiritual centre, 15 km form Baikal.

GATEWAYS

Aralam Wildlife Sanctuary (120 km from Baikal): Elephants, sloth, bears, sambars, mousedeer etc. can be found in this 55 sq.km sanctuary.

Muzhappilangad (105 km from Baikal): Kerala's only drive-in beach; 4 km long; a swimmer's paradise.

Parassinikadavu (68 km from Baikal): Famed for the Muthappan Temple, where Muthappan Theyyams are performed every morning and evening.

Wayanad (150 km from Baikal): Known for its picturesque hill stations, spice plantations, luxuriant forests; attractions include the Pookot Lake, Wayanad Wildlife Sanctuary and Edakkal Caves.

Kappad Beach (165 km from Baikal): Historic beach where Vasco da Gama landed on the 27 th of May, 1498.

Coorg (120 km from Baikal): Hill station famous for rolling hills, forests, coffee plantations.

Nagarhole Wildlife Sanctuary: 643 sq. km of rich and varied flora and fauna.

Kabini: 65 km form Nagarhole Wildlife Sanctuary; famous for the Kabini River Lodge, formerly a Maharajah's hunting lodge.

Sringeri: Famed as the Southern seat of the orthodox Hindu hierarchy.

Mookambika (210 km from Baikal): Famous for the Mookambika Temple, an important pilgrim centre of South India.

Gokarna: A Centre of Sanskrit learning; boasts of a beach.

Dharmasthala: Home to the famous Manjunatha Temple

Udupi (126 km from Baikal): Important Vaishnavite town.

2

PROMOTING TO CULTURE, HERITAGE AND TRADITION

At the broadest level, the natural and cultural heritage belongs to all people. We each have a right and responsibility to understand, appreciate and conserve its universal values.

Heritage is a broad concept and includes the natural as well as the cultural environment. It encompasses landscapes, historic places, sites and built environments, as well as bio-diversity, collections, past and continuing cultural practices, knowledge and living experiences. It records and expresses the long processes of historic development, forming the essence of diverse national, regional, indigenous and local identities and is an integral part of modern life. It is a dynamic reference point and positive instrument for growth and change. The particular heritage and collective memory of each locality or community is irreplaceable and an important foundation for development, both now and into the future.

At a time of increasing globalisation, the protection, conservation, interpretation and presentation of the heritage and cultural diversity of any particular place or region is an important challenge for people everywhere. However, management of that heritage, within a framework of internationally recognised and appropriately applied standards, is usually the responsibility of the particular community or custodian group.

A primary objective for managing heritage is to communicate its significance and need for its conservation to its host community and to visitors. Reasonable and well managed physical, intellectual and/or emotive access to heritage and cultural development is both a right and a privilege. It brings with it a duty of respect for the heritage values, interests and equity of the present-day host community, indigenous custodians or owners of historic property and for the landscapes and cultures from which that heritage evolved.

DYNAMIC INTERACTION

Domestic and international tourism continues to be among the foremost vehicles for cultural exchange, providing a personal experience, not only of that which has survived from the past, but of the contemporary life and society of others. It is increasingly appreciated as a positive force for natural and cultural conservation. Tourism can capture the economic characteristics of the heritage and harness these for conservation by generating funding, educating the community and influencing policy. It is an essential part of many national and regional economies and can be an important factor in development, when managed successfully.

Tourism itself has become an increasingly complex phenomenon, with political, economic, social, cultural, educational, bio-physical, ecological and aesthetic dimensions. The achievement of a beneficial inter-action between the potentially conflicting expectations and aspirations of visitors and host or local communities, presents many challenges and opportunities.

The natural and cultural heritage, diversities and living cultures are major tourism attractions. Excessive or poorly-managed tourism and tourism related development can threaten their physical nature, integrity and significant characteristics. The ecological setting, culture and lifestyles of host communities may also be degraded, along with the visitor's experience of the place.

Tourism should bring benefits to host communities and provide an important means and motivation for them to care for and maintain their heritage and cultural practices. The involvement and cooperation of local and/or indigenous community representatives, conservationists, tourism operators, property owners, policy makers, those preparing national development plans and site managers is necessary to achieve a sustainable tourism industry and enhance the protection of heritage resources for future generations.

ICOMOS, the International Council on Monuments and Sites, as the author of this Charter, other international organisations and the tourism industry, are dedicated to this challenge.

MAIN OBJECTIVES OF THE CHARTER

The Objectives of the International Cultural Tourism Charter are:

* To facilitate and encourage those involved with heritage conservation and management to make the significance of that heritage accessible to the host community and visitors.
* To facilitate and encourage the tourism industry to promote and manage tourism in ways that respect and enhance the heritage and living cultures of host communities.
* To facilitate and encourage a dialogue between conservation interests and the tourism industry about the importance and fragile nature of heritage places, collections and living cultures, including the need to achieve a sustainable future for them.
* To encourage those formulating plans and policies to develop detailed, measurable goals and strategies relating to the presentation and interpretation of heritage places and cultural activities, in the context of their preservation and conservation.

In addition:

* The Charter supports wider initiatives by ICOMOS, other international bodies and the tourism industry in maintaining the integrity of heritage management and conservation.
* The Charter encourages the involvement of all those with relevant or at times conflicting interests,

responsibilities and obligations to join in achieving its objectives.

* The Charter encourages the formulation of detailed guidelines by interested parties, facilitating the implementation of the Principles to their specific circumstances or the requirements of particular organisations and communities.

PRINCIPLES OF THE CULTURAL TOURISM CHARTER

First Principle

Since domestic and international tourism is among the foremost vehicles for cultural exchange, conservation should provide responsible and well managed opportunities for members of the host community and visitors to experience and understand that community's heritage and culture at first hand.

The natural and cultural heritage is a material and spiritual resource, providing a narrative of historical development. It has an important role in modern life and should be made physically, intellectually and/or emotively accessible to the general public. Programmes for the protection and conservation of the physical attributes, intangible aspects, contemporary cultural expressions and broad context, should facilitate an understanding and appreciation of the heritage significance by the host community and the visitor, in an equitable and affordable manner.

Individual aspects of natural and cultural heritage have differing levels of significance, some with universal values, others of national, regional or local importance. Interpretation programmes should present that significance in a relevant and accessible manner to the host community and the visitor, with appropriate, stimulating and contemporary forms of education, media, technology and personal explanation of historical, environmental and cultural information.

Interpretation and presentation programmes should facilitate and encourage the high level of public awareness and support necessary for the long term survival of the natural and cultural heritage.

Interpretation programmes should present the significance of heritage places, traditions and cultural practices within the past experience and present diversities of the area and the host community, including that of minority cultural or linguistic groups. The visitor should always be informed of the differing cultural values that may be ascribed to a particular heritage resource.

Second Principle

The relationship between Heritage Places and Tourism is dynamic and may involve conflicting values. It should be managed in a sustainable way for present and future generations. Places of heritage significance have an intrinsic value for all people as an important basis for cultural diversity and social development. The long term protection and conservation of living cultures, heritage places, collections, their physical and ecological integrity and their environmental context, should be an essential component of social, economic, political, legislative, cultural and tourism development policies.

The interaction between heritage resources or values and tourism is dynamic and ever changing, generating both opportunities and challenges, as well as potential conflicts. Tourism projects, activities and developments should achieve positive outcomes and minimise adverse impacts on the heritage and lifestyles of the host community, while responding to the needs and aspirations of the visitor. Conservation, interpretation and tourism development programmes should be based on a comprehensive understanding of the specific, but often complex or conflicting aspects of heritage significance of the particular place. Continuing research and consultation are important to furthering the evolving understanding and appreciation of that significance.

The retention of the authenticity of heritage places and collections is important. It is an essential element of their cultural significance, as expressed in the physical material, collected memory and intangible traditions that remain from the past. Programmes should present and interpret the authenticity of places and cultural experiences to enhance the appreciation and understanding of that cultural heritage. Tourism development and infrastructure projects should take account of the aesthetic, social and cultural dimensions, natural and cultural landscapes, bio-diversity characteristics and the broader visual context of heritage places. Preference should be given to using local materials and take account of local architectural styles or vernacular traditions.

Before heritage places are promoted or developed for increased tourism, management plans should assess the natural and cultural values of the resource. They should then establish appropriate limits of acceptable change, particularly in relation to the impact of visitor numbers on the physical characteristics, integrity, ecology and biodiversity of the place, local access and transportation systems and the social, economic and cultural well being of the host community. If the likely level of change is unacceptable the development proposal should be modified.

There should be on-going programmes of evaluation to assess the progressive impacts of tourism activities and development on the particular place or community.

Third Principle

Conservation and Tourism Planning for Heritage Places should ensure that the Visitor Experience will be worthwhile, satisfying and enjoyable. Conservation and tourism programmes should present high quality information to optimise the visitor's understanding of the significant heritage characteristics and of the need for their protection, enabling the visitor to enjoy the place in an appropriate manner.

Visitors should be able to experience the heritage place at their own pace, if they so choose. Specific circulation routes may be necessary to minimise impacts on the integrity and physical fabric of a place, its natural and cultural characteristics.

Respect for the sanctity of spiritual places, practices and traditions is an important consideration for site managers, visitors, policy makers, planners and tourism operators. Visitors should be encouraged to behave as welcomed guests, respecting the values and lifestyles of the host community, rejecting possible theft or illicit trade in cultural property and conducting themselves in a responsible manner which would generate a renewed welcome, should they return. Planning for tourism activities should provide appropriate facilities for the comfort, safety and well-being of the visitor, that enhance the enjoyment of the visit but do not adversely impact on the significant features or ecological characteristics.

Fourth Principle

Host communities and indigenous peoples should be involved in planning for conservation and tourism.

The rights and interests of the host community, at regional and local levels, property owners and relevant indigenous peoples who may exercise traditional rights or responsibilities over their own land and its significant sites, should be respected. They should be involved in establishing goals, strategies, policies and protocols for the identification, conservation, management, presentation and interpretation of their heritage resources, cultural practices and contemporary cultural expressions, in the tourism context. While the heritage of any specific place or region may have a universal dimension, the needs and wishes of some communities or indigenous peoples to restrict or manage physical, spiritual or intellectual access to certain cultural practices, knowledge, beliefs, activities, artefacts or sites should be respected.

Fifth Principle

Tourism and conservation activities should benefit the host community. Policy makers should promote measures for the equitable distribution of the benefits of tourism to be shared across countries or regions, improving the levels of socio-economic development and contributing where necessary to poverty alleviation. Conservation management and tourism activities should provide equitable economic, social and cultural benefits to the men and women of the host or local community, at all levels, through education, training and the creation of full-time employment opportunities.

A significant proportion of the revenue specifically derived from tourism programmes to heritage places should be allotted to the protection, conservation and presentation of those places, including their natural and cultural contexts. Where possible, visitors should be advised of this revenue allocation. Tourism programmes should encourage the training and employment of guides and site interpreters from the host community to enhance the skills of local people in the presentation and interpretation of their cultural values. Heritage interpretation and education programmes among the people of the host community should encourage the involvement of local site interpreters. The programmes should promote a knowledge and respect for their heritage, encouraging the local people to take a direct interest in its care and conservation.

Conservation management and tourism programmes should include education and training opportunities for policy makers, planners, researchers, designers, architects, interpreters, conservators and tourism operators. Participants should be encouraged to understand and help resolve the at times conflicting issues, opportunities and problems encountered by their colleagues.

Sixth Principle

Tourism promotion programmes should protect and enhance Natural and Cultural Heritage characteristics. Tourism promotion programmes should create realistic expectations and responsibly inform potential visitors of the specific heritage characteristics of a place or host community, thereby encouraging them to behave appropriately.

Places and collections of heritage significance should be promoted and managed in ways which protect their authenticity and enhance the visitor experience by minimising fluctuations in arrivals and avoiding excessive numbers of visitors at any one time. Tourism promotion programmes should provide a wider distribution of benefits and relieve the pressures on more popular places by encouraging visitors to experience the wider cultural and natural heritage characteristics of the region or locality.

The promotion, distribution and sale of local crafts and other products should provide a reasonable social and economic return to the host community, while ensuring that their cultural integrity is not degraded.

TOURISM FOR OTHER PURPOSES

Medical tourism or medical travel, is the act of traveling to other countries to obtain medical, dental, and surgical care. The term was initially coined by travel agencies and the media as a catchall phrase to describe a rapidly growing industry where people travel to other countries to obtain medical care. Leisure aspect of traveling may be included on such a medical travel trip. It includes medical services (inclusive of elective procedure and complex specialised surgeries) like knee/hip replacement, heart surgery, dental procedures and different cosmetic surgeries. Many companies like Medical Excursions, Inc. inspect the overseas facilities and then help the North Amercian patients to find qualified affordable and high class medical service providers.

The View

A combination of many factors has led to the recent increase in popularity of medical travel: the high cost of healthcare in industrialized nations, the ease and affordability of international travel, and the improvement of technology and standards of care in many countries of the world.

A large draw to medical travel is the convenience in comparison to that of other countries. Some countries that operate from a public health-care system are so taxed that it can take a considerable amount of time, to get needed medical care. The time spent waiting for a procedure, such as a hip replacement, can be a year or more in Britain and Canada; however, in Singapore, Bangkok or Bangalore, a patient could feasibly have an operation the day after their arrival. Reasons pushing medical travel include lower healthcare costs as well as the search for medical expertise and safety. According to research found in an article by the University of Delaware publication, Daily:

"The cost of surgery in Bolivia, Argentina, India, Thailand or South Africa can be one-tenth of what it is in the United

States or Western Europe, and sometimes even less. A heart-valve replacement that would cost US$200,000 or more in the U.S., for example, goes for $10,000 in India-and that includes round-trip airfare and a brief vacation package. Similarly, a metal-free dental bridge worth $5,500 in the U.S. costs $500 in India or Bolivia, a knee replacement in Thailand with six days of physical therapy costs about one-fifth of what it would in the States, and Lasik eye surgery worth $3,700 in the U.S. is available in many other countries for only $730. Cosmetic surgery savings are even greater: A full facelift that would cost $20,000 in the U.S. runs about $2,500 in South Africa or $ 2,300 in bolivia."

To understand the phenomenon of Medical travel, we can compare the average costs of cosmetic surgeries between the industrialized nations and the most popular countries in latin america which are specialized in medical tourism and cosmetic surgery tourism (Argentina, Bolivia, Brazil, Costa Rica, India, Mexico). All the prices have been provided us by the offices affiliated with the ministries of health in USA, Europe (France, Spain, Switzerland), Argentine, Bolivia, brazil, Costa Rica, India, and Mexico.

Medical tourists can come from anywhere in the world and may seek essential healthcare services such as cancer treatment and brain and transplant surgery as well as complementary or 'elective' services such as aesthetic treatments (cosmetic surgery).

Popular Medical travel worldwilde destinations are: Singapore, India, Thailand, Brunei, Cuba, Hong Kong, Hungary, India, Israel, Jordan, Lithuania, Malaysia, The Philippines, Thailand, Singapore, and recently, UAE.

Popular Cosmetic Surgery travel destination are: Argentina, Bolivia, Brazil, Costa Rica, Mexico and Turkey.

In Europe Belgium and Poland are also breaking into the business. South Africa is taking the term "medical tourism" very literally by promoting their "medical safaris": Come to see African wildlife and get a facelift in the same trip. However, feelings towards medical tourism are not always positive. In places like the US, where most have insurance and access to quality health care, medical tourism is viewed as risky. In some parts of the world, wider political issues can influence where medical tourists will choose to seek out healthcare; for example, in late 2006 some patients from the Middle East were choosing to travel to Singapore or Hong Kong for health care rather than to the USA.

While the tourism component might be a big draw for some Southeast Asia countries that focus on simple procedures, India is positioning itself the primary medical destination for the most complex medical procedures in the world. India's commitment to this is demonstrated with an ever growing number of hospitals that are attaining the US Joint Commission International accreditation.

Singapore positions itself as a medical hub where healthcare services, medicine, biomedical research and pharmaceutical manufacturing converge. Singapore has made international news for many complex surgeries in specialties such as neurology, oncology and organ transplants procedures. Currently Singapore boasts the largest number of US Joint Commission accredited hospitals in the region.

On the other hand, in South America, countries such as Argentina, Bolivia, Brazil lead on plastic surgery medical skills relying on the vast experience their surgeons have in treating the style-obsessed. It is estimated that 1 in 30 Argentinians had taken plastic surgery procedures, making this population the most operated in the world after the US and Mexico.

In Bolivia the situation is impressive. According to the "Sociedad Boliviana de Cirugia Plastica y Reconstructiva", more that 70% women who belong to the middle and upper class had taken plastic surgery procedure. There are companies emerging to offer global healthcare options that will allow North American patients to take full advantage of dramatic reductions in air travel and access world class healthcare at a fraction of the cost. Companies that focus on 'Medical Value Travel' typically will have experienced nurse case managers to assist patients with pre-and post-travel medical issues. They will also help provide resources for follow-up care upon the patient's return. While these services will initially be of interest to the self-insured patient, several studies indicate that the rapid growth of Health Savings Accounts will also drive interest to healthcare in other countries.

Because standards are everything when it comes to healthcare, there is a parallel issue around hospital accreditation. Potential medical tourists may be assisted in making their choices by whether or not hospitals have been assessed and accredited by reputable external accreditation bodies. In the USA, JCI (Joint Commission International) fulfills such a role, while in the United Kingdom and Hong Kong, the Trent Accreditation Scheme is a key player.

INDIAN SCENARIO

India is one of the most famous destinations in the world for medical tourists. It is known in particular for heart surgery and hip resurfacing, areas of advanced medicine in which India is generally considered a global leader. Probably no country has been in the news for medical tourism than India in 2005-06, and the government and private hospital groups both seem committed to a goal of making the subcontinent a world leader in the industry. Indian medical industry's main appeal is low-cost treatment. Most estimates claim treatment costs in India start at around a tenth of the price of comparable treatment in America or Britain. Morever Indian Hospitals also provides more personalized care than available in west.

For example, in April Madras Medical Mission, a Chennai-based hospital, successfully conducted a complex heart operation on an 87-year-old American patient at a reported cost of $8,000 (£4,850) including the cost of his airfare and a month's stay in hospital. The patient claimed that a less complex operation in America had earlier cost him $40,000. Take the rising popularity of "preventive health screening". At one private clinic in London a thorough men's health check-up that includes blood tests, electro-cardiogram tests, chest x-rays, lung tests and abdominal ultrasound costs £345 ($574). By comparison, a comparable check-up at a clinic operated by Delhi-based healthcare company

Max Healthcare costs $84. A lady from Vero beach, FL, who was featured in CBS 60 min in April 2005, went to India for hip surgery. In USA only hip replacements are possible, but India allows hip resurfacing that does not need the full hip replacement rather saves part of the hip to achieve the same result as the hip replacement. Shyamvaran 00:57, 16 January 2007 (UTC). Escorts Heart Institute and Research Center in Delhi and Faridabad, India performs nearly 15,000 heart operations every year, and the post-surgery mortality rate is only 0.8 percent, which is less than half of most major hospitals in the United States.

Medical Tourism in India is one of the best options available to people across the globe. Millions come to India every year to get treated and then enjoy their recuperative holidays across India. People from different walks of life cut across America, United Kingdom, Pakistan, Sri Lanka, Europe, Maldives, Germany and numerous other countries come to India to have their treatments done with peace of mind.

India provides world class medical facilities with hospitals and specialized multi specialty health centers providing their expertise in the areas of Cosmetic Surgery, Dental care, Heart Surgeries, Coronary Bypass, Heart Check up, Valve replacements, Knee Replacements, Eye surgeries, Indian traditional treatments like Ayurvedic Therapies and much more, practically covering every aspect of medicine combining modern treatments with traditional experience. Estimates of the value of medical tourism to India go as high as $2 billion a year by 2012. In 2003, Indian finance minister Jaswant Singh called for India to become a "global health destination".. However, the biggest stumbling block preventing the rapid growth of India as a healthcare destination is its poor infrastructure and lack of quality hotels.

SINGAPORE

Singapore's healthcare services built on a heritage of excellent quality, safety and trustworthiness, coupled with advanced research and international accreditation, and is Asia's leading medical hub.

Nine hospitals and two medical centres in Singapore have obtained Joint Commission International (JCI) accreditation. JCI is the main hospital accreditation agency in the United States. Many of these patients come from neighbouring countries such as Indonesia and Malaysia. However, patient numbers from Indo-China, South-Asia, the Middle East and Greater China to Singapore are seeing fast growth. On top of that, patients from developed countries such as United States also choose Singapore as their medical travel destination for relatively affordable quality healthcare services in a clean cosmopolitan city for a peace of mind.

Singapore made news for many complex and innovative procedures such as the separation of conjoined twins and tooth-in-eye surgery. The successful separation of the 10-month-old nepalese conjoined twins in 2001 puts Singapore's medical expertise onto the World's headlines. Singapore has since accomplished many more milestones both in Asia and in the world arena. Recently, Singapore also hosted the first International Medical Travel Conference (IMTC) from 12th-15th December 2006. The four-day event attracted participants and media from 21 countries, setting pace and platform for the development of the budding medical travel industry. The conference aims to bring together thought leaders to examine some of the fundamentals, issues and challenges involved in the burgeoning international medical travel industry.. Curiously however major media did not pay attention to this awkwardly managed event. However, up to late 2006 Singapore Hospitals have only chosen to accredit themselves through Joint Commission International (JCI), a US-based group, and this approach may have little appeal to potential health tourists based in other parts of the world. In time, Singapore Hospitals may look towards other European or Asian-based systems of hospital accreditation in an attempt to broaden their credibility and appeal.

THAILAND

Medical tourism is a growing segment of Thailand's tourism and health-care sectors. Lower labor costs translate into significant cost savings on procedures, compared to hospitals in the United States, and a higher, more personalized level of nursing care than Westerners are accustomed to receiving in hospitals back home. In 2005, one Bangkok hospital took in 150,000 treatment seekers from abroad. In 2006, medical tourism was projected to earn the country 36.4 billion baht.

One patient who received a coronary artery bypass surgery at Bumrungrad International hospital in Bangkok said the operation cost him US$12,000, as opposed to the $100,000 he estimated the operation would have cost him at home in the US.

Hospitals in Thailand are a popular destination for other Asians. Another hospital that caters to medical tourists, Bangkok General Hospital, has a Japanese wing and Phyathai Hospitals Group has interpreters for over 22 languages, besides the English speaking medical staff. When Nepal Prime Minister Girija Prasad Koirala needed medical care in 2006, he went to Bangkok.

While it is not commonly known outside Thailand, the modern Thai medical system had its origins in the United States when Prince Mahidol of Songla, the King's father, earned his MD degree from Harvard Medical School in the early 20th century. Prince Mahidol and another member of the Thai Royal Family paid for an American medical education for a group of Thai men and women.

Prince Mahidol also convinced the Rockefeller Foundation to provide scholarships for Thai citizens to study medicine and nursing. Funds from the Rockefeller Foundation were also used to help build modern medical training facilities in Thailand. The men and women who studied medicine and nursing as a result of Prince Mahidol's efforts became the first educators for the modern Thai medical system.

Today many Thai physicians hold US professional certification. A number of Thai hospitals have relationships with facilities in the US. The US Consular information sheet gives the Thai healthcare system high marks for quality, particularly facilities in Bangkok. In Thailand, there is modern infrastructure, with clean, safe streets. According to the US Consular information sheets, the crime rate in Bangkok is lower than that of many US cities. Personal safety is another factor to consider when traveling abroad both for vacation as well as healthcare. Thailand offers everything from cardiac surgery to organ transplants at a price much lower than the US or Europe, in a safe, clean environment.

Thailand has long been a destination for medical tourists, and has a growing number of hospitals with JCAHO accreditation. Over one million people per year travel there for everything from cosmetic surgery to cutting edge cardiac treatment. Don Ho, the famous Hawaiian entertainer, recently received cutting-edge adult stem cell cardiac treatment at a Bangkok hospital. Six weeks later he had recovered sufficiently from his nonischemic cardiomyopathy and was able to return to the stage.

MEDICAL TRAVEL: RISKS AND REWARDS

Medical tourism does carry risks that local medical procedures do not. Should complications arise, patients might not be covered by insurance or be able to seek adequate compensation via malpractice lawsuits, though it should be noted that the malpractice insurance is a considerable portion of the cost in the West.

For some living in remote rural areas, travel to another country is almost as expensive as travel to a large city in their own country.

Nations such as India or Thailand have different infectious diseases, and different prevalence of the same diseases, than home nations such as the US, Canada, UK. Exposure to foreign diseases without having built up natural immunity can be a hazard for weakened individuals, specifically for gastrointestinal diseases (e.g Hep A, amoebic dysentery, bacteria) which could weaken progress, mosquito transmitted diseases, and influenza, TB, etc. (75% of South Africans have latent TB)

Also, travel soon after surgery can increase the risk of complications, as can vacation activities. For example, scars will be darker and more noticeable if they sunburn while healing. Long flights can be bad for those with heart (thrombosis) or breathing related problems (low oxygen environment), not to mention uncomfortable.

However, because in poor tropical nations diseases run the gamut, doctors seem to be more open to the possibility of any disease, including HIV, TB, and typhoid, there are cases in the West where patients were consistently misdiagnosed for years because it is perceived to be "rare" in the West, a famous case of the misdiagnosis and death of a CDC researcher from TB, something that few would rule out in India or Thailand.

ASIA PACIFIC TOURISM INDUSTRY

The Asia and Pacific region will be the focus of the worldwide tourism industry in the new millennium. Over the last decade, tourist arrivals and receipts rose faster than any other region in the world, almost twice the rates of industrialized countries. Between 1980 and 1995, tourist arrivals and receipts in the Asia Pacific region rose at an average annual rate of 10% and 15% respectively, higher than any region in the world (World Tourism Organization 1996a). Statistics from the World Tourism Organization (WTO) for 1996 show that tourist arrivals and receipts accounted for a 15.2% and 19.4% share of the world's total respectively, a significant increase from 1985 as shown in Tables I and 2 (WTO 1997a). The Asia Pacific region has been gaining market share at the expense of the Americas and European regions, which saw a decline in their respective shares during the same period. The WTO 1996b) projects that by the year 2010, the region will surpass the Americas to become the world's number two tourism region, with 229 million arrivals. It is an indication that the growth of tourism in the Asia Pacific region in the next decade will be nothing short of spectacular.

Mass travel, which first began in the 1950s when millions of Americans and Europeans traveled the world, has blossomed in Asia. The region is now regarded as a major generator and receiver of tourism. A wealthy new middle class of Asians are taking to the skies and joining their European and American counterparts on their pleasure, business, and adventure trips around the globe. The rapid growth of the tourism industry has been attributed to a number of factors including among others, strong economic growth, increase in disposable income and leisure time, easing of travel restrictions, successful tourist promotion, and a recognition by the host governments that tourism is a powerful engine of growth and a generator of foreign exchange earnings.

It is the purpose of this paper to provide a basic discussion of the economic importance of tourism and review the major trends that shaped the growth and development of the tourism industry in the Asia Pacific region. A comparison of the tourism industry performance will also be made between selected Asia Pacific countries, and with other regions of the world, to highlight the trends and changes. The definition of the Asia Pacific region in this paper corresponds to the definition used by the WTO which includes North-East Asia, South-East Asia, and Oceania.

ECONOMIC IMPORTANCE OF TOURISM IN ASIA PACIFIC

Tourism is one of the most important sectors in the economies of Asia Pacific countries. Currently, tourism is the most important sector and major source of foreign exchange earnings in Thailand, Australia, and New Zealand. It is ranked second in Hong Kong, Malaysia and the Philippines, and ranked third in Singapore and Indonesia. For example, in New Zealand, the tourism industry employs more than 200,000 people, with projections of a 14% annual growth till the year 2000 (Chan 1995). In Hong Kong, tourism employs 12% of the workforce and contributes about 7% to the economy (Boxall 1996). The tourism sector in Thailand supports over 1.5 million jobs and contributes 5% to the economy (Asian Business 1996). Tourism is also gaining importance in China.

By the year 2000, China expects to receive 55 million visitors with foreign exchange earnings of US$14 billion, which will contribute 5% to China's economy, making tourism one of the most significant components of the national economy (Beria 1996). In Singapore, the healthy overall balance of payments is attributed to the huge surplus achieved by the tourism sector which contributes about 10% to the economy (International Monetary Fund 1996a). Despite Singapore's open economy, and its vulnerability to external shocks and import leakages, tourism has made a significant contribution to output, employment, and income.

Based on 1988 input-output tables, Khan et al. (1995) estimated that tourism contributed 11.9% to Singapore's GDP (Gross Domestic Product) in 1992, while employment accounted for 13.4% of the labor force. The employment effect of a million dollars in tourist expenditures would create 25 new jobs. The results its showed that every dollar of tourist expenditure would generate S$1.97 of output and S$1.05 in income. The income multiplier for tourism was larger when compared to Hong Kong, Indonesia and Malaysia, while the tourism output multiplier was greater relative to other sectors of the Singapore economy.

Comparisons with previous studies (Schymyck 1983; Toh and Low 1990) showed an increase in the contribution of tourism over time, a strong indication of the significance of tourism in the Singapore economy.

The estimated economic impact of tourism is also significant in South Korea. According to Lee and Kwon (1995), the total impact of tourism receipts of US$4.7 billion in 1993, generated US$11.7 of output, US$2.4 billion in income, and created 350,000 full time jobs. The secondary impacts were also found to have a considerable effect on the economy. The findings suggested that tourism should be promoted as a strategic export industry.

It is no surprise that the key to the success of tourism in the Asia Pacific region is a clear recognition by the host governments of the important role of tourism in the economic development of the country. Tourism serves as an important means to increase economic growth, raise the quality of life, create employment, and improve the overall balance of payments by helping to offset deficits in other sectors. Many Asia Pacific countries show a net surplus in their tourism balance of payment account.

Japan, Taiwan, and South Korea are major tourist generating countries in the region and this is reflected by the deficits in their respective travel balance of payments accounts. Mak and White (1992) attributed the travel account deficits for these high income countries to a higher allocation of disposable income to leisure travel. The relaxation of travel restrictions in Taiwan also had a significant impact on its travel account, due to the large increase in outbound travel. On the other hand, China, Thailand, and Singapore are major receivers of tourists, enjoying a huge surplus. As a percentage of exports, tourism contributes more than 13/n to the economies of Australia, New Zealand, and Thailand, again reflecting its ranking as the top export. Its contribution to the GDP is significantly greater in Singapore (10%) and Hong Kong (7%).

Almost all Asian nations are committing substantial manpower and resources to attract more arrivals whose expenditures represent significant contributions to national income and foreign exchange earnings. For example, Singapore has unveiled a new tourism blueprint titled "Tourism 21" that is expected to turn the nation into a world class tourism business center and the tourism capital of the East. Plans call for increasing arrivals and receipts by 6.4% and 6.6% annually to 10 million and US$11.4 billion, respectively, by the year 2000 (Boey 1996).

Even Indonesia and Malaysia have raised their commitments towards developing the tourism sector. Indonesia plans to make tourism the nation's number one foreign exchange earner by the year 2004, when arrivals will hit 11 million and receipts reach US$15 billion from current levels of 4.3 million and US$5.4 billion, respectively (Travel Trade Gazelle 1997). In the current Seventh Malaysia Plan, which ends in the year 2000, a number of strategies were formulated to turn tourism into a top revenue earner for the country. Millions of dollars will be allocated for tourism infrastructure in an effort to increase arrivals and receipts to 12.5 million and US$6.3 billion, respectively, by the end of this decade (Pacific Area Travel Association News 1996). With increasing competition for the tourist dollar, the national tourism organizations of New

Zealand, Thailand, Australia and Hong Kong, among others, have also allocated an increase in tourism funding to tap the emerging tourism markets that promise new income and employment opportunities.

Growth Factors

A number of factors are responsible for the rapid growth and development of the tourism industry in the Asia Pacific region. These include the strong economic growth, increase in income, breakdown of political barriers, easing of travel restrictions, liberalization of air transport, and focused marketing campaigns. These factors are expected to accelerate the growth of tourism over the next decade.

Economic Growth

The rapid growth of the tourism industry is a reflection of the region's booming and diversified economies. Economic growth has ranged between an average of 6% to 9% in the last decade, in contrast to 3% to 4% growth achieved by the rest of the world. Only the industrialized countries of Australia, Japan, and New Zealand show a lower rate of growth than the rest of the region. China, which has achieved double-digit growth over the last 5 years, is poised to become one of the world's largest economies and surpass Japan in the next decade. The region is expected to maintain its growth at a rate between 6% to 8% over the next decade (IMF 1996b).

Strong economic growth in Asia is attributed to a focus on market reforms, export oriented industries, stable currencies, diversification of the economy, and massive injection of foreign capital. Billions of dollars are being poured into the tourism infrastructure to accommodate a burgeoning Asian tourism industry. This has intensified trade, investment, and travel within the region and with the rest of the world. Asian governments have also sought to avoid extremes of inflation and unemployment, and are keeping budget deficits small or running surpluses. It is no wonder that the region has attracted much attention from the rest of the world regarding its success. The opening up of Indochina, Myanmar, and China to tourism, and given the increasing number of companies setting u p bases and new businesses in the region the volume of business travel will rise. This will provide ample marketing opportunities for travel-related businesses.

Income and Leisure Time

As a result of strong economic growth, disposable incomes have soared in Asian countries and along with it, the propensity to travel. Leisure consciousness has been enhanced with travel no longer seen as a luxury. In fact, it is now seen as an affordable commodity to be enjoyed by all who choose to engage in a variety of leisurely pursuits. Some Asians may see travel as a status symbol, while others see it as relief from the pressures of work. The introduction of a 5-day workweek in China will provide Chinese residents with more leisure time that will likely be devoted to travel.

A number of Asian countries have recorded significant growth in real per capita income over the last Syears with Singapore (7.3%), Thailand (6.8%), China (10.3%), 5. Korea (6.7%), and Indonesia (7.1%) showing the highest growth (IMF 1997). Rising incomes have created a middle class of sophisticated and affluent Asians who are better educated, have more disposable income, and who appreciate the value of leisure. Research by Mak and White (1992) has shown travel propensity and tourism spending to be positively correlated a ed with per capita income among the major Asia Pacific countries. This means that increases in income levels will enable a greater proportion of Asians to travel overseas. Unlike previous generations, this generation of primarily young travelers are intent on enjoying the fruits of their labor.

Although price conscious, they still demand high qualify products. Since Asians are more likely to travel in groups and families, more travel products and services, such as tour packages that incorporate activities, must be designed to cater to their needs. This may include travel to exotic places, soft-adventure travel, cruises, and sports related tours, among others. Disposable incomes will continue to rise, and thus fuel the demand for leisure travel. The trend among Asia Pacific countries is towards more frequent regional holidays to various destinations and resorts within the region.

Political Stability and Breakdown of Political Barriers

In recent years, the Asia Pacific region has become politically more stable than it has ever been, especially in the Philippines, where tourism was adversely affected by terrorism, civil strife, and natural disasters in the last decade. However, the political, social and economic reforms of the current government have reversed the fortunes of the tourism industry. Tourism investments in the Philippines over the last 3 years were estimated at U5$6.27 billion, with a large portion of the funds allocated towards resort development. To encourage more investment, the Philippines Department of Tourism is urging financial institutions to provide funding to investors involved in tourism-related projects (Shaw 1997).

Investors are showing confidence not only in the Philippines but also in Vietnam, Indonesia, and China. These nations, which were off-limits to foreigners at one time, are witnessing rapid hotel and resort developments. Even areas which were closed or long considered inaccessible in parts of China and Indonesia are now open to tourism. The opening of borders to both inbound and outbound travel, and the breakdown of political barriers, will provide tourists with opportunities to pursue their leisure interests. For example, South Korea's normalization of relations with China also is expected to boost arrivals from Seoul to major cities in China when non-stop air traffic routes are inaugurated.

RELAXATION IN TRAVEL RESTRICTIONS

Historically, the demand for and freedom to travel increases when travel restrictions are lifted or eliminated. With strong demand for travel, a number of Asia Pacific countries have lifted some travel restrictions. The lifting of restrictions in South Korea and Taiwan in the late 1980s, for example, contributed to a surge in the demand for outbound travel. More recently, the Taiwanese government's open door policy and the institution of a 5-day visa-free entry program to 15 countries also helped to increase arrivals to Taiwan by 10% in 1995 over the previous year (Wieman 1996a). Similarly, the Malaysian government's decision to allow tourists a 3-day visa-free stay in Malaysia, and Indonesia's granting of unilateral visa-free entry are steps in the right direction The general trend is towards a reduction of travel barriers to promote tourism.

LIBERALIZATION IN AIR TRANSPORT

Traditionally, Asian countries have safeguarded their national flag carriers to protect them from foreign competition. However, the situation is changing as governments realize that such restrictive policies are counterproductive to tourism. Singapore and Taiwan have already signed open skies agreements with the United States and similar agreements are expected between the U.S. and Malaysia, S. Korea and New Zealand (Dhaliwal 1997). Liberalization of air transport will only serve to enhance trade and tourism growth in the region. It will to lead to more multilateral open skies agreements between countries.

In other parts of the region, Thailand and Australia are showing more tourism growth as a result of liberalized internal aviation policies. Indonesia, the Philippines and South Korea have followed suit with similar aviation policies. Indonesia's limited open skies policy invites foreign airlines to fly to new international destinations and participate in code sharing agreements with Indonesian airlines.

As a result of liberalized air policies in the Philippines, new international gateways have emerged, and more inter-island services initiated.

This will save travel time, increase convenience, and enable the promotion of more resorts in the islands. Liberalization of aviation policies have also sparked the creation of new carriers and subsidiaries of major carriers such as Silkair (Singapore), Dragonair (Hong Kong), and Sempati (Indonesia). These airlines have launched new routes to secondary destinations, especially in China, Indonesia, Thailand, and Malaysia, to serve the emerging and growing tourism market in secondary cities.

Technological Development

Technological developments have significantly impacted the travel industry in the Asia Pacific region and will continue to do so over the next decade. Developments in large and more fuel efficient aircraft such as the Boeing 777, Boeing 747, and Airbus A340 have lowered operating costs, increased airline seat capacity, and raised the comfort and safety of air travel. These aircraft facilitate travel over longer distances and fly non-stop over trans-Atlantic and Pacific routes. Lower operating costs, coupled with cheaper airfares, have reduced the cost of travel, thereby making air travel the dominant mode of travel in the region. Most of the new wide bodied jets built over the next decade will be delivered to Asia Pacific airlines to meet their increasing demand for capacity.

Technological developments are also impacting the way in which the product is delivered to the customer. Ticketless travel will find its way into the major hubs in Asia this year. Singapore Airlines will introduce ticketless travel on selected regional routes while Malaysian Airlines will introduce it on domestic routes. Air New Zealand and Ansett Australia are also planning ticketless travel by the end of this year. Ticketless travel will speed up customer service, provide convenience, improve efficiency, and decrease distribution costs Ticketless travel can save airlines up to 30% of their distribution costs if it is implemented and standardized successfully (Klyne 1997). With the availability of computer-based interactive information and product buying systems, tourists can view the facilities and destinations on the Internet, video, or CD-ROM and make direct purchases. The National Tourism Organizations (NTOs) of the Asia Pacific countries have also created custom-made destination promotion pages on the World Wide Web in order to reach a global audience. New technological developments and production efficiencies will continue to create more leisure time that will be devoted to travel.

Focused Marketing and Themed Campaigns

In light of the increasingly competitive situation in the Asia Pacific region, traditional methods of marketing a destination to the masses has yielded to more focused marketing segmentation strategies and themed campaigns.

Thailand started the trend towards international and nationwide events when it launched "Visit Thailand Year 1987" to celebrate the Thai King's 60th birthday. The success of the campaign was reflected in visitor arrival figures, which jumped 24% in 1987 (Corben 1996). Since then, the success of nationwide campaigns have been emulated all across Asia. In 1997, China will organize a second "Visit China Year 1997" to complement its recovery of sovereignty of Hong Kong. The theme for the campaign is" Visit China-A Completely New Experience" with major events planned throughout the country. These marketing campaigns are designed to enhance the destination image by focusing on the rich cultural, historical, and natural heritage of the country.

Through creative and innovative p roduct differentiation strategies, each country has created a diverse destination product with a unique guest appeal that will enrich the visitor experience, provide quality, and maximize the value of the visitor's leisure time. Increased emphasis will be placed on niche marketing, whereby specific market segments are identified through visitor profile studies and then targeted by matching the destination product to appeal to the segment.

For example, in 1995, the Korea National Tourist Corporation used its "Discover Korea: A Different Asia" campaign to emphasize the differences that South Korea had to offer over other Asian countries; its unique traditional culture, delicious cuisine, exceptional shopping, and four distinct seasons.

For the Japanese market, the theme was "Korea: The Nearest Country" capitalizing on its proximity to Japan. The success of the campaign was reflected in tourism receipts which jumped 46.6% over 1994 (Price 1995). Capitalizing on this trend, Malaysia has developed a new "Malaysia: Fascinating Destinations" theme to showcase eight different destinations within the country, each with its own attraction and appeal.

The campaign is aimed at the North American, European, East Asian, and Australian markets. To complement existing promotional campaigns, some Asian countries have entered into joint marketing ventures and cooperative endeavors with neighboring countries and other NTOs.

For example, Singapore and Indonesia jointly promote Bintan Island in Indonesia, with plans for more initiatives covering other Indonesian islands. Singapore and Indonesia have also identified seven target markets in the U.S., Europe, and Asia in which both countries will spend US$800,000 over the next 2 years to promote both destinations (Business Times 1996). NTOs have also forged alliances with the private sector to promote destinations. For example, by setting up an alliance with major travel agencies in South Korea, the New Zealand Tourism Board was able to design and promote New Zealand tour packages aimed at the mature traveler from S. Korea. Palmer and Bejou (1995) noted that alliances between the private and p ublic sectors will attract more visitors that can benefit both sectors.

The value of forming alliances has also been recognized in tourism marketing (Gunn 1988; Stevens 1988). Joint promotions and marketing with members of ASEANTA (Association of South East Asian Nations Tourism Organization) and travel missions led by PATA (Pacific Area Travel Association) have also been successful. Both organizations have been instrumental in promoting the travel interests of members through trade shows, seminars, education and training, research, and destination marketing and sales promotion. For example, the collaborative efforts of ASEANTA paid off during" Visit ASEAN Year 1992," when visitor arrivals increased 9.5% to a record 21.86 million (WTO 1996a).

SPACE TRAVEL AND TOURISM

According to current reports in the media, travelling to outer space should become possible for everyone by the beginning of the next century. In April 1998, the newspaper Berlin Morgenpost reported that the international Hilton Hotel corporation is planning the construction of a 5-star hotel, the "Lunar Hilton," on the Moon. A team of British architects was commissioned to develop plans for the gigantic building project.

The luxury hotel with 5000 beds and a height of 325 metres provides its own beach at its private "ocean," and should be equipped with all the amenities one can expect from a first class hotel.

However, the short-term realisation of this utopian project of the Hilton Group will most likely take a little more time, and for the first half of the 21st century it must be regarded as pure science fiction. Apart from the technical feasibility of some of the construction plans, economic analyses performed by DLR and the Technical University of Berlin show that the transportation of humans and building materials to the Moon would be extraordinarily expensive, even if very optimistic economic conditions in space operations are assumed. With the announcement of its spectacular project, the Hilton Corporation competes with three Japanese corporations, Shimizu, the construction firm Nishimatsu, and Obayashi, all of which have already invested millions into futuristic colonising concepts for the moon.

Life-cycle cost analyses performed in [ESA99, REICHERT97b/c/d] for the planet Mars indicate, that the transportation of humans would require ticket prices in the range of hundreds of millions of dollars, even if very favourable economic conditions in space operations are assumed. In addition, one must consider that after the successful completion of the Apollo program no transportation infrastructure is currently available that would allow humans to be transported beyond the Earth orbital. The creation of such a new infrastructure would require investments of billions of dollars. The Moon and Mars are therefore not likely to play a role in international tourism in the first half of the next century, although Mars represents one of the most promising travel destination because of its many similarities to Earth and its potential of possible former life forms.

Therefore future space tourism will focus for a long time on Earth orbit which can be reached more easily. It is likely, that the space tourism business is initiated by very short suborbital flights, followed by short Earth orbital tourism in advanced, reusable spacecraft which allow several orbits around

Earth. Before extended stays in space hotels will become a reality in the far future, touristic trips to existing orbital facilities (e.g. the international space station) might represent an intermediate step.

Already since the mid-sixties, several important analyses of Earth orbital space tourism have been carried out [EHRICKE67]. Various scenarios of transportation and accommodation of tourists in space have been analysed in the frame of industrial research in Japan, increasingly over the last 10 years [COLLINS97, MATSUMOTO97]. In the United States, NASA and the American "Space Transportation Association " have completed a study of the feasibility of space tourism with some promising results [O'NEIL97] in 1998.

Furthermore, DASA (DaimlerChrysler Aerospace) investigates touristic spacecraft and space hotel concepts and supported the first international symposium on space tourism in the spring of 1997, which took place in Bremen (Germany) and attracted more than 100 experts from around the world. The symposium also found a significant echo in the media. Moreover, in 1998/99, the general feasibility and economics of space tourism played also a considerable role in an ESA study under the lead of DLR [ESA98, ESA99, REICHERT98]. All of these activities indicate that space tourism is gaining more and more attention and significance. Today, it is already possible to book atmospheric parabolic flights in aeroplanes for the short-term simulation of zerogravity, and to reserve future passenger flights into suborbital space, even though the technology for the latter has not been developed yet.

THE INDUSTRIAL SIGNIFICANCE

According to an estimate of the World Travel Tourism Council, annual global expenditures in the terrestrial tourism sector amount to about 3400 billion US dollars for the year 1995. Tourism thus globally represents one of the largest industries.

If it would be possible to shift only a few percent of the worldwide terrestrial tourist expenditures to a future space tourism market, this could double the civil space budgets to 60 billion dollars. This would create up to half a million new jobs also in the high technology space industry, if it is assumed that a sales volume of $50000 to $250000 creates one job.

If a space tourism business can be established in the future, the scientific and operational know-how-globally gained after decades of research and experience in manned space flight (e.g. by astronaut training centers or institutions of aerospace medicine)-could be applied to the space flight preparation and medical supervision of future space tourists.

Furthermore, touristic spaceflights could be planned, controlled and monitored by existing space operation centers in Europe, the USA or Russia. As soon as a space tourism market is established, large commercially oriented industrial conglomerates will cooperate in strategic alliances to operate and expand the space tourism business comparable to the terrestrial tourism and telecommunications industries.

The main motivation for an industrial investment in the space tourism sector will be the potential of very high achievable profits, which can be expected due to multi-billion dollar market potential.

OPEN MARKET

As soon as the "space ticket" can be purchased for some $10000-in the best of all cases a ticket price comparable to that of a transatlantic flight with the Concorde-one can expect that a global space tourism market will be established.

This has been confirmed by first national and international polls and market analyses (e.g. in the US, Japan, Europe) which indicate that a remarkable segment of clients would be already willing to make considerable financial commitments for short trips into space.

For example, 4.3% of all Germans are willing to pay several $10000-which is roughly comparable to an annual income-for a space trip [ABITZSCH97]. This could be a ticket price which might be achievable with future generations of spacecraft, and it is comparable to the cost of a vacation on a cruise ship which already attracts a steady clientele.

The expected number of passengers for a space trip as a function of the ticket costs according to international polls performed in the US, Japan, and Europe. With current costs of several ten million dollars to transport a human into space, space tourism is not affordable and finds no acceptance in the public.

However, with declining space travel ticket prices the situation will change. Once a ticket price of $ 1000 is obtainable, a passenger volume of about 20 million is expected, and even with a ticket price of $ 50000 a passenger rate of 1 million per year can be expected. [ABITZSCH97]. Nevertheless, the above mentioned polls have to be critically assessed with respect to their accuracy and credibility. Therefore, more detailed and representative polls and market research in this area have to be carried out.

Generally, any average person in good health and with appropriate preparation is able to go on a space trip. NASA, for example, just recently decided to send 77-year old former astronaut and Senator John Glenn into space with the Space Shuttle. He took part in important medical research experiments from which especially the older generation will profit.

FUTURE MANNED SPACE TRANSPORTATION SYSTEM

The fact that tourist space travel has not been established yet is mostly due to the high costs of manned space travel. The transportation of a passenger into orbit, for example with the Russian rocket launcher Soyuz still costs several $10 million. Therefore, alternative and less expensive space transportation system concepts have to be identified.

Already in 1979, a manned Space Shuttle was proposed in [DURST79], with a cabin module designed to offer a seat capacity for 74 passengers. The costs for this design were calculated in 1997 to be $3.6 million per passenger, assuming a launch rate of 12 flights per year [KOELLE97].

A further reduction of the costs is only expected by the development of advanced, reusable single-staged spacecraft. An example of such a spacecraft is the Japanese design for the single staged Kankoh-Maru launcher [COLLINS97]. This model with a capacity of 50 passengers is propelled by oxygen/hydrogen engines and is supposed to be operated like regular airplanes on conventional airports.

The launch costs for this design are estimated in [KOELLE97] to be $300000 per passenger (assuming 10 launches per year) and and in [ESA98] to be about $50000 to $100000 (optimistically assuming 1 launch per day). The illustration shows the Japanese single staged launcher in comparison to a Boeing 747 and 737.

A further considerable cost reduction-ticket prices ranging from $10000 to $100000-can therefore be only expected by the development of future generations of launchers, which have extremely high launch rates, are fully reusable and are operated with a minimum maintenance effort, comparable to today's aircraft fleets in the commercial airline business. The X-33 Space Shuttle Successor-a one billion-dollar development program initiated by NASA, can be considered as a first step to lower the transportation cost into space by using a single stage to orbit launching system for the first time.

According to the American company Zegrahm suborbital flights will play a major role, already in the next decade, as a precursor to initiate touristic space trips. These short space trips either consist of a vertical ascent into space or end after one orbit around Earth with a landing at the departure airport. Although the advanced technology for suborbital flights is not developed yet, it is already possible to make reservations for such space trips for the beginning of the next decade at a ticket price of about $100000.

However, the past experience shows, that the new development of high technology launchers generally requires long periods of research and testing and also investments typically in the range of several billion dollars. Taking these circumstances into account, the cost calculations and especially the short time frame for the first suborbital flights already for the beginning of the next decade appears very optimistic. Moreover, the first X-prize (promising $10 million prize for the first private manned rocket, which is launched to an altitude of 100 kilometer) candidates ran out of business.

Another project aims at the same objective: the proposed Ascender spaceplane which is designed to perform several flights per day with a crew of 4 members. Ascender is equipped with two Williams-Rolls FJ44 turbofans and a Pratt & Whitney RL10 rocket engine. After take-off from a conventional runway it performs a subsonic ascent to an altitude of 8 kilometre on jet power by using its two turbofans. Afterwards the rocket engine is ignited which lifts the spaceplane to an altitude of about 100 km. After re-entry into the atmosphere the spaceplane returns to the departure runway. The price per passenger is estimated [ASHFORD97] to be $ 5000 within the next 10 to 20 years. This cost estimate must be critically assessed, and appears too optimistic, especially in comparison with military jets with one flight hour costing up to several $10000. Furthermore, up to now, the RL10 rocket engine is not designed to be operated fully reusable and several times a day.

This might significantly increase the cost per flight and indicates that a costly development program has to be initiated to modify the RL10 engine according to the requirements of the Ascender spaceplane. Finally, Ascender 's maximum take-off weight of only about 4000 kg seems very optimistic and too low to fulfil the mission requirements. Nevertheless, the general Ascender spaceplane approach looks promising and could result in an important technological development program, which leads to a single stage to orbit precursor spacecraft for Europe.

For this reason a first rough return on investment analysis has been carried out for the suborbital scenario in [ESA98, ESA99]. Space tourism is expected to be carried out by commercial companies which expect a profit from their business. Furthermore, in general, initial investments for the development and production have to be refinanced. The profit as a function of the operational year including and excluding financing costs, assuming a fare per passenger of $50000. If the financing costs are neglected, a first profit can be achieved in the 9th operational year which increases to about $36.6 billion in the 30th operational year. Considering financing costs, the date of the first profit shiftes to the 11th year and increases to about $34 billion in the 30th operational year.

This decreased profit is caused by financing costs, which sum up to about $2.5 billion within the 30 year life cycle. The date of the first profit could be even shifted to earlier years, if the repayment of the development and production costs is spread over a longer period. Because of the relatively early return of i nvestment and the high achievable profits, the suborbital flights scenario generally looks very promising from an economic standpoint.

This is also confirmed by the fact, that international polls indicate, that the assumed ticket price of $50000 could lead to more than one million passengers per year [ABITZSCH97]. Due to the fact, that the fleet of 10 spaceplanes is only capable of transporting 43800 passengers per year, a further extension of the suborbital flights business seems very likely with decreasing ticket costs. However, it should kept in mind that the achieved profit mainly depends on low operation costs per flight (currently not state of the art) and the ability to realise the Ascender spaceplane with very low mass budgets as designed by [ASHFORD97].

A completely different design approach is implemented in the concept of the single stage ALLTRA-M1 rocket of the German FAR research group, which could also represent a promising X-prize candidate [FAR99]. A capsule, which can accommodate up to 3 crew members is mounted on top of the rocket, which is able to reach an altitude of at least 100 kilometres during a vertical ascent.

The ALLTRA-M1 rocket has a total mass of only about 10 tons and has almost the dimensions of a garage. The rocket is equipped with a hybrid propulsion system, in which liquid oxygen (in the central tank) is burned up with ordinary solid plastics in the lateral boosters. The hybrid propulsion system represents an interesting propulsion alternative between the classical solid and liquid/liquid propulsion systems. Its simple design, generous production tolerances and environmentally friendly and inexpensive fuels, possibly produced from recycled materials, make them a good candidate for low-cost high power propulsion systems. Thus a complete refuelling of the ALLTRA-M1 rocket costs only about $5000 and a 2-staged rocket concept could even reach a stable orbit around Earth. However, the overall economy, the atmospheric re-entry with acceptable G-loads, the soft landing and the general reusability still have to be demonstrated for the ALLTRA-M1 rocket in further studies.

Space Hotels

In order to provide longer touristic stays in Earth orbit, concepts for space hotels have been investigated worldwide. In Japan, several designs for large-scale space hotels were analysed in the context of industrial studies like the Shimizu space hotel illustrated [MATSUMOTO97]. It has a total mass of 8000 tons and offers all amenities and entertainment opportunities, one can expect from such a giant hotel complex. It is difficult to imagine from a current standpoint, that this giant hotel complex can be financed, built up and constructed in the near future. However, this sophisticated hotel concept might represent the second generation of space hotels maybe in the second half of the 21st century.

A different design philosophy is considered in the Space Hotel Berlin concept, which was evaluated to some extend at DLR in the context of an ESA study [ESA98, ESA99]. For this concept, mainly existing technologies are used by connecting modified habitat modules derived from the International Space Station (e.g. COF) as "apartments" to a circular ring-structure.

Rotating the circular structure with different velocities, creates a wide variety of artificial gravity levels. With regard to mass and costs, the Space Hotel Berlin is about comparable to the International Space Station. In case of a 100 percent rate of capacity utilisation, first rough life cycle cost analyses indicate that the accommodation of tourists seems possible at a price of about $100000 per overnight stay. This depends on the assumed life time of the space hotel complex, ranging from 10 to 30 years [ESA98, ESA99]. However, these costs do not include financing cost (for prefinancing the development and production phase), a profit for a commercial company and the expensive

Earth to LEO transportation of the tourists. This means, that a space hotel can be realised at the earliest, as soon as future generations of launchers provide extreme cost-efficient tickets, which are decreased by a factor of about hundred. Moreover, a further reduction of the space hotel's costs have also to be achieved by a more optimised design.

The major subsystems of one basic element, of which the Space Hotel Berlin concepts consists during the first build-up phase. The central subsystem is a cylindrical "apartment"-module with a large panoramic window which is capable to accommodate about 4 tourists. Connected to the module is a solar array which provides in combination with a rechargeable battery pack sufficient electrical energy for the flight phases when the space hotel enters into the Earth's shadow for about 40 minutes.

Furthermore, a multifunctional connecting node, which can be entered by humans, is docked at the apartment module. This node provides five further docking ports which can be used, if needed in subsequent build-up phases, to connect additional apartment modules. For safety reasons each node has its own rescue capsule, which can be used in emergencies for the immediate return of the tourists back to Earth. With respect to the main apartment axis, the connecting node is 30o aligned, which causes the circular structure of the Space Hotel Berlin with a capacity of about 50 tourists. An artist view of the Space Hotel Europe concept, which is derived from the circular structure of theSpace Hotel Berlin to simplify the rendezvous/docking manoeuvres and to improve the living conditions.

Fascination of Space Travel

The fact, that a significant portion of the public is willing to spend a lot of money on space trips proofs that these are regarded as very promising and fascinating. The confrontation with the high technology of space missions, the heroic myth of astronauts, and the possibility of orbiting planet Earth in just a little more than 80 minutes with a speed of about 30000 kilometres per hour (compared to the 80 days needed a hundred years ago) will represent for each tourist an unforgettable adventure and event. Furthermore, for the first time in his life, the tourist in a space hotel will experience an entirely different environment.

Depending on the rotational velocity of the Space Hotel Berlin various levels of artificial gravity can be obtained, ranging from customary terrestrial gravity (1G) to Mars gravity (1/3 G) and even Lunar gravity (1/6 G), i.e. a human being will weigh only one sixth of his or her earthly weight. In the central node of the Space Hotel Berlin there will be nearly zero gravity. Here the tourist can experience weightlessness. How does one behave if one can not get from A to B in a normal way and "above" or "below" are without meaning. Many of the questions that astronauts were asked-how they manage eating, sleeping, and personal hygiene-can be explored by tourists themselves.

The zerogravity area also offers fascinating opportunities for entirely new sorts of entertainment, games and sports. For example a ball game in zero-gravity and three-dimensional space. Or one can imagine a swimming pool.

The water would not be in a basin, but would float as wobbly water bubbles in space, some of which are several meters in diameter, and one can swim and dive through them. One can imagine that some tourists may want to use the zero-gravity zones for future medical therapies: This could represent a first step towards a future space hospital.

Furthermore, the Coriolis force, which only appears within rotating systems, will baffle the tourist, since it will push him, like a magic force, into a certain direction, depending on his direction of movement.

Probably, the predominant part of the vacation will be spent with the breathtaking view each tourist will have from the panoramic window of each apartment onto the blue home planet from a distance of 400 kilometres.

Even if initially concentrating on his home city and country, soon the tourist will discover earth with its thin and precious atmosphere and a wide variety of picturesque structures on its surface as a totality without national borders.

On the other hand, the view of the infinite expanse of outer space will dramatically symbolise that we owe our human existence, history and future a singular, beautiful, tiny "grain of sand" which we call Earth.

After returning to Earth, the consciousness of many tourists may have changed; it will be expanded and globalised with many potentially positive social consequences, which could help, for example, to lower the dangers for environmental pollution, local conflicts, and war.

Once space tourism is affordable to the broad public, space activities-especially manned space programs-will develop and increase in a way that is hardly imaginable today. A wide variety of space station concepts have been investigated for decades and first concepts for gigantic, circular cities in orbit are available. Perhaps many humans increasingly will harbour the wish to visit the more remote planetary worlds of Mars and of the Earth's Moon some day, according to the Russian space pioneer Ziolkowksy who proclaimed around the year 1900: "Earth is the cradle of humanity, but one cannot always remain in the cradle."

ECO-TOURISM: A NEW FORM OF TOURISM

Eco-tourism focuses on local cultures, wilderness adventures, volunteering, personal growth and learning new ways to live on our vulnerable planet. It is typically defined as travel to destinations where the flora, fauna, and cultural heritage are the primary attractions.

Responsible eco-tourism includes programs that minimize the adverse effects of traditional tourism on the natural environment, and enhance the cultural integrity of local people. Therefore, in addition to evaluating environmental and cultural factors, initiatives by hospitality providers to promote recycling, energy efficiency, water re-use, and the creation of economic opportunities for local communities are an integral part of eco-tourism.

Historical, biological and cultural conservation, preservation, sustainable development etc. are some of the fields closely related to Eco-Tourism. Many professionals have been involved in formulating and developing eco-tourism policies. They come from the fields of Geographic Information Systems, Wildlife Management, Wildlife Photography, Marine Biology and Oceanography, National and State Park Management, Environmental Sciences, Women in Development, Historians and Archaeologists, etc.

Eco-tourism is considered the fastest growing market in the tourism industry, according to the World Tourism Organization with an annual growth rate of 5% worldwide and representing 6% of the world gross domestic product, 11.4% of all consumer spending-not a market to be taken lightly

Definitions, Views, Statements and Objectives: Tourism is changing rapidly as nature, heritage, and recreational destinations become more important, and as conventional tourism is forced to meet tougher environmental requirements.

This presents a challenge to government and private enterprise to develop new approaches to the tourism market. Successful tourism must benefit local populations economically and culturally to give them incentives to protect the natural resources which create the attraction. Strategies must be economically feasible if private investors are to support the projects.

Our goal is to enable people to enjoy and learn about the natural, historical and cultural characteristics of unique environments while preserving the integrity of those sites and stimulating the economic development opportunities in local communities.

Specifically, we believe that successful eco-tourism projects must:

- effectively promote the preservation of entire local ecosystems, not just individual species, vistas or sites;
- be economically viable in order to attract financing and be sustainable:
- be well planned, financed, managed and marketed in order to meet the stringent environmental and recreational demands of a true eco-tourism development.

International Eco-Tourism

Eco-tourism is cultural tourism (a cross-cultural experience), nature tourism (assisting with conservation programmes), a travel-learn experience (discover how we are coping with modernity), a little bit of soft adventure (just being here is an adventure), and benefiting the well-being of indigenous peoples.

Western Samoa, National Eco-tourism Programme: In an era of heightened environmental consciousness and accessibility to exotic locales, countries are busily promoting their natural resources as lures for tourists. The trick with eco-tourism is to preserve the natural resources while also promoting them and accommodating volumes of tourists.

Businesses are creating camps and eco-lodges, and natural resource managers are designing trails and tours.

Most of the popular eco-travel destinations have fragile eco-systems, however, so it is important to maintain a careful balance between preservation and promotion--"sustainable development"--in order to ensure the long-term health of both the eco-systems and the tourism economies.

Science and the Environment

Tourism Concern advocates :

1. Tourism that is just, yielding benefits that are fairly distributed.
2. Tourism that is participatory, recognising the rights of residents.
3. Tourism that is sustainable

Tourism Concern: The term eco-tourism was coined by Héctor Ceballos-Lascuràin in 1983, and was initially used to describe nature-based travel to relatively undisturbed areas with an emphasis on education.

The concept has, however, developed to a scientifically based approach to the planning, management and development of sustainable tourism products and activities. It is an enlightening, participatory travel experience to environments, both natural and cultural, that ensures the sustainable use, at an appropriate level, of environmental resources and, whilst producing viable economic opportunities for the tourism industry and host communities, makes the use of these resources through conservation beneficial to all tourism role players. It is not a marketing ploy, nor is it scenic or nature-based travel. It is an approach that creates a variety of quality tourism products that are:

- environmentally/ ecologically sustainable
- economically viable
- socially and psychologically acceptable

The result of which reflects:

- an integrated and holistic approach to product development
- capacity building in host communities
- a sense and uniqueness of place
- commitment to the greening of the tourism industry.

What is Sustainable Tourism?

It provides a lot of information to tourists. Travelers not only learn about the destination, they learn how to help sustain its character while deepening their own travel experiences. Residents learn that the ordinary and familiar may be of interest and value to outsiders.

It supports integrity of place. Destination-savvy travelers seek out businesses that emphasize the character of the locale in terms of architecture, cuisine, heritage, aesthetics, and ecology. Tourism revenues in turn raise local perceived value of those assets.

It benefits residents. Travel businesses do their best to employ and train local people, buy local supplies, and use local services.

It conserves resources. Environmentally aware travelers favor businesses that minimize pollution, waste, energy consumption, water usage, landscaping chemicals, and unnecessary nighttime lighting.

It respects local culture and tradition. Foreign visitors learn about and observe local etiquette, including using at least a few courtesy words in the local language. Residents learn how to deal with foreign expectations that may differ from their own.

It does not abuse its product. Stakeholders anticipate development pressures and apply limits and management techniques to prevent the "loved to death" syndrome. Businesses cooperate to sustain natural habitats, heritage sites, scenic appeal, and local culture.

It strives for quality, not quantity. Communities measure tourism success not by sheer numbers of visitors, but by length of stay, money spent, and quality of experience. It means great trips. Satisfied, excited visitors bring new knowledge home and send friends off to experience the same thing-which provides continuing business for the destination.

Concept of Eco-tourism

Eco-tourism is "responsible travel to natural areas that conserves the environment and sustains the well-being of local people." Sometimes it is defined as a sub-category of sustainable tourism or a segment of the larger nature tourism market.

It includes an interpretation/learning experience, is delivered to small groups by small-scale businesses, and stresses local ownership, particularly for rural people.

What is the difference between eco-tourism and nature-based travel?

While nature-based tourism is just travel to natural places, eco-tourism provides local benefits-environmentally, culturally and economically. A nature-based tourist may just go bird watching; an ecotourist goes bird watching with a local guide, stays in a locally operated ecolodge and contributes to the local economy.

Where does Sustainable Tourism fit in?

Sustainable Tourism embraces all segments of the industry with guidelines and criteria that seek to reduce environmental impacts, particularly the use of non-renewable resources, using measurable benchmarks, and to improve tourism's contribution to sustainable development and environmental conservation

Sustainable Eco-tourism:

- Minimizes environmental impacts using benchmarks
- Improves contribution to local sustainable development
- Requires lowest possible consumption of non-renewable resources
- Sustains the well-being of local people
- Stresses local ownership
- Supports efforts to conserve the environment
- Contributes to biodiversity

Ecosystem: A dynamic complex of plant, animal, fungal and microorganism communities and their associated non-living environment interacting as an ecological unit.

Eco-tourism: Responsible travel to natural areas which conserves the environment and sustains the livelihood of local people.

Eco-tourism Activities: Activities included in a tour that are designed to entertain clients and are coordinated by a professional guide or interpreter. Over 80 activities have been listed for eco-tourism, such as birdwatching, hiking, diving, kayaking, participating in cultural events, photography, and mountaineering.

Eco-tourism Product: A combination of resources, activities, and services, which are sold and managed through professional tour operators.

Eco-tourism Resources: Natural and cultural features that attract visitors, such as landscapes, endemic or rare flora and fauna, cultural festivals, and historical monuments.

Eco-tourism Services: Tourism services such as transportation, food, lodging, guiding and interpretation services which cause minimal damage to the biological and cultural environments and promote a better understanding of the natural and cultural history of an area.

Stakeholders: Individuals who have a vested interest in development, including community members; environmental, social, and community NGOs; natural resource, planning, and government officials; hotel owners, tour operators, guides, transportation providers, and representatives from other related services in the private sector.

Sustainable Development: Development that meets the needs and aspirations of the current generation without compromising the ability to meet those of future generations.

Principles of Sustainable Tourism

Increasing evidence shows that an integrated approach to tourism planning and management is now required to achieve sustainable tourism. It is only recently that there has been a growing recognition of the importance of combining the needs of traditional urban management (transportation, land use planning, marketing, economic development, fire and safety etc.) with the need to plan for tourism.

Some of the most important principles of sustainable tourism development include:

- Tourism should be initiated with the help of broad-based community-inputs and the community should maintain control of tourism development.
- Tourism should provide quality employment to its community residents and a linkage between the local businesses and tourism should be established.
- A code of practice should be established for tourism at all levels-national, regional, and local-based on internationally accepted standards. Guidelines for tourism operations, impact assessment, monitoring of cumulative impacts, and limits to acceptable change should be established.
- Education and training programmes to improve and manage heritage and natural resources should be established.

3

ROLE IN SUSTAINABLE DEVELOPMENT

INTRODUCTION

A primary challenge of local governance, both today and in decades ahead, is to steer increasingly external, global forces on local development so that development achieves the shared vision of the local population. In cities, towns and villages throughout the world, the primary responsibility for this steering process rests with the institution of local government and its diverse local authorities.

As providers of social services, builders of economic infrastructure, regulators of economic activity, and managers of the natural environment, local authorities have many direct instruments at their disposal to influence development. Yet in addition to their direct roles in the development process, perhaps the most important role that local authorities can play in a global economy is that of facilitator among the diverse interests seeking to influence the direction of local development.

Only with such a facilitator can a community of diverse interests define a shared vision and act consistent with this vision.

The role of local authorities as facilitators in the development process is reinforced through municipal international cooperation (MIC). With globalisation, the governance challenges facing local authorities in different parts of the world have increased in their similarities, transcending the national political and economic systems upon which different communities rely. These shared challenges of governance have instigated thousands of local authorities to establish municipal international cooperation projects and to join international local government organisations (LGOs) to advocate for local self-governance and control over the development process.

Even prior to the UN Conference on Environment and Development, but particularly since the adoption of Agenda 21, many local authorities and their LGOs have focused on the unique challenges of governance for sustainable development. At the local level, sustainable development is achieved by steering local development activities to simultaneously achieve three objectives:

* increased local social welfare;
* greater, and more equitably distributed, local economic wealth; and
* enhanced integrity of local ecosystems.

Thousands of local authorities, in partnership with their communities and supported by MIC activities, have instigated Local Agenda 21 processes to create a shared vision for local development that is consistent with the sustainable development concept. In response to these visions, local authorities have been adapting their practices and activities to steer local development along the sustainable development path. Local Agenda 21 processes, in conjunction with decentralisation policies originating at the national level, are transforming local governance and reorienting the process of local development in communities throughout the world.

Tourism is one of the many external forces influencing the direction and options for local development. The question of whether tourism can be sustainable-that is, whether it can contribute to local sustainable development-is rightfully addressed in the context of the Local Agenda 21 process.

A truly legitimate and practical discussion on sustainable tourism must take place in and with the communities that are being influenced by tourist industry development. It must create accountability of the tourism industry to locally-defined development visions. This paper provides an general call for the tourism industry, through both its local and transnational agents, to join and support the Local Agenda 21 processes in communities where tourism is a fundamental development force.

The true proof of "sustainable tourism" will be the sustainable development of local communities that serve as tourist destinations. It is time for the sustainable tourism debate to focus on this challenge. Local authorities worldwide welcome the leadership of the UN Commission on Sustainable Development, and the interest of the tourism industry, to reduce tourism's negative impacts and to increase the positive contribution of tourism business and consumption activity to local sustainable development.

Initiatives of Industry

Main Hurdels

Tourism is a recognised global industry-one of the largest industries in the world. Like any global industry, tourist business activities can have considerable impact on local development trends. The local impacts of the tourism industry are diverse and are often unique to the tourism sector.

Tourist activities, as traditionally defined by the tourism industry, fundamentally involve the transportation and hosting of the tourism consumer in a local community, i.e., "tourist destination," where the tourist product is consumed. No other global industry structures itself in such a way that the consumer is brought to the product, rather than the product being delivered to the consumer in his or her own community. This structural difference produces unique social impacts upon the local tourist community, including the interruption of local customs and lifestyles, the spread of infectious diseases, changes in local demographics, and changes in local housing and labor markets.

The primary product of tourism is not something produced by the industry. The product is often the heritage, wealth, and expected legacy of the community that serves as the tourist destination. The business activity of the tourism industry is to promote the "salable" or appealing aspects of the community, transport non-residents into the community, manage the hospitality for and guide the activities of these visitors, and provide them with goods and services to purchase during their stay. If these business activities degrade the community's heritage and wealth, then the community suffers more directly than the consumer, who can return to his or her own community without responsibility for or awareness of the impacts of his tourist activities.

Tourism activities can, in particular, degrade the social and natural wealth of a community.

The intrusion of large numbers of uninformed foreigners into local social systems can undermine pre-existing social relationships and values. This is particularly a problem where tourism business is centered in traditional social systems, such as isolated communities or indigenous peoples.

Tourism in natural areas, euphemistically called "eco-tourism," can be a major source of degradation of local ecological, economic and social systems. The intrusion of large numbers of foreigners with high-consumption and high-waste habits into natural areas, or into towns with inadequate waste management infrastructure, can produce changes to those natural areas at a rate that is far greater than imposed by local residents. These tourism-related changes are particularly deleterious when local residents rely on those natural areas for their sustenance. Resulting economic losses can encourage socially deleterious economic activities such as prostitution, crime, and migrant and child labour.

Solutions

Solutions to adverse tourism impacts are to be found in the shared interest of local communities, tourism businesses, and tourism consumers to maintain the natural wealth and social heritage of the tourist destination. In the first instance, therefore, an institutional mechanism must be established, relative to each destination, to articulate and develop this sense of shared interest. To secure the legitimacy of these mechanisms, the participation of all interested local groups or interests must be guaranteed. Dialogue must take place in an open and transparent way. Experience demonstrates that if dialogue among interested parties is to have a real impact on development, it must generate accountability among these parties with regards to future investments, practices and policies. Consensus or decisions arising from dialogue must be reflected in institutional action. Only through such accountability can interests maintain a commitment to continued dialogue and a common agenda for local tourism development.

Experience demonstrates that this accountability should be reciprocal between individual or private interests and societal or public interests. Without such reciprocal accountability, local communities are typically forced to choose, in conflict, between private and public benefits, even if ample "win-win" development choices exist. On the one hand, accountability requires that property owners are provided with opportunity to retain the economic value of their property, either through sale or income generating activity.

On the other hand, private market relationships, including property ownership, do not provide sufficient basis for social accountability related to "public goods," including ecological integrity and social heritage. Private property titles do not recognise the concepts of ecological integrity or social heritage. Excessive reliance upon private property ownership as a guide in development has in fact contributed to the deterioration of public goods.

Within such a framework of accountability, numerous instruments are available to guide local tourist development on a sustainable path. These instruments include:

* heritage preservation requirements for site developments and building designs;
* programs to exchange land and development rights from non-suitable to suitable development areas;
* private heritage and green space stewardship programs;
* tax benefits accruing to property owners exercising sustainable development practices;
* tourism taxes and development fees to support construction and maintenance of required infrastructure.

However, without true commitment to the sustainable tourism agenda, these instruments are not themselves sufficient to prevent the steady erosion, by legally sanctioned private actions, of local natural wealth and social heritage.

Therefore, support from the international, national, provincial and local levels of industry and government, is essential to the success of this agenda.

Agencies and Partnerships for Change

Fortunately, in more than 2,000 communities in 64 countries Local Agenda 21 partnership forums already exist to serve as a mechanism for sustainable tourism dialogue. Where these forums are weak or have not yet addressed tourism issues, the tourist industry, local government organisations (LGOs) and concerned NGOs can serve as a catalyst for dialogue.

A particular opportunity exists in those countries where Local Agenda 21 national campaigns (in more than 20 countries) or where National Councils for Sustainable Development (NCSDs-in about 70 countries) have been established. NCSDs can play a key role in providing country-level support to local review of the sustainable tourism agenda. Through their international facilitating body, the Earth Council, a comprehensive effort between industry, NGOs, LGOs and NCSDs can be established. Of additional interest at the local level is the potential role of local tourism offices or Convention and Visitor Bureaus (CVBs) that have been created through public-private partnerships to promote local tourist attractions.

Where motivated to support sustainable tourism development, the CVBs could serve as facilitators of working groups, within the context of Local Agenda 21 activities, on sustainable tourism development. Where CVBs or their related international body(ies) have made no express commitment to sustainable development, local authorities, as primary funders of CVBs, are in an excellent position to mobilise their awareness and support.

Internationally, alliances between LGOs and various tourism industry trade associations, trade unions and consumer organisations can support awareness raising and local demonstration projects that may serve as models for other local communities on a country or regional basis.

CONSUMER BEHAVIOR TO PROMOTE SUSTAINABLE TOURISM

Problems

Tourism-related consumption has three stages of impact. First, prior to departure, tourists purchase travel-related clothing and equipment, which may be produced under conditions that undermine the social and ecological sustainability of the producing communities. Second, when tourists travel long distances to tourist destinations, they create considerable atmospheric pollution and other impacts on the global environment. Third, upon arrival at the tourist destination, tourists often continue their accustomed habits of consumption, even though these destinations may not have the infrastructure required to manage those consumption patterns. This paper will focus on the second and third stages of impact.

In addition to high altitude emissions from long distance air travel, air travel produces considerable negative local environmental impacts, including ground level emissions of VOCs and particulates, disposal of fuel, hazardous chemicals and solid waste, noise pollution, and wildlife and habitat disruption. Marine dumping of wastes from cruise ships is an increasing concern.

However, with nearly 600 million international travelers in 1997, surprisingly little public information is available on the environmental and social impacts of long distance travel. For instance, individual travelers receive far greater information about the impacts of their local automobile use than of their air or cruise ship transportation. Motor vehicle pollution is typically more highly regulated than aircraft and ship pollution.

Following arrival at tourist destinations, the tourism industry typically strives to host tourists according to the standards and amenities of their country of origin. These hospitality standards mimic-and encourage-the high consumption lifestyles of developed countries. For instance, luxury hotel rooms, with high levels of energy and water consumption, are given the highest rankings or "stars" in international hotel rankings. These "luxury" consumption standards, using current technologies, are themselves globally unsustainable (i.e., in an equitable world).

The most immediate observable impacts of introducing these high consumption practices into lower consumption communities are:

* degradation of local water and soil quality, with direct impacts on local health and economies, as a result of the lack of adequate water, drainage, waste water, and waste management infrastructure to manage the higher volumes of waste produced by higher levels of consumption;
* reduced access by local residents to land, housing and marine resources through, among other things, reallocation of these community resources to foreign tourist residents and inflation of local prices;
* destruction of traditional sources of income.

Solutions

The most direct way to reduce the adverse impacts of tourism-related travel is to increase opportunities for people to engage in appealing tourism activities in their own cities, regions or countries. In various cities of the world, this local tourism concept is known as "green tourism."

Green tourism-in contrast to "eco-tourism," which relies on travel to distant locations-seeks to provide recreational attractions and hospitality facilities to local people within their local regions, thereby reducing tourism-related travel. While green tourism has the positive economic effect of stimulating local economic activity, it reduces the flow of foreign currency to developing nations-and any resulting economic benefits that may accrue to developing towns and cities from these revenue flows. However, short of definitive actions by the tourism industry and host countries/communities to reduce the negative environmental impacts of foreign travel and the negative social impacts of foreign tourist enclaves in developing nations, green tourism advocates will continue to build support among tourism consumers.

Solutions to tourism-related pollution in the travel and tourism industry are technologically available. Overcoming economic barriers to their implementation may require government regulation, the development of economic instruments, and industry self-regulation.

The industry has every opportunity to institute voluntary initiatives and self-regulation to address green tourism advocates and those calling for government regulation. The growing effort among international hotel chains, for instance, to offer guests the option of reusing their bedroom towels and linens demonstrates the ability of the industry to respond in one area of impact.

However, more comprehensive efforts are required to tangibly resolve accelerating environmental and social impacts.

In this regard, the establishment of formal environmental management systems (EMSs) in each business establishment provides a way for tourism businesses to identify their adverse social and environmental impacts and to institute a programme for continuous reductions of those impacts. EMS registration programmes such as ISO 14001 and European EMAS regimes offer extensive guidance to tourism businesses, and deserve the active support of international tourism industry associations.

Ultimately, the solution to adverse environmental impacts arising from local tourist consumption is the establishment of waste reduction programs and appropriate waste management systems and infrastructure, particularly in developing country destinations.

Again a choice exists between voluntary and regulatory measures. National governments and tourism businesses, which receive disproportional economic benefits from tourism, share an interest in maintaining tourismrelated hard currency inflows, and should either directly provide such infrastructure or ensure that funds are made available to local authorities for this purpose. Without such support, powers should be provided to local authorities to increase local revenues from tourism, through local airport taxes, hotel and service taxes, and development fees, to finance infrastructure construction and maintenance. Only through such economic instruments can the public costs of tourism activity be "internalised" in the local tourist economy.

Local revenue measures need to be carefully coordinated across municipal jurisdictions on a regional basis to ensure coordinated infrastructure development. Without a coordinated regional infrastructure development approach, pollution from communities without infrastructure can undo the environmental benefits of infrastructure investments in neighboring communities. Where statutory regional planning bodies do not exist to provide coordination, Local Agenda 21 forums may provide a flexible mechanism for multi-jurisdictional coordination.

Tourist businesses can make a significant voluntary contribution to resolving the social costs of tourism by:

* providing local resident employment and training opportunities, including in traditional trades and crafts;
* establishing purchasing guidelines that favor local goods and services procurement;
* making donations and investments in local recreational facilities, parks, cultural facilities and security operations (which also serve to improve local tourist amenities as well);
* establishing local profit-sharing arrangements.

Failing necessary voluntary measures, local governments can institute economic incentives and regulatory measures to reward best practices and prevent severe social impacts that need to be resolved at public expense.

Ultimately, in the face of private establishments that demonstrate no long-term commitment to maintaining the preconditions for tourism-which include public safety, environmental quality, infrastructure maintenance, and economic justice-local authorities need to use all powers available to protect the cultural and environmental wealth that make an attractive tourist destination.

Agents and Partnerships for Change

A partnership approach to addressing negative impacts of tourism consumption requires, above all, assumption of responsibility and voluntary action by the tourism industry. For example, within the framework of a voluntary EMS approach, partnerships can be established between local governments, airport authorities, regional air quality agencies, airlines, trade unions, NGOs and resident associations to develop an action programme to reduce local airport pollution. Following the model of the "Responsible Care" programme in the chemical industry, these partnerships could be supported by international travel and tourism organisations and related industry associations.

Measures to reduce high altitude pollution by aircraft require similar initiatives by the industry and government at the national and international levels.

Of critical importance is the creation of mechanisms to inform and involve tourism consumers in making educated choices about their activities as tourists in distant tourist destinations. Ideally, these efforts would ensure that tourism consumers, as with industry, begin to recognise and understand tourist destinations as living communities that deserve their support and respect.

Communications from tourism consumers to tourism industry and to local authorities about their desire to reduce the adverse impacts of their tourism activities can be essential to mobilising changes in industry and government practices.

International consumer advocacy organisations and trade unions can play an important role in informing consumers about tourism development activities that violate basic principles of sustainable development. Provision of such information to LGOs can facilitate local authority responsiveness to identified problems.

Other actions to reduce the adverse local impacts of tourism consumption at local tourist destinations can be developed within the context of the Local Agenda 21 activities outlined in sections B and D.

PROMOTING BROAD-BASED SUSTAINABLE DEVELOPMENT

Problems

Many of the technologies and measures required for sustainable development in the tourism sector are clear. Resources exist within the tourism industry-which annually generates hundreds of billions of dollars-to apply these technologies and to make development within the sector more equitable. However, as the experiences of hundreds of local authorities demonstrate, through their engagement in broad-based sustainable development planning through Local Agenda 21, the appropriate application of technologies and resources requires effective and truly accountable development partnerships. If industry and government are to protect and sustain the social, cultural and environmental wealth that attracts tourists, they must build more ambitious and committed partnerships to plan, manage and invest in this wealth.

In this respect, the primary barrier to sustainable development through tourism is an over reliance on market mechanisms to guide tourism development and consumption decisions. The market-which treats cultural and environmental wealth as free, "public goods" and which responds to degradation of this wealth as a "free rider"-provides instruments to guide development, but is insensitive to many requirements of sustainable tourism. Furthermore, in a global market such as tourism, the problem of "leakage", whereby the economic benefits of local tourism activity flow out of the local community and country back to a foreign corporate headquarters, is another indication of the inadequacy of simple market-driven approaches.

Sustainable tourism development requires a partnership among the stakeholders of the local tourist destination. This partnership must use both market and non-market instruments to implement a shared sustainable development vision. Without such a partnership, advocacy for sustainable development becomes a conflictive struggle between an industry which seeks to respond only to market forces and a public sector which, when accountable, acts to protect public goods and wealth for future generations. Therefore, the key problem at this stage of the "sustainable tourism" debate is the creation of tangible, working local partnerships. These local partnerships must be encouraged and supported by national governments and industry, and not undermined by "higher level" agreements. To succeed, local residents and their local authorities need to more fully recognise the significant adverse impacts of tourism development and must be informed about opportunities for reducedimpact tourism development. Tourism businesses need to recognise and support the social conditions (e.g., security, public health) and the cultural and environmental wealth that make a community an attractive tourist destination.

Solutions

The UN Commission on Sustainable Development has repeatedly recognised Local Agenda 21 planning as an effective partnership mechanism for implementing Agenda 21 in cities and local communities. Experience with Local Agenda 21 activities in hundreds of communities since 1990 has highlighted a number of principles for effective sustainable development planning.

These principles can also provide the basis for effective partnerships for sustainable tourism planning and development in local tourist destinations. These partnerships can be established either within or independent from existing Local Agenda 21 activities.

The principles for Local Agenda 21 planning are as follows:

* Participation and Transparency, that involves local residents, representing all major groups of society, in Local Agenda 21 planning and makes information aboutsustainable development easily available to the general public.
* Partnerships that build collective responsibility for planning, decision making,problem solving, project implementation and evaluation.
* Accountability that holds all partners answerable for their actions.

* Systemic Approach that addresses the underlying causes of social, economic and ecological problems in an integrated way, focusing on the entire systems that are affected, rather than only problem symptoms.
* Ecological Limits, that are defined by Earth's carrying capacity and that serve as the limits for development.
* Equity and Justice, that are secured locally through the provision of equal opportunities and human rights, and globally through development cooperation partnerships between developed and developing nations.
* Concern for the Future, that requires long-term planning and action that addresses both immediate needs and long-term trends.

These principles can be applied, in working partnerships, to evaluate and improve efforts to address sensitive tourism development issues, such as:

* inequitable distribution of tourism revenues and "leakage" of revenues to foreign shores;
* displacement of pre-existing local settlements by tourism developments;
* equal access to local coastal and recreational resources and controversies over uses and long-term protection of those areas;
* concerns related to lack of foreign tourist sensitivity to cultural traditions and sites.

Local Partnerships for Change

The primary partnerships for sustainable tourism development will be local partnerships, addressing the unique development goals and needs of each community. Where Local Agenda 21 activities are underway, a Sustainable Tourism Working Group could be established within the existing Local Agenda 21 planning structures to facilitate planning and action.

Notwithstanding the primacy of local partnerships, the transnational nature of tourism requires transnational partnerships to support sustainable tourism planning activities at the local and national levels. The Local Agenda 21 process has established a new mechanism for such transnational partnership, called "Local Agenda 21 Charters." Initiated by the Netherlands Ministry of Foreign Affairs, in cooperation with the International Union of Local Authorities, the International Council for Local Environmental Initiatives, and Towns & Development, the Local Agenda 21 Charters process provides a mechanism for local communities to factor issues of global responsibility within their Local Agenda 21 activities. Two local authorities, typically on a North-South and East-West basis, establish a "Charter" agreement that specifies areas of mutual support to jointly address relevant issues of global equity and sustainability. Presently, 20 local authorities have established the first Local Agenda 21 Charters.

Ultimately, tourism consumers must be rallied to the sustainable tourism agenda, thereby shaping both the market and public policy. Tourism consumers in existing Local Agenda 21 communities may find the Local Agenda 21 Charters mechanism useful in supporting sustainable development in popular tourist destinations. Existing "twinning" or "sister city" relationships with cities that are located in tourist regions can provide the basis for a possible Local Agenda 21 Charters relationship.

COASTAL AREAS AND THEIR IMPACTS

Problems

Economic development activities in any sensitive natural area pose a particular challenge for sustainable development. Coastal areas host the most productive marine ecosystems and serve as spawning grounds for the oceans. The degradation of coastal areas in many countries, with the resulting impacts upon coastal settlements and fisheries, justifies strict local controls on further coastal development.

Coastal zones are dynamic in nature, responding to daily tidal changes as well as long term events such as sea level rising. This dynamic quality offers a defense from extreme weather events. Rigid infrastructure from coastal development can inhibit the ability of coastal ecosystems to respond to changes. Since coastal areas are the most highly populated regions on Earth, their protection requires unique attention and the effective management of numerous competing interests.

In many coastal areas, tourism development is destroying or marginalising dwindling habitats for marine animals and spawning fish, as well as the livelihoods of traditional fishing families and villages.

Unregulated water sport activities and machinery are adding to this toll. Lack of effective waste water treatment for tourist facilities is making a significant contribution to coastal water pollution. Excessive private tourist development is denying equitable human access to beaches and coastal waters, cutting off local populations from their coastal heritage. Inappropriate development in high risk storm areas is costing families, local economies and governments billions of dollars annually.

Solutions

As a first measure towards the sustainable management of coastal areas, governments at all levels, working in partnership with private foundations and investors, should establish designated coastal areas where development will be forever restricted. Protection of these areas should be stringently enforced. In areas where coastal development can be socially and environmentally justified, tourism development should be designed as a form of low-impact economic activity relative to other development alternatives.

The reputation and viability of the sustainable tourism concept depends upon the definition and implementation of clear management objectives for each coastal area. These objectives should clearly designate ecologically and socially/culturally sensitive areas as well as high risk areas.

Appropriate tourism uses should be designated for each area according to levels of sensitivity and risk. Education programs should be established to inform tourists about these management objectives.

The aims of any sustainable tourism development in coastal areas should be to:

* recognise the economic value of existing coastal ecosystems, towns and heritage sites by providing opportunity for local revenue-generation through managed tourist use of these areas;
* design tourism developments, in cooperation with local stakeholders, to suit the unique ecological and social characteristics of each coastal site;
* use tourism investment to develop and upgrade the watershed, solid waste and waste water management systems for coastal cities and towns;
* ensure equitable access to coastal areas by all people, with a specific emphasis on using tourism development as a means to upgrade and manage traditional social uses, for example, through the designation of special natural/cultural heritage sites.

In addition sound planning and management to achieve the above aims, the following opportunities for low-impact tourism development could be considered:

* application of low-impact building and transportation designs, materials and technologies;
* control of waste production through recycling and efficiency measures;
* co-investment by the tourism industry, government and local residents to upgrade existing settlements and urban infrastructure, including drainage and sewerage infrastructure.

Local Agenda 21

The planning and management of coastal development typically requires the cooperation of local stakeholders-including property owners, residents, local business groups, and local authorities-and government agencies at the national and sub-national levels. In general, some institutional mechanism will need to be established to facilitate cooperation and consensus-building among these actors. As coastal areas typically extend beyond the jurisdictions of individual local authorities, regional coastal management agencies are often established through inter-municipal cooperation or sub-national action to provide effective multi-jurisdictional coordination. Alternatively, private foundations or regional/national NGOs have frequently been used as a mechanism for coastal area planning. Under ideal circumstances, tourism industry representatives, including property owners, will be directly involved in coastal planning and management schemes. In such cases, the tourism industry, in particular transnational businesses, needs to make a good faith commitment not to circumvent local/regional planning and management discussions by directly lobbying national government for special permissions and considerations.

Ultimately, actions to reduce the adverse impacts of tourism on coastal areas will reflect the principles of Local Agenda 21 planning outlined earlier.

RURAL TOURISM AND SUSTAINABLE DEVELOPMENT

Rural tourism is a segment of the total tourist industry which is particularly important in Hungary, in a country with no spectacular natural attractions, without seaside, high mountains, rainforest or herds of exotic animals. However, its attractive cultural landscapes with small villages, thermal springs, rivers and lakes, combined with the traditional hospitality, are able to offer pleasant experiences to the kind of tourist who is looking for relaxation and recreation in a calm setting. On one hand, rural tourism development can play an important role in the diversification of the Hungarian tourist supply and in the creation of a more complex and colourful country image. On the other hand, rural tourism is not only the end, but the means to stimulate economic growth, to increase the viability of underdeveloped regions, and to improve the living standards of local populations.

If rural tourism is to fulfil all these roles, it has to be developed in a way that ensures the long-term sustainability of the resources and that of the development progress itself. But what is a sustainable way of development in rural tourism ? How can sustainability be monitored and promoted in rural destinations ? This paper attempts to answer these questions by presenting the current situation of Hungarian rural tourism through indicators that are considered to be relevant for this type of tourism.

THE CONCEPT OF RURAL TOURISM

Rural tourism is an old and a new phenomenon at the same time. Interest in countryside recreation started to grew already in the 19th century as a reaction to the stress of the increasing urbanisation and industrialisation. The rural scene was admired by poets and artists. The new railway companies transported more and more tourists to the countryside. However, the rural tourism of our era is different: the number of tourists involved has increased significantly and tourism has developed in all types of countryside instead of being limited to areas of exceptional scenic beauty.

Though it seems to be simple to define rural tourism as "tourism that takes place in the countryside", this definition does not include the complexity of the activity and the different forms and meanings developed in different countries. According to a broader definition, "rural tourism includes a range of activities, services and amenities provided by farmers and rural people to attract tourists to their area in order to generate extra income for their businesses" (Gannon, 1988, in te Kloeze, 1994).

If this broader concept is accepted, rural tourism covers not only farm tourism or agritourism (which is generally what rural tourism means for most people), but also special interest nature holidays, touring in rural areas and residential tourism, and the services include-besides accommodation-events, festivities, outdoor recreation, production and sale of handicrafts and agricultural products, etc.

The term "rural tourism" has different meanings in different countries. In Finland, for example, it usually means renting out cottages to visitors or providing catering services in the countryside. In Hungary, a special term of "village tourism" exists, indicating that only activities and services provided in villages are included in this kind of tourism (as we will see later, village tourism typically covers low-priced accommodation, involvement in agricultural or other local activities is not common). In Slovenia, the most important form of rural tourism is tourism on family farms, where guests stay either with the farmer family or in a guest house, but visiting farms to have a meal and explore the farmyard is also popular (Verbole, 1995).

In the Netherlands, the rural tourist product means especially camping on the farm, with most farm services being linked to route-bound activities as cycling, walking or horse-riding (Peters et al, 1994). In Greece, the main provision of rural tourism product is bed and breakfast with accommodation in traditionally furnished rooms and with traditional breakfasts often based on home-made products. Complementary activities-currently still on a limited scale-include restaurants and refreshment facilities or the organisation of cultural and recreational activities (Turner, 1993).

Rural tourism is one of the main priorities of tourism development in many European countries, including Hungary. The market for rural holidays is growing at the same time as the future of many rural regions is uncertain, due to changes in agricultural practice (including the effects of the Common Agricultural Policy in the EU) or the increasing attractiveness of urban living standards.

Rural tourism seems to be an appropriate tool to revitalise the declining rural areas and to ensure their sustainable future by job retention or even job creation, increased job diversity, service retention, farm support, broadened cultural provision, landscape and nature conservation or the maintenance of rural arts and crafts as tourist attractions.

Rural tourism often provides an incentive (and part of the necessary funding) for infrastructural development, which then contributes to the growth of other economic activities in rural areas. A specific benefit of rural tourism development can be the increasing number of opportunities for social interaction for local people who often live relatively isolated lives in agricultural communities (Swarbrooke, 1996).

RURAL TOURISM AND SUSTAINABILITY

Rural tourism is often considered to be intrinsically sustainable, for it attracts small number of visitors, there is no need for extensive infrastructural development, tourists are usually genuinely interested in the local culture and traditions. One of the main attraction of rural holidays is the personal interaction with local residents, so hosts and guests are able to share ideas and knowledge, and consequently tourism can fulfil its role as the "industry of peace", as a tool of mutual understanding.

Nevertheless, if rural tourism development is analysed on a deeper level, certain doubts arise concerning intrinsic sustainability. The most significant issue to be investigated is the economic profitability of rural tourist services, since the demand is often seasonal, the occupancy rates are low and the investment required for creating or improving facilities for tourists is often high. In most rural tourist destinations it is quite unlikely that tourism can be viable as a sole source of income. Rural tourism can usually be only one of the income-generating alternatives in a region, so its role in sustainable development is highly influenced by the performances of other economic sectors (especially agriculture).

Concerning environmental sustainability, experiences suggest that considerable investment needs to be undertaken in the environmental management of vulnerable natural assets in order to make rural tourism in any sense sustainable. Tourists are usually most attracted by the industrially least developed regions, which are particularly sensitive to human interference. In addition, managed agricultural landscapes do not always meet the expectations of tourists based on the images of "traditional rural" landscapes represented in the tourist literature and in promotional materials.

Tourism development also influences the socio-cultural characteristics of rural destinations, both in positive and negative way (Keane & Quinn, 1990; Peters et al, 1994). As positive impacts, the following can be mentioned: rural tourism usually encourages better use of the available resources (like land, labour, capital, natural and cultural attractions), brings about socio-economic change, contributes to heritage protection and the conservation of the rural environment, provides more social contact for local people and increases their chance to learn about other cultures. As negative impacts, tourism in rural areas changes or damages the rural landscape and the natural and cultural values of a given region, rearranges social stratification (this can also be interpreted as a positive change in certain cases), puts additional pressure on the local community, changes their rhythm of life, threatens their privacy or results in the inauthentic presentation of local customs and traditions, adapted to the tourists' wishes.

SUSTAINABLE DEVELOPMENT OF TOURISM

The concept of sustainable development was introduced by the World Commission on Environment and Development in the Brundtland Report in 1987, defining sustainable development as "development that meets the needs of the present without compromising the ability of future generations to meet their own needs". Tourism is one of the foremost economic activities around the world, having transported more than 617 million people internationally and generated 448 billion USD in receipts in 1997 (WTO, 1998). It is a major economic force, having generated in 1996 an estimated 3,153.3 billion USD in gross output, creating employment for app. 255 million people, producing app. 10.7 per cent of world gross domestic product, investing app. 766 billion USD in new facilities and equipment annually, and contributing more than app. 653.3 billion USD to global tax revenue (WTTC, 1996).

The volume and significance of tourism clearly shows that it is not enough to develop new forms of "alternative" tourism in order to minimise the negative and maximise the positive impacts of tourism development. The whole sector must be developed and managed in a way that it does not damage the natural and socio-cultural environment and this is the responsibility of the worldwide tourism industry.

Though the Brundtland report made no special reference to tourism, since its publication, the role of tourism in the process of continuously misusing the Earth's resources has been analysed and the concept of sustainable tourism appeared.

Sustainable tourism has several-often seriously debated-definitions. According to the definition of the Federation of Nature and National Parks, sustainable tourism is "all forms of tourism development, management and activity that maintain the environmental, social and economic integrity and well-being of natural, built and cultural resources in perpetuity" (FNNP, 1993). A publication by the Tourism Concern and the World Wide Fund for Nature defines sustainable tourism as tourism which "operates within natural capacities for the regeneration and future productivity of natural resources; recognises the contribution that people and communities, customs and lifestyles, make to the tourism experience; accepts that these people must have an equitable share in the economic benefits of tourism; and is guided by the wishes of local people and communities in the host areas" (Tourism Concern & WWF, 1992). Though the existing definitions usually differ in their focus or level of elaborateness, the main message of the Brundtland Report seems to be more and more accepted by the tourism industry all over the world. However, the notion of sustainability is a very complex one and it has many ramifications (Mowforth & Munt, 1998).

Ecological sustainability, which means that tourism development does not cause irreversible changes in a given destination's ecosystem, is the most commonly accepted dimension, since there is an obvious need all over the world to protect natural resources from the negative impacts of tourism activities. The general growth of environment-awareness has significantly contributed to this trend. Social sustainability refers to the ability of a community to absorb tourism (both the industry and the tourists themselves) without the creation of social disharmony.

Cultural sustainability in the context of tourism assumes that a given community is able to retain or adapt their own distinctive cultural traits against the pressure of both the so-called "tourist culture" and the "residual culture" of the visitors (Jafari, 1987). Economic sustainability refers to a level of economic gain from tourism that is sufficient to provide an appropriate income for the local community (compared to the inconvenience caused by the activities of the tourism sector) and to cover all the costs of any special measure taken to satisfy the tourists (thus a precondition of economic sustainability is the attractiveness of an area and the perceived high quality of its tourist supply: without being in a competitive position in the world market, no destination can be economically sustainable).

The different aspects of sustainability do not compete, but must be seen as equally important. High level of economic profitability must not be considered as a tool to cover over the damage done to social or natural resources, but the relative fragile nature of these latter must not create a planning environment where economic considerations are not being taken (properly). Sustainable tourism development has to be economically viable and naturally and culturally sensitive at the same time. As we could see, inappropriate tourism development results in increasing stress on destinations and consequently in negative changes in the destinations' physical, economic and socio-cultural characteristics. In order to avoid or minimise unfavourable impacts, decision-makers must be aware of all the factors that play a role in the development process. In the measurement of the progress that an individual destination is making towards sustainable tourism development, sustainability indicators are commonly accepted as one set of useful tools.

SUSTAINABILITY INDICATORS

"Indicators measure information with which decision-makers may reduce the chances of unknowingly taking poor decisions" (WTO, 1996). In other words, indicators are a set of useful measures of those factors that are important to the decision-makers (the relative significance of these factors depend on their relevance to the development objectives of a given destination, and on their importance to tourists). "Indicators are both a tool for management today and an investment in the future, since they reduce the risk of inadvertent damage to the resource base on which the [tourist] industry depends" (WTO, 1996).

Based on different guidelines and recommendations (Tourism Concern & WWF, 1992; McCool & Watson, 1994; Murphy, 1994; Howie, 1996; Swarbrooke, 1996; WTO, 1996; Mowforth & Munt, 1998), the indicators suggested for the purpose of this study are the following:

Table: Indicators of Sustainability in Rural Tourism

	Indicator	Measure
1.	Stress	- Number of visitors/tourists (per annum/ season)
2.	Social stress	- Ratio of visitor/tourist numbers to local population (per annum/season)
3.	Attractiveness	- List of natural and cultural resources - Rate of attractiveness of natural and cultural resources
4.	Planning process	- Existence of local/regional plan for development
5.	Tourism planning process	- Existence of local/regional plan for tourism development
6.	Area protection	- Category of protection - Percentage of protected area compared to the whole territory of the destination
7.	Local involvement	- Ratio of the number of locally owned tourist businesses to the total number of tourist businesses
8.	Local control	- Existence of formal measures (public hearing, community meeting, local referendum) to ensure local control over development planning and implementation
9.	Employment	- Number of jobs created in tourism (full-time equivalent) - Ratio of local employee number to the number of guest workers
10.	Tourism contribution to the local economy	- Proportion of total tax income generated by tourism only

11. Economic diversity	-	Share of different economic activities in the total tax income
12. Energy consumption	-	Ratio of renewable energy sources to non-renewable energy sources (consumption)
13. Waste management	-	Percentage of households with proper sewage system
	-	Percentage of waste receiving treatment
14. Education and training	-	Percentage of local people involved in tourism with professional training and education
	-	Distribution of tourism employees by education
	-	Percentage of tourism employees (and local people) participating in on-the-job training in a given time period
15. Local satisfaction	-	Overall perception of tourism's impacts in local community
16. Tourist satisfaction	-	Overall satisfaction of tourists concerning the quality and the value/price ratio of the complex tourist product
	-	Percentage/change of repeat visits compared to first-time visits

RURAL TOURISM DEVELOPMENT IN HUNGARY

Rural tourism in Hungary started to develop already in the last century, and this kind of tourism became popular very soon. Before the Second World War, holidays taken in rural areas accounted for 35-45% of all holidays (Kovács, 1993).

However, the rural tourism of that period entirely disappeared after 1945 and the reorganisation of the market faces significant obstacles: the lack of an institutional framework, the bad financial situation and the relative underdevelopment of those regions which possess the most attractive resources for tourism development, the little interest on behalf of professional tourist organisations (since rural tourism development promises only low profitability) and the lack of business and hospitality skills and the ageing of the local residents.

The development of rural tourism has been included (and often emphasised) in regional development plans since the 1960's, without too much success (Kõszegfalvi, 1991). Tourism development has been concentrated in a few areas of the country (mainly located at natural waters, around thermal springs and in the mountains) and traditional rural tourism was somehow "lost" in the meantime.

It has to be added that the majority of the Hungarian population living in urban areas still has relatives in the countryside, so VFR is an existing form of rural tourism, but as the motivations are different (to visit relatives, not to become familiar with farming communities' lifestyle or to learn about local crafts and customs), on their behalf a demand for an organised supply of rural tourist products is basically non-existent. So these tourists do not contribute significantly to the economic development of the visited areas, but the fact that they do pay visits to certain rural destinations limit their demand for any further holidays of this kind. In other words, their need for staying in a rural environment is mostly satisfied by their relatives without any expenses (except travel costs), so very often they are not willing to spend any additional amount of money on similar holidays in other rural areas of the country.

An other important factor to consider is that the majority of middle-class Hungarian families (i.e. the segment typically most interested in rural tourism) have their own small holiday homes somewhere in the countryside where they can spend weekends and (part of) their summer holidays. The main motivation for spending leisure time in these holiday homes is relaxation and, for most owners, very small-scale agricultural production (growing fruits and vegetables for their own consumption). Of course, this kind of residential tourism contributes to the development of infrastructure in the given areas, and also to the retention of certain services (especially retailing).

On the other hand, the ownership of non-locals restricts (both physically and financially) the opportunities of local people to buy real estate, and the holiday home owners have different infrastructural and social needs than the local residents (e.g. they are not likely to support the local school, because their children go to school in their permanent residence).

New attempts to revitalise the traditional type of tourism started mainly in the 1980's, especially in the least developed areas of the country. Some small areas can present significant success, but in general the progress so far has not met the expectations. Besides the earlier presented obstacles, the domestic image of rural holidays (cheap, aimed for the least affluent, relatively boring) does not help either to attract Hungarian visitors to rural areas. In order to change this image, the Hungarian Tourism Corp. started a campaign in 1997 to promote domestic (including rural) holidays.

One of the consequences of all the above described tendencies is that most destinations developing (or planning to develop) rural tourism expect to receive mainly foreign visitors, as opposed to the general European trends. In Western Europe rural tourism is one of the growing segments of tourism, more and more Western Europeans seek to enjoy holiday experiences in the countryside (Swarbrooke, 1996). Since Eastern Europe in general is more rural than Western Europe (both considering the level of urbanisation and industrialisation, and the socio-cultural characteristics of the societies), so it is most likely to attract a growing number of visitors from the West, if the rural tourist product is appropriately developed and promoted.

In Hungary at the moment, foreign tourists are mostly interested in two types of rural tourism: first, in accommodation in the vicinity of popular tourist destinations (being motivated by the much lower prices), second, in folklore programmes and horse-shows in the "puszta" (traditionally in the Great Plain in the Eastern part of the country, but nowadays horse-shows are organised also around Lake Balaton, the second most popular tourist destination of Hungary, in order to spare tourists the trouble of taking a long trip to the original "puszta"). The development of all the other types of rural tourism (including active nature holidays or participation in farm activities) is still in an early stage.

Unfortunately, the "cheap" domestic image and the low international demand are also expressed in the prices of the rural tourist services, and, consequently, in the contribution of rural tourism to the local economies. Compared to the volume of the labour invested, the profitability of rural tourism is very low in Hungary, despite the exclusivity and uniqueness of certain products (Kovács, 1993). So for those who have the necessary capital to invest in a larger-scale product, there is no real incentive to be involved in this economic activity, and the communities do not realise the profit that they expect (and that would enable them to further develop and diversify their supply in order to modify the existing "low-price-low quality" image).

Considering the further development of rural tourism in Hungary, a controversial issue is that whose interests should be prioritised. At first glance, it seems to be obvious that one of the preconditions of sustainable tourism development is the long-term consideration of local residents' interests. From this point of view, the process of modernisation, urbanisation and agricultural change should be supported also by tourists, since local residents have all the right to acquire the same level of infrastructural development and comfort as people living in urban areas. But if this argument is accepted and rural areas develop the similar way as cities, this kind of development means changes in the overall landscape, the settlements' visual image and in the way of life of local residents, and these changes are not always welcome by tourists. In Hungary we can experience that tourists are looking for the traditional village atmosphere which means for them small thatched houses with white walls, geraniums in the windows, sweep-pole well, domestic animals, etc., so they prefer the conservation of the traditional village life even against local communities' wishes for development.

SUSTAINABILITY IN HUNGARIAN RURAL TOURISM

As we could see earlier, sustainability is a complex notion, being determined by economic, ecological and socio-cultural factors. The indicators presented in this paper might act as useful measures of those factors that together contribute to sustainable rural tourism development. In order to draw a picture of the present nature of Hungarian rural tourism, the analysis of the development process and the characteristics of the sector might be useful. There are, however, several limitations in an analysis of this kind, mainly because of the lack of accurate data. The following conclusions are mostly drawn from estimates and experiences, not from statistics, because they are simply not available. These conclusions are consequently rather subjective, though they represent the opinion of several experts and rural tourist entrepreneurs, besides that of the authors.

Analysing all the indicators, we have a relatively complex picture. The interpretation of different measures may also differ, since some indicators are of very subjective character (like local satisfaction-a person who has direct economic benefit from tourism is most likely to accept a higher number of tourists without any annoyance than someone who has to suffer all the negative consequences of tourism without benefiting) and a given quantitative value of an indicator can be evaluated in different ways by different persons. How to decide for example what percentage of an area should be protected in order to ensure the highest degree of sustainability ? If only ecological sustainability is to be achieved, then preferably the total area should be protected. But if social sustainability is considered as well, then local residents should have the opportunity to continue traditional recreational activities, e.g. fishing or angling, or the settlement should have the space to grow if the population grows, which are not always compatible with the ecological principles of protection (Ungár, 1998).

Stress-measured as the number of visitors/tourists in a given destination-is not threatening the sustainable future of Hungarian rural tourism at the moment. If we consider only those destinations which meet the definition of rural tourism presented earlier in this paper (Gannon, 1988, in te Kloeze, 1994) and do not include the well-developed holiday resorts which are actually located in the countryside, but cannot be considered as rural areas due to their high level of urbanisation, then the number of visitors/tourists is much lower than what local communities would find as appropriate. In Hungary, there are app. 2000 beds registered in rural tourism and the average occupancy rate is less than 10% (Gál, 1998). Seasonality is characteristic to the demand, but without causing any additional stress yet (in the future, if the number of tourists significantly increases, the temporal coincidence of the tourist season and the main agricultural jobs might lead to tension, but this is far from being an issue yet). Consequently, social stress is non-existent, which could be considered as a positive factor, but since it is derived from the very low level of demand (and not from the balanced distribution of visitors in space and time), it cannot be considered as a favourable indicators of sustainability.

Most of the areas of Hungary, where rural tourism is part of the general local or regional development plans, possess various natural and cultural attractions. Among these, the most important ones are the clean natural environment, the thermal springs, the hospitality of the local people, the gastronomy, the rural lifestyle, and, to a certain extent, the preserved traditions and heritage. On the other hand, the old architectural styles that made our villages so distinctive are disappearing, the construction boom in the '60s and '70s resulted in relatively similar village appearances all over the country, less and less young people know and practice the old traditions, and the general modernisation has changed the rural lifestyle. As we could see earlier in this paper, the interest of tourists looking for authentic rural experiences very often conflict with the interest of locals looking for urban comfort. Certain attractions typical of rural tourism, like the opportunity for participation in farm activities or involvement in the hosts' everyday life, are missing in the majority of destinations (though, fortunately, these latter attractions are man-made, so can be developed in the future). Altogether, the overall attractiveness of the rural areas in Hungary is acceptable, the potential for rural tourism development seems to be existing, but there is a need for a marketing approach in the development of complex tourist products, and for further diversification and development of attractions based on the needs of different tourist segments. Local and regional plans for general development exist in all rural tourist destinations, since they are required by the law. Tourism planning is far less common, especially in those areas where rural tourism is in an early stage of development. Among the reasons for not having tourism development plans, we can find the lack of educated and experienced planners or that of a common will on behalf of the local residents, the negative previous experiences concerning tourism development plans (more plans have been written than implemented, outsider experts have often created unaccomplishable plans) or simply the lack of financial resources. The existing plans very often focus on the economic aspects of the development process, disregarding future ecological or socio-cultural consequences of the proposed actions. The necessity of a regional approach is being accepted relatively slowly: at the present low level of demand, destinations usually see each other as competitors, not as potential cooperation partners.

Protected areas of higher category have a better chance to attract visitors than others. At the moment, in the first half of 1998, Hungary has nine National Parks and countless local protected areas and further attempts are made in order to increase the territory of these areas by establishing new National Parks. The precious natural and cultural resources of these Parks (diverse flora and fauna, rare species, geological formations, typical domesticated animals, cultural landscapes, cultural heritage) serve as the basis of rural tourism development in the nearby villages (the scattered structure of the Hungarian National Park system-all but one park consist of several pieces of protected land-facilitates the involvement of these commmmunities). In general, rural tourism benefits of the existence of National Parks (lower categories of protected areas play a less significant role in the success of tourism), and the current ratio of protection can be considered as appropriate from an overall aspect of sustainability (i.e. a balance between ecological, economic and social interests seems to be achieved.

Since rural tourism development is typically low-scale and locally managed in Hungary, the involvement rate of local people is high, though it depends on how the term "local people" is defined. Especially in the smallest, least developed villages, it is quite common that the people originally living in the area have moved to bigger villages or to towns, in order to get a job or provide better education for their children. Their houses have often been bought by people from cities who looked for relaxation in natural environment or who decided to save the dying old villages. Many small-scale rural tourist businesses are managed by these people, who, by origin, are not local, but, by their commitment and their efforts made to help a settlement or a region survive, must be evaluated as locals. Their involvement, objectives and intentions are very similar to those of the local people, so their contribution must be considered as beneficial for the sustainability of rural tourism development. The ownership of non-locals (in the above mentioned sense) in Hungarian rural tourism is not common, mainly because of the low potential profitability (it is more characteristic to the established tourist resorts like the ones around Lake Balaton).

Since the demand for rural tourism is relatively low in Hungary, the number of jobs created by this activity is not high at the moment, but the diversification of the attractions and services could induce a significant growth in this field in the near future. At the moment, rural tourism mainly provides additional income for rural families (as part-time activity particularly for the female population) and contributes to the development of pluriactivity (i.e. when a family or an individual carries out more than one type of job). The supplementary income generated by rural communities can help the development of the infrastructure or social services as well, and the perceived potential of economic development (by tourism as a catalyst) can make an area more attractive, thus more viable in the long term. Since rural tourism is a relatively new phenomenon in Hungary (not considering now the period before 1945), this is more of an expectation than a fact at the moment.

Consequently, the contribution of rural tourism to the local economy is relatively low in most rural destinations, at least in terms of registered financial income. This is partly due to the presence of grey economy (facilitated by the lack of a well-established institutional framework and the informal nature of the rural tourist services). There are no reliable statistics on the actual incomes from rural tourism, and the ratio of taxes generated by tourism to the total amount of taxes does not accurately reflect the share of the industry. (This fact also affects our knowledge of the economic diversity of an area- but even without proper statistics it can be stated that in the least developed villages rural tourism is often the only economic activity with a growth potential). Besides the financial results, rural tourism development generally improves the quality of life in the destinations (by providing broader personal contacts, by motivating people to take better care of their environment or indirectly, by assuring preference to an area in national development projects).

Environmental factors, like energy sources or waste management, are usually rather neglected in rural tourism development. Even if attempts are made to provide proper sewage or waste treatment systems all over the country, these attempts are related to tourism only in the most frequented destinations with the most urgent environmental problems (like at Lake Balaton). The utilisation of renewable energy sources is generally not an issue (when it is, the reason is mostly increased environment-consciousness, not a perceived threat of a growing number of tourists exploiting the non-renewable energy sources). For most destinations, the main priority is to provide the tourists with all the comfort they need (e.g. bathrooms). Given the present low level of demand, it seems to be totally impossible that one day masses of tourists would threaten the ecological balance of any rural destination. On the other hand, the fact that rural tourism has started to develop quite recently in Hungary, provides an opportunity for the country to adopt other regions' experiences in order to avoid mistakes made elsewhere. The stricter environmental regulations of the European Union also affect the general economic development process in Hungary, which can be beneficial for the ecological balance of rural tourism as well.

In tourism development in general, training and education of the labour force is one of the necessary requirements of sustainability. Since in rural tourism many local residents without formal tourism education are involved, their education on the main issues of sustainability must form part of the overall development process. In Hungary, the failure of several rural tourism development projects could have been strongly related to the lack of market knowledge and marketing skills. Because in many cases even the basic knowledge of running a business is missing, there is typically no specific need for studying or implementing the principles of sustainable development. The issue of sustainability usually emerges only in those heavily frequented areas where the negative impacts of tourism can already be detected.

Though there are exceptions, local people in general are far from being satisfied by rural tourism development. The main factors behind this dissatisfaction are the gap between the expected and the realised profitability, the relatively slow growth of the sector, the related bureaucracy, the lack of significant support from the state. Other contributing factors were the lack of marketing and business skills of the local people, the lack of domestic demand and the overstatement of the local resources and attractions. Especially at the beginning of the development process, hopes were high, large numbers of tourists were expected to come and spend generously, but reality has not lived up to the expectations of the communities involved. Nowadays, a more cautious development phase is in stage, the cooperation between villages and regions improves, more thorough planning takes place, the people involved are eventually gathering the necessary knowledge, skills and experiences.

On the other hand, those tourists who actually take part in rural holidays in Hungary, are usually satisfied with the quality of their experiences. Both among Hungarians and foreigners, there is a relatively high proportion of repeat visitors. Their satisfaction indicates that the product itself is perceived as of good quality by that narrow segment of customers that is attracted by it. The only problem concerning sustainability is the low level of demand: no matter how satisfied customers are, if-at least in short run-their demand cannot ensure economic sustainability for the visited areas. (In the long run, word of mouth promotion may increase interest in rural recreation and the overall image of rural holidays may be changed as well.)

Conclusions

By the general analysis of the sustainability of rural tourism development in Hungary, an attempt was made to present the complex nature of the activity. Though rural tourism has the potential to be one of the most effective tools of regional development, it has not grown up to the expectations so far, due to several interrelated reasons described earlier in the paper.

The next step in the research of this topic will be the detailed assessment of one or several rural tourist destinations in Hungary through the presented sustainability indicators. A study of this kind would serve various purposes: it would help to test the usefulness, the appropriateness and the applicability of these indicators in the analysis of the sustainability of rural tourism, and it would contribute to the understanding of what different interest groups (including local community members, tourists, ecologists or businessmen) perceive as sustainable rural tourism development. A better understanding of these perceptions would help the planning of a rural tourism that is able to satisfy the needs of most groups for now and in the future.

4

PRESENT SCENARIO

Trends in Arrivals and Receipts

Economic growth, increasing competition, easing of travel restrictions, and aggressive promotion strategies adopted by the NTOs contributed to the growth in arrivals in 1996. Most of the Asia Pacific countries saw an increase in arrivals. Japan, which experienced a drop in arrivals in 1995 due to its lack of appeal, increasing cost, and strong currency, rebounded in 1996 with a 22% growth in arrivals. South Korea failed to meet its target of 4 million arrivals. The decline in arrivals were attributed to rising costs of vacationing in the country. Japan, which is S. Korea's largest market, accounting for over 40% of all visitors, declined 8.4% to 1.52 million visitors. Many Japanese visitors also chose to visit Hong Kong before the hand over to China. Malaysia experienced a decline in arrivals, primarily from its Asian markets, due to health-related concerns of a cholera outbreak. Political stability in the Philippines, easing of restrictions in China, concerns over the hangover of Hong Kong to China, and improving economic conditions in Australia and Indonesia, led to double-digit growth rates in arrivals in these countries.

Paralleling the growth in arrivals, tourism receipts also showed significant growth for most of the Asia Pacific countries, especially for Japan, Australia, and New Zealand, which exceeded 20%. Higher receipts were also recorded for Hong Kong, China, Indonesia, and the Philippines. On the other hand, South Korea and Singapore saw a decline in receipts, due to increasing cost concerns. The strong Singapore currency, a declining length of stay, and growing competition from regional destinations contributed to the decline. Tourism receipts for Asia Pacific countries are expected to grow at a faster rate than arrivals, due to rising affluence and increased spending by visitors.

Outbound Travel

In 1996, the Asia Pacific region surpassed North America for the first time in generating visitors. Outbound travel grew 8% to record 94 million international visitors, while North Americans made 92 million trips abroad. The Asia Pacific region received 74% of the visitors generated, followed by Europe (14%), and the Americas (10%). It is a dramatic increase from the 69% share recorded in 1985 (WTO 1997b).

Falling airfares, high cost of domestic travel in some countries, rising affluence, increase in business travel, and more competitive packages, contributed to increasing number of Asians traveling overseas to regional destinations (Mak and White, 1992). Intraregional travel, which is characterized by more frequent short-haul trips, has been growing at a higher rate than long-haul travel. Between 1985 and 1995, intraregional travel grew at an average annual rate of 12%, compared to 10% for long-haul travel (WTO 19971,). Japan by far, is still the largest tourist generating market in the region, but the emerging markets of China, S. Korea, Hong Kong, Taiwan, Singapore, and Thailand, are generating most of the region's new international travelers.

The increase in demand for travel has created new marketing opportunities in eco-tourism, adventure travel, dive travel, cruises, golf tours, arts and entertainment, and meetings and incentives, among others. Tourism marketers must focus on attracting these high yield markets by differentiating their products and customizing them to individualized needs. Since the Asia Pacific region covers a great diversity of cultures, lifestyles and preferences, more innovative and creative marketing strategies have to be designed for each source market of visitors. The increasing sophistication the Asian visitors also requires travel products to offer quality, comfort, convenience, relaxation, independence, and unique learning experiences that maximize the value of their leisure time.

Future Perspective

The Asia Pacific region will still maintain its status as the fastest growing region in the world and most forecasts point to the region's healthy long-term prospects. The WTO's (1996b) forecast reveals the region emerging as the world's number two region behind Europe in 2010 with 229 million international arrivals, growing at an annual rate of 7.6%. The rapid growth of tourism will create new marketing opportunities in the cruise line industry, timesharing, meetings and incentives, eco-tourism, and dive travel. Japan will continue to be the principal visitor generating market, while China has the potential to be the next major visitor generating market.

Major events that will boost the status of the region include the Commonwealth Games in Malaysia in 1998, the 2000 Olympic Games in Sydney and soccer's World Cup in Korea and Japan in 2002. Forecasts by the World Travel and Tourism Council (1995) for the Asia Pacific region reveal that by the year 2005, travel and tourism will generate US$1.9 trillion in gross output, and account for 11.6% of GDP. Further, the industry will create an additional 105 million new and indirect jobs. To support this growth, US$553 billion in capital investments will be needed for the infrastructure and superstructure.

Strong economic growth will continue to increase disposable incomes and stimulate the desire to travel. This will increase the demand for air travel which is expected to grow at an annual rate of 8.6% till 2000 and 7.1% from 2000 to 2010. By 2010, the Asia Pacific region will control half of the world's total passenger traffic. Japan will dominate the traffic with over 90 million passengers, followed by Hong Kong, China, and Singapore. The fastest growing travel markets by 2000 will be Vietnam, China, Taiwan, Indonesia, and Thailand (Air Transport Action Group 1995). To accommodate the demand for air travel, airlines in the region will take delivery of more than US$100 billion worth of aircraft. As of March 1996, Asia

Pacific airlines had firm orders and options for a total of 575 aircraft (Muqbil 1996). New airports are opening in Hong Kong, Korea, and Malaysia, while expansions in Singapore and Indonesia will help to alleviate capacity and congestion problems. Billions of dollars will be spent in capital investments to meet the increasing demands of a burgeoning tourism and hotel industry. Joint promotions and alliances between NTOs and the private sector, will create a stronger collective tourism product that will increase arrivals and enhance tourism growth.

Finally, the recent devaluation of the regional currencies will also have major implications for the tourism industry in the region. Inbound travel will increase as visitors will be attracted by the higher purchasing power in countries where currencies have been devalued. More specifically, visitor expenditures will increase as a result of a higher length of stay and attractive prices. In the short term, devaluation may have some negative impact on outbound travel and operating costs, but the long-term benefits will outweigh the costs.

TOURISM INFORMATION MANAGEMENT

Information management is the handling of information acquired by one or many disparate sources in a way that optimizes access by all who have a share in that information or a right to that information.

Through the 1970s this was largely limited to files, file maintenance, and life cycle management of paper and a small number of other media. With the proliferation of information technology starting in the 1970s, the job of information management took on a new light. No longer was information management a simple job that could be performed by almost anyone. An understanding of the technology and the theory behind it became necessary, as information was ever more stored via electronic means. By the late 1990s when information was regularly disseminated across computers and other electronic devices, information managers found themselves tasked with increasingly complex devices. With the latest tools available, information management has become a powerful resource for organizations.

Context: Information Management (IM) is characterised by the phrase 'Getting the right information to the right person at the right place at the right time'. It does, not, however, address the question of what constitutes the 'right information'. This omission can be addressed through the philosophy of Informational management (IaM). IaM is characterised by the phrase, 'Knowing what information to gather, knowing what to do with information when you get it, knowing what information to pass on, and knowing how to value the result' {adapted from G.Russell Swanborough}. This identifies the 'right information' and the resulting whole solution is worth more than the sum of its parts.

Following the behavioural science theory of management, mainly developed at Carnegie Mellon University and prominently represented by Barnard, Cyert, March and Simon, most of what goes on in organizations is actually decision making and information processes. The crucial factor in the information and decision process analysis is thus individuals' limited ability to process information and to take decisions under these limitations.

According to March and Simon (1958), organizations have to be considered as cooperative systems with a high level of information processing and a vast need for decision making at various levels. They also claimed that there are factors that would prevent individuals from acting strictly rational, in opposite to what has been proposed and advocated by classic theorists. Instead, they proposed that any decision would be sub-optimum due to the bounded rationality of the decision-maker. Instead of using the model of the economic man, as advocated in classic theory, they proposed the administrative man as an alternative based on their argumentation about the cognitive limits of rationality. While the theories developed at Carnegie Mellon clearly filled some theoretical gaps in the discipline, March and Simon did not propose a certain organizational form that they considered especially feasible for coping with cognitive limitations and bounded rationality of decision-makers. Through their own argumentation against normative decision-making models, i.e. models that prescribe people how they ought to choose, they also abandoned the idea of an ideal organizational form.

In addition to the factors mentioned by March and Simon, there are two other considerable aspects, stemming from environmental and organizational dynamics. Firstly, it is not possible to access, collect and evaluate all environmental information being relevant for taking a certain decision at a reasonable price, i.e. time and effort (Hedberg, 1981). In other words, following a national economic framework, the transaction cost associated with the informating process is too high. Secondly, established organizational rules and procedures can prevent the taking of the most appropriate decision, i.e. that a sub-optimum solution is chosen in accordance to organizational rank structure or institutional rules, guidelines and procedures (Mackenzie, 1978; Mullins, 1993), an issue that also has been brought forward as a major critique against the principles of bureaucratic organizations.

According to the Carnegie Mellon School and its followers, information management, i.e. the organization's ability to process information, is at the core of organizational and managerial competencies. Consequently, strategies for organization design must be aiming at improved information processing capability. Jay Galbraith (1977, p 49 ff.) has identified five main organization design strategies within two categories- increased information processing capacity and reduced need for information processing.

A. Reduction of information processing needs
   1. Environmental management
   2. Creation of slack resources
   3. Creation of self-contained tasks
B. Increasing the organizational information processing capacity
   1. Creation of lateral relations
   2. Vertical information systems

Environmental Management: Instead of adapting to changing environmental circumstances, the organization can aim at modifying its environment. Vertical and horizontal collaboration, i.e. cooperation or integration with other organizations in the industry value system are typical means for reducing uncertainty. An example for reducing uncertainty in the relation with the prior or demanding stage of the industry system is the concept of Supplier-Retailer collaboration or Efficient Customer Response.

Creation of slack resources. In order to reduce exceptions, performance levels can be reduced, thus decreasing the information load on the hierarchy. These additional slack resources, required to reduce information processing in the hierarchy, are representing an additional cost to the organization and the choice of this method is clearly depending on the alternative costs of other strategies. Creation of self-contained tasks. Achieving a conceptual closure of tasks is another way of reducing information processing. In this case, the task-performing unit has all the resources required to perform the task. This approach is concerned with task (de-)composition and interaction between different organizational units, i.e. organizational and information interfaces.

Creation of lateral relations. In this case, lateral decision processes are established that cut across functional organizational units. The aim is to apply a system of decision subsidiarity, i.e. to move decision power to the process, instead of moving information from the process into the hierarchy for decision-making. Investment in vertical information systems. Instead of processing information through the existing hierarchical channels, the organization can establish vertical information systems. In this case, the information flow for a specific task (or set of tasks) is routed in accordance to the applied business logic, rather than the hierarchical organization.

Following the lateral relations concept, it also becomes possible to employ an organizational form that is different from the simple hierarchical information. The Matrix organization is aiming at bringing together the functional and product departmental bases and achieving a balance in information processing and decision making between the vertical (hierarchical) and the horizontal (product or project) structure.

The creation of a matrix organization can also be considered as management's response to a persistent or permanent demand for adaptation to environmental dynamics, instead of the response to episodic demands.

Management Information System

Management Information Systems is a general name for the academic discipline covering the application of people, technologies, and procedures-collectively, the information system-to business problems.

This field is directly linked to management by objectives (MBO) and to the monitoring of key performance indicators (KPI). It can also help in processing specific information for decision making (for example analyze customer behavior).

Some Confusions between MIS and IT: In business, information systems support not only business processes and operations, but also decision-making and competitive strategies, which are the fields of MIS.

As an area of study, MIS is sometimes referred to, in a restrictive sense, as information technology management. The study of information systems is usually a commerce and business administration discipline. It frequently involves software engineering, but also distinguishes itself by concentrating on the integration of computer systems with the aims of the organization.

The area of study should not be confused with computer science which is more theoretical in nature and deals mainly with software creation, and not with computer engineering, which focuses more on the design of computer hardware. IT service management is a practitioner-focused discipline centering on the same general domain.

Potential Benefits of MIS Investments: Investing in information systems can pay off for a company in many ways.

1. an investment can support a core competency.
2. It can enhance distribution channel management.
3. Such an IT investment can help build brand equity.

4. IT investment can boost production processes (2). Information systems allow a company flexibility in its output level.
5. Implementing IT experience can leverage learning curve advantages.
6. IT investment can impact mass customization production processes.
7. Leverage IT investment in computer aided design (1).
8. It can mean expanded E-commerce.
9. Information systems leverage stability.

Human Resource Management

Human Resource Management Systems (HRMS, EHRMS), Human Resource Information Systems (HRIS), HR Technology or also called HR modules, shape an intersection in between human resource management (HRM) and information technology. It merges HRM as a discipline and in particular its basic HR activities and processes with the information technology field, whereas the planning and programming of data processing systems evolved into standardised routines and packages of enterprise resource planning (ERP) software. On the whole, these ERP systems have their origin on software that integrates information from different applications into one universal database. The linkage of its financial and human resource modules through one database is the most important distinction to the individually and proprietary developed predecessors, which makes this software application both rigid and flexible.

THE HR FUNCTIONS

All in all, the HR function is still to a large degree administrative and common to all organizations. To varying degrees, most organisations have formalised selection, evaluation, and payroll processes. Efficient and effective management of the "Human Capital" Pool (HCP) has become an increasingly imperative and complex activity to all HR professionals. The HR function consists of tracking innumerable data points on each employee, from personal histories, data, skills, capabilities, experiences to payroll records. To reduce the manual workload of these administrative activities, organisations began to electronically automate many of these processes by introducing innovative HRMS/HCM technology. Due to complexity in programming, capabilities and limited technical resources, HR executives rely on internal or external IT professionals to develop and maintain their Human Resource Management Systems (HRMS). Before the "client-server" architecture evolved in the late 1980s, every single HR automation process came largely in form of mainframe computers that could handle large amounts of data transactions. In consequence of the high capital investment necessary to purchase or program proprietary software, these internally developed HRMS were limited to medium to large organisations being able to afford internal IT capabilities. The advent of client-server HRMS authorised HR executives for the first time to take responsibility and ownership of their systems. These client-server HRMS are characteristically developed around four principal areas of HR functionalities: 1) "payroll", 2) time and labour management 3) benefits administration and 4) HR management.

The payroll module automates the pay process by gathering data on employee time and attendance, calculating various deductions and taxes, and generating periodic paycheques and employee tax reports. Data is generally fed from the human resources and time keeping modules to calculate automatic deposit and manual chequc writing capabilities. Sophisticated HCM systems can set up accounts payable transactions from employee deduction or produce garnishment cheques. The payroll module sends accounting information to the general ledger for posting subsequent to a pay cycle.

The time and labor management module applies new technology and methods (time collection devices) to cost effectively gather and evaluate employee time/work information. The most advanced modules provide broad flexibility in data collection methods, as well as labour distribution capabilities and data analysis features. This module is a key ingredient to establish organisational cost accounting capabilities. The benefit administration module permits HR professionals to easily administer and track employee participation in benefits programs ranging from healthcare provider, insurance policy, and pension plan to profit sharing or stock option plans.

The HR management module is a component covering all other HR aspects from application to retirement. The system records basic demographic and address data, selection, training and development, capabilities and skills management, compensation planning records and other related activities. Leading edge systems provide the ability to "read" applications and enter relevant data to applicable database fields, notify employers and provide position management and position control.

Typically, HRMS/HCM technology replaces the four core HR activities by streamlining them electronically; 1) payroll, 2) time and labour management, 3) benefit administration and 4) HR management. While using the internet or corporate intranet as a communication and workflow vehicle, the HRMS/ HCM technology can convert these into web-based HRMS components of the ERP system and permit to reduce transaction costs, leading to greater HR and organisational efficiency. Through employee or manager self-service (ESS or MSS), HR activities shift away from paper based processes to using self-service functionalities that benefit employees, managers and HR professionals alike. Costly and time consuming HR administrative tasks, such as travel reimbursement, personnel data change, benefits enrolment, enrolment in training classes (employee side) and to instruct a personnel action, authorise access to information for employees (manager's side) are being individually handled and permit to reduce HR transaction time, leading to HR and organisational effectiveness. Consequently, HR professionals can spend fewer resources in managing administrative HR activities and can apply freed time and resources to concentrate on strategic HR issues, which lead to business innovation.

EHRMS Vendors: Vendors of popular EHRMS enterprise level software packages include: SAP, Oracle, PeopleSoft,

Lawson, and Infor. A wide variety of other software vendors VSO provide various subsets of enterprise level functionality. For example, basic time and attendance software packages provide employee timekeeping functionality while other vendors focus primarily on payroll processing.

Applic 8 (pronounced Applicate) of Switzerland is one of the sole vendors to provide a complete web-based payroll application for managing all payroll-related tasks and pertinent reporting, as well as HR-Intranet, a complete and collaborative application destined to empower all employees and managers to communicate and share all pertinent HR administration data such as absences, overtime, and official documents.

Open Source EHRMS' such as OrangeHRM are also available, however they lack end-to-end processes, functionalities and integration with common or open source ERP systems.

Information Technology Management

Information technology management (or IT management) is a combination of two branches of study, information technology and management.

Strictly speaking, there are two incarnations to this definition. One implies the management of a collection of systems, infrastructure, and information that resides on them. Another implies the management of information technologies as a business function.

The first definition stems from the practice of IT Portfolio Management and is the subject of technical manuals and publications of various information technologies providers; while the second definition stems from the discussion and formation of the Information Technology Infrastructure Library (ITIL).

The ITIL has been in practice throughout regions of the world mainly conducted by IT service providers consulting companies. The relative paucity in the use of the best practice set can be attributed to a lack of awareness among IT practitioners. However the lack of ready-to-use tools also presents a significant barrier. Some organizations that value such practices tend to engage consultants to introduce the practice. Such implementations can conflict with the home-grown culture due to a lack of internal buy-in. Other organizations implement the practices by spending resources to develop in-house tools.

Most in-house developed tools tend to focus on one or a few specific areas where the orgnizations feel the most pains. To reap the full advantages, tools will need to be integrated with the organization's IT data in the center.

THE KNOWLEDGE AGENDA

Momentum of Knowledge Awareness: The interest in knowledge as a strategic lever in business is not new. In the 1970s and 1980s there were great expectations that knowledge based computer systems ('expert systems') could harness knowledge to solve many business problems. That promise was only partially fulfilled and certainly not to the extent that workers in the field had hoped. In retrospect the problem was that developers focused too much on what has been described as "falling into the trap of trying to develop 'thinking machines' rather than using machines to augment human thinking" (Skyrme 1990).

The more general view of the pervasive role of knowledge in business activities, has evolved from a number of management writers and practitioners as portrayed by Amidon (1997) in her 'Wellsprings timelines'-hindsight, insight and foresight. This shows the evolution and convergence of thinking and writing about knowledge as a strategic focus, alongside other initiatives such as agile manufacturing, innovation and the learning orignization. In our discussions with managers during 1996 and early 1997, the two most important written influences cited were the ongoing series of articles by Stewart in Fortune (Stewart 1993, 1995), and of the book by Nonaka and Takeuchi (1995) The Knowledge Creating Company. The latter, in particular, has provided managers with a framework for distinguishing between explicit and tacit knowledge and the conversion processes between them. They describe explicit knowledge as that which: "can be expressed in words and numbers and can be easily communicated and shared in the form of hard data, scientific formulae, codified procedures or universal principles" and contrast it with tacit knowledge which "is highly personal and hard to formalise. Subjective insights, intuitions and hunches fall into this category of knowledge."

The four conversion processes they describe are:

- Tacit-to-tacit (socialisation)-where individuals acquire new knowledge directly from others;
- Tacit-to-explicit (externalisation)-the articulation of knowledge into tangible form through dialogue;
- Explicit-to-explicit (combination)-combining different forms of explicit knowledge, such as that in documents or on databases;
- Explicit-to-tacit (internalisation)-such as learning by doing, where individuals internalise knowledge from documents into their own body of experience.

Contribution of Knowledge to Business Success: Knowledge adds value to a business through its products, processes and people. The product contribution of knowledge is described by Davis and Botkin (1994). They describe six features of knowledge-based businesses:

1. The more you use knowledge-based offerings, the smarter they get.
2. The more you use knowledge-based offerings, the smarter you get.
3. Knowledge-based products and services adjust to changing circumstances.
4. Knowledge-based businesses can customise their offerings.
5. Knowledge-based products and services have relatively short life cycles.
6. Knowledge-based businesses enable customers to act in real-time.

Recent examples of the growing intensity of knowledge in products are the intelligent oil drill, which 'knows' the shape of the reservoir it is drilling, and the intelligent car, whose engine management systems can monitor performance of vital parts and 'knows' when they need servicing. These are examples of where knowledge can enhance the value of a product in the eyes of the customer. Another contribution of knowledge is that in business processes. Throughout industry there are examples of where individuals or departments are ostensibly carrying out the same process, but where the performance levels are quite different. Often it is the 'tacit' knowledge of the experienced person that makes the difference. The sharing of best practices from one part of an organization to another is therefore a key component of many knowledge management programmes. For example, Texas Instruments was able to save the equivalent of the investment in a new semiconductor fabrication plant, by sharing best practices between their existing plants (O'Dell 1996).

The value of knowledge as manifest in an organisations products, its intellectual capital (such as patents and licences), people (human capital) and processes (structural capital) is very evident when the book value of a company, as measured by traditional accounting methods, is compared with its market value, which takes into account the marketplace perception of intangible value not measured by accountants. For many high-tech companies (such as Microsoft) or knowledge intensive companies (such as biotechnology companies) this factor is ten or more to one. The net result is that as the value and contribution of knowledge becomes more evident, that organisations are investing in initiatives to manage and harness that knowledge. This means a systematic approach to managing the processes for creating and capturing it, classifying it and storing it, disseminating and using it.

State of Knowledge Practice: During 1996, as part of the research for a 500-page report on knowledge management, we investigated the state of knowledge management in various companies around the world (Skyrme and Amidon 1997). This included literature reviews, case study interviews and the results of an Ernst ∓ Young/Business Intelligence two continent survey (North America and Europe). The survey showed that nearly 90 per cent of senior managers believed that their organisations were in a knowledge-intensive business, whatever their industry. It also revealed different perceptions of the value of various activities and of the contribution of technology across different industries and functions. Our research showed that the following were common activities that were taking place in knowledge management initiatives:

- Creation of knowledge teams-people from all disciplines to develop the methods of knowledge management
- Sharing of best practices-from one part of the organization to another, through databases, but also through personal interaction and sharing events
- Development of knowledge databases-best practices, expert directories, market intelligence etc.
- Creation of Knowledge Centres-focal points for the development of knowledge skills, managing and enhancing knowledge databases and facilitating knowledge flow
- Collaborative Technologies-the use of Intranets (internal Internet) or groupware for rapid information access
- Intellectual Capital teams-to identify and audit intangible assets such as knowledge.

One shorthand way of summarising the knowledge movement, is to say that it is to get the right knowledge at the right place, at the right time. If this is done expeditiously, customer service can be improved through solving problems better, new products brought to market quicker, business processes continually improved, and innovative new ideas brought to commercialisation. What many practitioners have found, is that it the flow of knowledge that is important. This is where networked computer and communications technology plays an important role.

THE INTERNET REVOLUTION

The Evolution of Computing in the Workplace: One of the most widespread ways in that technology supports knowledge processes, is not through simple point solutions, such as expert systems or group decision support systems, but through enterprise wide information and knowledge sharing infrastructures. Groupware conferencing systems like Lotus Notes and Intranets were very evident.

If one traces the evolution of the contribution of information and communications technologies (ICT) in the workplace, the focus has changed over time. In the 1960s and 1970s the focus was on automating procedures. We even called the discipline data processing at the time. During the 1980s the leading edge was moving toward communications, most notably through electronic mail. At this time, online access to information through networks was also growing appreciably. Like manufacturing automation before, as we have gain the efficiencies in the office through automation of standard procedures (aided and abetted by BPR!) the locus of computer software development has shifted to support less structured activities, those of professional and managers. This is what I call the cognitive computing focus. We are trying to avoid the mistakes of the 'black box' mentality of earlier knowledge systems, and develop systems that augment and support the knowledge work of humans.

Of these, the one that is having the most profound impact is that of the Internet and related technologies. As noted earlier, to many it seems like a revolution, but I prefer to call it an evolution, since its use has been growing exponentially for many years. From a knowledge perspective the Internet has several characteristics that our research found was exploited in various knowledge programmes:

- It uses a communications standard protocol (TCP/IP) that is widely supported-this means that it is universally accessible from many locations and through many different computer platforms
- End-user software, such as electronic mail and World Wide Web browsers are universally available and are low cost (and often free)-this makes it cost effective to implement on an enterprise wide basis
- Internet access is widely available throughout the world, increasingly with international providers-this means that a company's employees, especially those that travel

a lot, can use the Internet rather like a corporate network; we found several organisations using a global service like CompuServe as a better option than building an in-house corporate network

- The World Wide Web. This provides a quick means of publishing information that can be shared on a worldwide basis: "every user is also a publisher". This universal repository of information means that information resources can be updated and widely shared at an attractive cost.

In fact, it can be said that it is the World Wide Web that made the Internet popular among most business users. We now have something akin to Doug Engelbart's notion of a 'docuverse'- a document universe that interlinks pages of information. I'm sure some of you still use Gopher, Verocia and Archie, but for most end-users, the Web represents the Internet.

Internet vs. Online: It is appropriate here to consider the many criticisms of the Internet that have been made to me by online service providers, who perhaps at the time did not want the Internet to be so successful (although they now have a different view that they are embracing it). First, there is often the criticism that "you get what you pay for", and since the "web is free" then the information is not worth much. In fact, many areas of useful information on the Web are not free-users pay for them, albeit usually on a 'pay-by-use' basis rather than an up front subscription as for many traditional online services. In fact, I have spent money on searched items and subsequently found I could have got the very same item for free on the Web! Second, the Internet is not secure. This is true if you are dealing with really sensitive information. But for most people seeking information and knowledge this is not a real issue.

Two criticisms that do have some validity are that it is slow and difficult to find information. Actually the Internet is very fast when you consider how quickly information can be retrieved from the vast databases that it holds. Obviously if you use a local CD-ROM or proprietary online service you can get information quicker, but if you look at the end-to-end time, from developing a search strategy to collecting information, and the time an end-user might have to spend briefing an intermediary, then the difference is often not that great.

Perhaps the most valid criticism is that the information is very variable in quality and the way it is organised. However, there are a number of resource sites that are building up categorised information and archive databases that compare favourably with online services. Online services have been perfecting their database techniques, their classification schemes and keywords for many years and provide a standard familiar interface to their disparate sources of information. Their value added comes in sourcing, classifying and refining information. This is worth a premium, but charges will undoubtedly have to come down to meet the increased availability of low cost information on the Internet.

In summary, the Internet is an incredible information source, and it has brought information directly to the end-users, without involving an intermediary such as a librarian or information professional. Furthermore, technology developments on the Internet will really improve matters in the near future. Examples include more intelligent search engines and intelligent software agents, that roam the net and bring back relevant information to your desk-top. This poses challenges for online providers and information professional alike. How can we serve the end-user better? How should we meet the opportunities and the challenge of the Internet? As is already happening, the world of online services and the Internet are converging. Users want the best of both worlds, the accessibility, universality, ease-of-use and low cost of the Internet combined with structured, organised and (in some cases) the exclusive information of online services.

The Knowledge Dimension: So far in this paper, the consideration of the Internet has been almost entirely to do with its information role. But by the time knowledge becomes encoded in a database, it is 'explicit' knowledge. In many respects effective sharing of tacit knowledge needs the face-to-face socialization process as described by Nonaka and Takeuchi. This is difficult over a distance although new technologies such as viedoconferencing are helping. If companies want to share the best knowledge they have to tap into experts wherever they happen to be-world-wide, inside or outside of the firm. The Internet here pays the role of enhancing remote access, through making the necessary connections and enhancing global communications. Users congregate in areas of shared interests, and start electronic conversations.

Electronic mail is the main way that this happens, but computer conferencing, such as with Lotus Notes, is popular in a corporate setting. However, knowledge sharing across organisational boundaries is increasingly required. Therefore, Internet facilities such as electronic mail discussion lists are a way that individuals working in dispersed multi-company teams, an increasingly common facet of organisational life, can converse together over a distance. The European Telework Development project is one example, where the project was originally formulated electronically, and where almost all of the day to day activities between 30 participants in 15 countries, takes place that way (Mitchell 1996). While there are a growing number of Web conferences, companies that are most developed in sharing and developing knowledge over electronic networks seem to prefer a fully functional groupware product such as Lotus Notes, now Web enabled through its Domino version.

Intranets: It is the ease of use that have made the use of Internet technology, such as browsers and search engines, of interest to companies wanting to share information. The advantages in a corporate setting of using Intranets (internal Internets) are similar to those that make use of the Internet attractive in external information access and communications. End-users are familiar with browser interfaces, information can be shared across different local area networks and computer platforms, and published information is instantly available over the whole network. Furthermore this information need not just be HTML (the Web mark-up language) documents, but can be in any number of common formats, such as word processed documents. Increasingly Intranets are also hosting transaction and database applications with the Web browser being the universal interface to different 'back-end' systems.

Thus an Intranet can connect everyone with everyone else, and can facilitate sharing of company information, and with Internet gateways external information. As with the Internet, the issues of organising and managing information becomes problematical. There is also the added tensions within an organisation of what is 'official' information and what 'informal'. Intranets are surfacing many organizational cultural issues, such as 'information politics'! (CIO 1996)

Knowledge Work Support

The ICT Contribution: In analysing knowledge work we found that information and communications technologies enhance knowledge processes and support knowledge workers in several ways:

- Ready access to organised information
- Better communications and interaction with fellow knowledge workers (either individually or in groups)
- Access to personal knowledge support tools (such as cognitive mapping tools)
- Use of specific point solutions (e.g. risk analysis in lending)
- Group decision support systems that facilitate decision making processes.

These represent combinations of person-to-computer and person-to-person interaction. Access to relevant information is not just though information databases. It is common to have information screens that support business process applications. For example, at insurance company CIGNA, the knowledge of their best experts has been incorporated into help screens in their underwriter's desk top system.

Support for the Knowledge Value Chain: The number of ways in which computers support knowledge work is very varied and makes planing for it quite difficult. We have developed half a dozen frameworks that position the various support mechanism along different dimensions. We share two of the here. The first is along a knowledge processing value chain.

First, computer support can make the input processes more effective. This means selecting information and knowledge that is relevant. Text summarising for, example extracts the key parts from a document, so that the reader can gain most of the sense in only a fraction of the original. British Telecom research has found that virtually no important meaning is lost with a 25 per cent abridgement of the original document. Data mining extracts new knowledge from existing data. It can find patterns that humans cannot, but considering many more dimensions and variables.

In terms of the knowledge base, what we found was an increasing emphasis of adding some context to the information. This might be a fuller description of the application of the information, an indication of the quality of the source, and many other little human touches that are often not found in formal databases, but which happen in day-to-day conversation. Some companies now add multimedia commentary e.g. the "expert speaks or demonstrates".

Finally, in terms of dissemination and use, as noted before it is the roll-out of Intranets and groupware that is having the most impact on knowledge management. The 'black box' expert systems, and other point solutions to knowledge problems, are growing in popularity for specific applications. However, Intranets and groupware are seen as a universal solution to the primary need for knowledge sharing, from best knowledge and expertise to the point of action, from those who have it, to those who need it.

It provides a foundation for the sharing of information or 'explicit knowledge' as encoded in databases and 'tacit' knowledge, as partially transmitted in email and other conversations. Often computer communications help make the connections between people, who subsequently follow up with "richer" communications methods, such as video conferencing or face-to-face. BP, for example, have rolled out videoconferencing as a key plank of their knowledge management initiative, in their virtual teamworking project. This allows experts and knowledge workers to communicate effectively and share 'tacit' knowledge without the need to travel.

Layers of Infrastructure: Another useful perspective on the role of ICT in knowledge management is the role of technology infrastructure. If, as noted, technologies that allow collaborative work, such as the Intranet and groupware, are needed, what are the building blocks to have a truly effective infrastructure. The 'stepping stones' that together build an enterprise-wide and inter-enterprise collaborative infrastructures.

Layered Elements of a Collaborative Technological Infrastructure: They represent ever complex layers of functionality:

- Connections-the ability to connect anyone into the network at any time. Portable computer and mobile phones are an example. One case we investigated, Buckman Laboratories, invests only in portable, not desk top, computers. A person's office is where their computer is, and wherever they can plug it into the international telephone system and the company network.
- Communications-establishing communications facilities such as electronic distribution lists, electronic meeting places (forums and discussion lists).
- Conversations-developing techniques and skills in conversing electronically; extracting meaning from ongoing threads of conversation. There is a role here for what is increasingly called a 'knowledge editor'.
- Collaboration-developing a toolcase of collaborative tools, or knowledge collaboration 'archetypes'; supplementing these with moderators who nurture the development of new knowledge through a wide range of contributions.

Not only are these technology layers, but they are process layers as well. The human and organisational factors become more important the higher the layer. Thus, BP found that for videoconferencing to work effectively, needed personal coaching when it was introduced.

If a knowledge support architecture is defined in terms of these levels, it clearly identifies the potential an organisation has to effectively create and share knowledge. Whether they realise this potential depends crucially on other factors, mostly organisational in nature.

Strategies for Success

Success Factors: Our research showed that the greatest inhibitor to knowledge sharing was inappropriate behaviours and organisational culture. The syndrome "knowledge is power" predominates too often. It is beyond the copse of this paper to go into the organisational and behavioural aspects, that were so important that they took two chapters of the six central chapters of our report (Skyrme and Amidon 1997). In summary, a number of recurring factors do stand out in a successful knowledge programme:

- A knowledge leader or champion-someone who actively drives the knowledge agenda forward, creates enthusiasm and commitment.
- Top management support-a CEO who recognises the value of knowledge and who actively supports the knowledge team in its work.
- A clear value proposition-identification of the link between knowledge and the bottom line business benefit; new measures of performance and appropriate rewards.
- A compelling vision and architecture-frameworks that drive the agenda forward.
- Effective information and knowledge management processes.

We will focus on the latter as it is the province of many information professionals. What we found was that those that were successful had successful developed a cooperative team that involved those with information management skills, IT knowledge (especially of Internet technologies) and change agents. However, we found a general lack of awareness among top management of the contribution of good information management. For example, identifying important knowledge is often an important starting point in a knowledge programme. Yet there was little appreciation that information resources management (IRM) through techniques such as information audit, could make a strong contribution.

Organisations are crying out for a systematic approach that gathers information, classifies it, adds value to it and supports the knowledge sharing process. We found that some of the management consultancies, whose business after all is "knowledge", were furthest ahead. Price Waterhouse, for example, not only have their Knowledge View SM database of best practices, but also have a taxonomy that aids sharing of information across business disciplines and industries, a knowledge centre, and many other features of good practice.

Implications for Information Professionals: The knowledge agenda and the growth of the Internet means that there is an opportunity to elevate the skills developed over many years in handling information to a higher level and become active in the knowledge agenda. Certainly the overall visibility of information professionals needs to be improved. On the one hand the Internet makes information more readily accessible to the end-user, thus to some extent by passing the need to get involved in mundane activities. On the other it has created a heightened awareness of what information is available, yet tools, such as search engines, may not be effectively used. Users are facing the information paradox-"drowning in data, yet short of intelligence". The implications for an information professional, that we draw from our analysis, are that you should:

1. Articulate the value added that good information management can bring to your organisation and its contribution to the bottom line.
2. Develop closer partnerships with the knowledge champions in your organisation. They need your skills and you might benefit from their current popularity among senior management!
3. Help the users help themselves. Provide more "how to" guides so that they can make more effective use of the only information resources at their disposal, including the Internet/Intranet as an information resource.

4. Be an active Internet/Intranet user yourself. Use email as a primary means of communication. Work in discussion lists and have your own groupware areas, one for peer knowledge sharing of best practice, and one for your client base.
5. Seek out best practice, wherever it is. When did you last benchmark your activities against a comparable activity externally?

Implications for Online Service Providers: The Internet is here to stay and growing in stature all the time. By now, most online service providers have recognised the inevitable and have strategies to embrace the Internet. However, they need to avoid the air of complacency that was evident a few years ago. The need for well organised information is as real as ever, but organisations will want to put it into their own frame of reference. The implications are therefore:

1. *Don't get Caught out with Technological Myopia in Future:* There are trend analysis techniques that help you identify what is coming and what wilt take hold. This is truer today as the Internet growth is fuelling significant investment into new software and technologies. Some of these technologies could really boost your product offering.
2. *Segment and Segment Again:* The days of the "one product serves all" are over. Marketers are taking of the ultimate segment of one. Discerning patterns of use by individual users (do some data mining!) and you can fine tune your offering and sell them more.
3. *Develop a Better Understanding and Closer Relationship with your End-user:* Understand more about knowledge work, and that information you provide does not stand-alone. It is part of a wider knowledge process. Thus new segmentation of information and new categories (e.g. problem categories) may be more useful than your existing ones.
4. *Re-evaluate Your Business Models and Pricing Strategy:* Organisations are sliming down and there's more

opportunities for 'pay-as-you-go' rather than up front subscriptions.

5. *Develop Hybrid Solutions:* This not only means combining CD-ROM with online, but also looking at human augmentation of your services. e.g. automatic email to subject matter experts, online video conferencing while browsing through information. The future will be in knowledge networks, not information networks.
6. *Conclusion:* This paper has drawn together two main strands of current management focus-the Internet and knowledge management. Each has a momentum of its own. However, in combination, they provide a powerful driving force for business and individual opportunities. We have summarised some highlights from our research into this interaction and indicated some of the ways in which information professionals and online service providers can exploit this convergence.

5

TOURISM AND MARKETING

MEANING AND DEFINITION

Almost every marketing textbook has a different definition of the term "marketing." The American Marketing Association (AMA) uses the following: "The process of planning and executing the conception, pricing, promotion, and distribution of ideas, goods, and services to create exchanges that satisfy individual and organizational objectives." From this definition, we see that:

- Marketing involves an ongoing process. The environment is "dynamic." This means that the market tends to change-what customers want today is not necessarily what they want tomorrow. For example, sales of beef are declining in the United States because consumers have become health oriented. Similarly, Tupperware parties are less popular today than they once were because there are fewer housewives who do not work outside the home.
- This process involves both planning and implementing (executing) the plan.
- Some of the main issues involved include:
  - o Marketers help design products, finding out what customers want and what can practically be made available given technology and price constraints.
  - o Marketers distribute products-there must be some efficient way to get the products from the factory to the end-consumer.

- o Marketers also promote products, and this is perhaps what we tend to think of first when we think of marketing. Promotion involves advertising-and much more. Other tools to promote products include trade promotion (store sales, coupons, and rebates), obtaining favorable and visible shelf-space, and obtaining favorable press coverage.
- o Marketers also price products to "move" them. We know from economics that, in most cases, sales correlate negatively with price-the higher the price, the lower the quantity demanded. In some cases, however, price may provide the customer with a "signal" of quality. Thus, the marketer needs to price the product to (1) maximize profit and (2) communicate a desired image of the product.
- o Marketing is applicable to services and ideas as well as to tangible products. For example, accountants may need to market their tax preparation services to consumers.

Reasons for studying marketing. There are several good reasons for studying marketing. First of all, marketing issues are important in all areas of the organization-customers are the reasons why businesses exist! In fact, marketing efforts (including such services as promotion and distribution) often account for more than half of the price of a product. As an added benefit, studying marketing often helps us become more savvy consumers. We will learn, for instance, that the per unit price of a bigger package is frequently higher than that of a smaller one, and that more expensive products are frequently not better in quality.

Criteria that must be met for marketing to occur. Several criteria must be met for marketing to occur:

- There must be two parties, each with unsatisfied needs or wants. This want, of course, could be money for the seller.
- Each must have something to offer. Marketing involves voluntary "exchange" relationships where both sides

must be willing parties. Thus, a consumer who buys a soft drink in a vending machine for 60¢ must value the soft drink, available at that time and place, more than the money. Conversely, the vendor must value the money more. (It is interesting to note that money is, strictly speaking, not necessary for this exchange to take place. It is possible, albeit a bit cumbersome, to exchange two ducks for a pair of shoes.)

- The parties must be able to communicate. This could be through a display in a store, an infomercial, or a posting one Bay.

The marketing vs. the selling concept. Two approaches to marketing exist. The traditional selling concept emphasizes selling existing products. The philosophy here is that if a product is not selling, more aggressive measures must be taken to sell it-e.g., cutting price, advertising more, or hiring more aggressive (and obnoxious) sales-people.

When the railroads started to lose business due to the advent of more effective trucks that could deliver goods right to the customer's door, the railroads cut prices instead of recognizing that the customers ultimately wanted transportation of goods, not necessarily railroad transportation. Smith Corona, a manufacturer of typewriters, was too slow to realize that consumers wanted the ability to process documents and not typewriters per se. The marketing concept, in contrast, focuses on getting consumers what they seek, regardless of whether this entails coming up with entirely new products.

The 4 Ps-product, place (distribution), promotion, and price-represent the variables that are within the control of the firm (at least in the medium to long run). In contrast, the firm is faced with uncertainty from the environment.

Marketing Environment

Elements of the Environment: The marketing environment involves factors that, for the most part, are beyond the control of the company. Thus, the company must adapt to these factors. It is important to observe how the environment changes so that a firm can adapt its strategies appropriately. Consider these environmental forces:

- *Competition:* Competitors often "creep" in and threaten to take away markets from firms. For example, Japanese auto manufacturers became a serious threat to American car makers in the late 1970s and early 1980s. Similarly, the Lotus Corporation, maker of one of the first commercially successful spreadsheets, soon faced competition from other software firms. Note that while competition may be frustrating for the firm, it is good for consumers. (In fact, we will come back to this point when we consider the legal environment). Note that competition today is increasingly global in scope.
- *Economics:* Some firms in particular are extremely vulnerable to changes in the economy. Consumers tend to put off buying a new car, going out to eat, or building new homes in bad times. In contrast, in good times, firms serving those needs may have difficulty keeping up with demand.
- *Political:* Businesses are very vulnerable to changes in the political situation. For example, because consumer groups lobbied Congress, more stringent rules were made on the terms of car leases. The tobacco industry is currently the target of much negative attention from government and public interest groups. Currently, the desire to avoid aiding the enemy may result in laws that make it more difficult for American firms to export goods to other countries.
- *Legal:* Firms are very vulnerable to changing laws and changing interpretations by the courts. Firms in the U.S. are very vulnerable to lawsuits. McDonald's, for example, is currently being sued by people who claim that eating the chain's hamburgers caused them to get fat. Some impacts of the legal environment:
- Firms are significantly limited in what they can do by various laws-some laws, for example, require that disclosures be made to consumers on the effective interest

rates they pay on products bought on installment. A particularly interesting group of laws relate to antitrust. These laws basically exist to promote fair competition among firms. Some principles involved here include:

- o *Collusion:* Firms may not "conspire" to fix prices (agree that they will not sell below an agreed upon price) or reduce services.
- o *Predation:* Firms may not sell their products below their cost of production for the purpose of driving competitors out of business so that they, themselves, can raise prices when competition is reduced.
- o *Market Share:* Firms which have an unacceptably large market share may be "broken" up by court order so that many smaller firms will be around to compete. (This is what happened to AT&T, and at times, IBM has been worried about this prospect).
- o *Tying*: A firm that controls a valuable product may not require the consumer to buy a more commonplace one to get the scarce product. For example, Intel controls many of the newest microprocessors (e.g., Pentium IV). Intel also makes motherboards for computers; however, motherboards are made by a lot of firms. Intel would be thought to abuse its effective monopoly power if it required consumers to buy a motherboard in order to get its newest chips.

- *Technological:* Changes in technology may significantly influence the demand for a product. For example, the advent of the fax machine was bad news for Federal Express. The Internet is a major threat to travel agents.
- *Social:* Changes in customs or demographics greatly influence firms. Fewer babies today are being born, resulting in a decreased demand for baby foods. More women work outside the home today, so there is a greater demand for prepared foods. There are more unmarried singles today. This provides opportunities for some firms (e.g., fast food restaurants) but creates

problems for others (e.g., manufacturers of high quality furniture that many people put off buying until marriage). Today, there are more "blended" families that result as parents remarry after divorce. These families are often strapped for money but may require "duplicate" items for children at each parent's residence.

Environmental scanning helps the firm understand developments in the market. Such developments may involve changes in the market place due to social trends (e.g., Gerber, a manufacturer of baby products, faces a serious challenge with declining U.S. birth rates), technology (e.g., VCR makers are threatened by DVD players), or new or potential competitors (e.g.,

Internet service providers are being threatened by increasing marketing efforts from MSN). Note that environmental scanning must be performed continuously, since environmental change does not cease.

ECONOMIC CYCLES

The economy goes through cycles. In the late 1990s, the U.S. economy was quite strong, and many luxury goods were sold. Currently, the economy is somewhat weak, and many firms are facing the results.

Car makers, for example, have seen declining profit margins (and even losses) as they have had to cut prices and offer low interest rates on financing. Generally, in good economic times, there is a great deal of demand, but this introduces a fear of possible inflation. In the U.S., the Federal Reserve will then try to prevent the economy from "overheating." This is usually done by raising interest rates. This makes businesses less willing to invest, and as a result, people tend to make less money. During a recession, unemployment tends to rise, causing consumers to spend less.

This may result in a "bad circle," with more people losing their jobs due to lowered demands. Some businesses, however, may take this opportunity to invest in growth now that things can be bought more cheaply.

Strategic Planning and the Marketing Process

Plans and planning. Plans are needed to clarify what kinds of strategic objectives an organization would like to achieve and how this is to be done. Such plans must consider the amount of resources available. One critical resource is capital. Microsoft keeps a great deal of cash on hand to be able to "jump" on opportunities that come about. Small startup software firms, on the other hand, may have limited cash on hand. This means that they may have to forego what would have been a good investment because they do not have the cash to invest and cannot find a way to raise the capital. Other resources that affect what a firm may be able to achieve include Trademarks/ brand names: It would be very difficult to compete factors such as: Patents: It would be difficult to against Coke and Pepsi in the cola market. compete against Intel and AMD in the microprocessor market since both these People: firms have a number of patents that it is difficult to get around. Even with all of Microsoft's money available, it could not immediately hire the Distribution: Stores have space people needed to manufacture computer chips. for only a fraction of the products they are offered, so they must turn many away. A firm that does not have an established relationship with stores will be at a disadvantage in trying to introduce a new product.

Plans are subject to the choices and policies that the organization has made. Some firms have goals of social responsibility, for example. Some firms are willing to take a greater risk, which may result in a very large payoff but also involve the risk of a large loss, than others.

Strategic marketing is best seen as an ongoing and never-ending process. Typically:

- The organization will identify the objectives it wishes to achieve. This could involve profitability directly, but often profitability is a long term goal that may require some intermediate steps. The firm may seek to increase market share, achieve distribution in more outlets, have sales grow by a certain percentage, or have consumers evaluate the product more favorably. Some organizations have objectives that are not focused on monetary profit-e.g., promoting literacy or preventing breast cancer.

- An analysis is made, taking into consideration issues such as organizational resources, competitors, the competitors' strengths, different types of customers, changes in the market, or the impact of new technology.
- Based on this analysis, a plan is made based on tradeoffs between the advantages and disadvantages of different options available.
- This strategy is then carried out. The firm may design new products, revamp its advertising strategy, invest in getting more stores to carry the product, or decide to focus on a new customer segment.
- After implementation, the results or outcome are evaluated. If results are not as desired, a change may have to be made to the strategy. Even if results are satisfactory, the firm still needs to monitor the environment for changes.

LEVELS OF PLANNING AND STRATEGIES

Plans for a firm can be made at several different levels. At the corporate level, the management considers the objectives of the firm as a whole. For example, Microsoft may want seek to grow by providing high quality software, hardware, and services to consumers. To achieve this goal, the firm may be willing to invest aggressively.

Plans can also be made at the business unit level. For example, although Microsoft is best known for its operating systems and applications software, the firm also provides Internet access and makes video games. Different managers will have responsibilities for different areas, and goals may best be made by those closest to the business area being considered. It is also more practical to hold managers accountable for performance if the plan is being made at a more specific level. Boeing has both commercial aircraft and defense divisions. Each is run by different managers, although there is some overlap in technology between the two. Therefore, plans are needed both at the corporate and at the business levels.

Occasionally, plans will be made at the functional level, to allow managers to specialize and to increase managerial accountability. Marketing, for example, may be charged with increasing awareness of Microsoft game consoles to 55% of the U.S. population or to increase the number of units of Microsoft Office sold. Finance may be charged with raising a given amount of capital at a given cost. Manufacturing may be charged with decreasing production costs by 5%.

The firm needs to identify the business it is in. Here, a balance must be made so that the firm's scope is not defined too narrowly or too broadly. A firm may define its goal very narrowly and then miss opportunities in the market place. For example, if Dell were to define itself only as a computer company, it might miss an opportunity to branch into PDAs or Internet service. Thus, they might instead define themselves as a provider of "information solutions."

A company should not define itself too broadly, however, since this may result in loss of focus. For example, a manufacturer of baking soda should probably not see itself as a manufacturer of all types of chemicals. Sometimes, companies can define themselves in terms of a customer need. For example, 3M sees itself as being in the business of making products whose surfaces are bonded together. This accounts for both Post-It notes and computer disks.

A firm's mission should generally include a discussion of the customers served (e.g., Wal-Mart and Nordstrom's serve different groups), the kind of technology involved, and the markets served.

Several issues are involved in selecting target customers. We will consider these in more detail within the context of segmentation, but for now, the firm needs to consider issues such as:

- The size of various market segments;
- How well these segments are being served by existing firms;

- Changes in the market-e.g., growth of segments or change in technology;
- How the firm should be positioned, or seen by customers. For example, Wal-Mart positions itself as providing value in retailing, while Nordstrom's defines itself more in terms of high levels of customer service.

The Boston Consulting Group (BCG) matrix provides a firm an opportunity to assess how well its business units work together. Each business unit is evaluated in terms of two factors: market share and the growth prospects in the market. Generally, the larger a firm's share, the stronger its position, and the greater the growth in a market, the better future possibilities. Four combinations emerge:

- A star represents a business unit that has a high share in a growing market. For example, Motorola has a large share in the rapidly growing market for cellular phones.
- A question mark results when a unit has a small share in a rapidly growing market. The firm's position, then, is not as strong as it would have been had its market share been greater, but there is an opportunity to grow. For example, Hewlett-Packard has a small share of the digital camera market, but this is a very rapidly growing market.
- A cash cow results when a firm has a large share in a market that is not growing, and may even be shrinking. Brother has a large share of the typewriter market.
- A dog results when a business unit has a small share in a market that is not growing. This is generally a somewhat unattractive situation, although dogs can still be profitable in the short run. For example, Smith Corona how has a small share of the typewriter market.

Firms are usually best of with a portfolio that has a balance of firms in each category. The cash cows tend to generate cash but require little future investment. On the other hand, stars generate some cash, but even more cash is needed to invest in the future-for research and development, marketing campaigns, and building new manufacturing facilities. Therefore, a firm may take excess cash from the cash cow and divert it to the star. For example, Brother could "harvest" its profits from typewriters and invest this in the unit making color laser printers, which will need the cash to grow. If a firm has cash cows that generate a lot of cash, this may be used to try to improve the market share of a question mark. A firm that has a number of promising stars in its portfolio may be in serious trouble if it does not have any cash cows to support it. If it is about to run out of cash-regardless of how profitable it is-is becomes vulnerable as a takeover target from a firm that has the cash to continue running it.

A SWOT ("Strengths, Opportunities, Weaknesses, and Threats") analysis is used to help the firm identify effective strategies. Successful firms such as Microsoft have certain strengths. Microsoft, for example, has a great deal of technology, a huge staff of very talented engineers, a great deal of experience in designing software, a very large market share, a well respected brand name, and a great deal of cash. Microsoft also has some weaknesses, however: The game console and MSN units are currently running at a loss, and MSN has been unable to achieve desired levels of growth. Firms may face opportunities in the current market. Microsoft, for example, may have the opportunity to take advantage of its brand name to enter into the hardware market. Microsoft may also become a trusted source of consumer services. Microsoft currently faces several threats, including the weak economy. Because fewer new computers are bough during a recession, fewer operating systems and software packages.

Rather than merely listing strengths, weaknesses, opportunities, and threats, a SWOT analysis should suggest how the firm may use its strengths and opportunities to overcome weaknesses and threats. Decisions should also be made as to how resources should be allocated. For example, Microsoft could either decide to put more resources into MSN or to abandon this unit entirely. Microsoft has a great deal of cash ready to spend, so the option to put resources toward MSN is available. Microsoft will also need to see how threats can be addressed. The firm can earn political good will by engaging in charitable acts, which it has money available to fund. For example, Microsoft has donated software and computers to schools. It can forego temporary profits by reducing prices temporarily to increase demand, or can "hold out" by maintaining current prices while not selling as many units.

Criteria for effective marketing plans. Marketing plans should meet several criteria:

- The plan must be specific enough so that it can be implemented and communicated to people in the firm. "Improving profitability" is usually too vague, but increasing net profits by 5%, increasing market share by 10%, gaining distribution in 2,000 more stores, and reducing manufacturing costs by 2% are all specific.
- The plan must be measurable so that one can see if it has been achieved. The above plans involve specific numbers.
- The goal must be achievable or realistic. Plans that are unrealistic may result in poor use of resources or lowered morale within the firm.
- The goals must be consistent. For example, a firm cannot ordinarily simultaneously plan improve product features, increase profits, and reduce prices.

Consumer Behaviour

Consumer behavior involves the psychological processes that consumers go through in recognizing needs, finding ways to solve these needs, making purchase decisions (e.g., whether or not to purchase a product and, if so, which brand and where), interpret information, make plans, and implement these plans (e.g., by engaging in comparison shopping or actually purchasing a product).

Sources of influence on the consumer. The consumer faces numerous sources of influence. Often, we take cultural influences for granted, but they are significant. An American will usually not bargain with a store owner. This, however, is a common practice in much of the World. Physical factors also influence our behavior. We are more likely to buy a soft drink when we are thirsty, for example, and food manufacturers have found that it is more effective to advertise their products on the radio in the late afternoon when people are getting hungry. A person's self-image will also tend to influence what he or she will buy-an upwardly mobile manager may buy a flashy car to project an image of success. Social factors also influence what the consumers buy-often, consumers seek to imitate others whom they admire, and may buy the same brands. The social environment can include both the mainstream culture (e.g., Americans are more likely to have corn flakes or ham and eggs for breakfast than to have rice, which is preferred in many Asian countries) and a subculture (e.g., rap music often appeals to a segment within the population that seeks to distinguish itself from the mainstream population). Thus, sneaker manufacturers are eager to have their products worn by admired athletes. Finally, consumer behavior is influenced by learning-you try a hamburger and learn that it satisfies your hunger and tastes good, and the next time you are hungry, you may consider another hamburger.

Consumer choices are often influenced dramatically by values. Some consumers, for example, seek to "fit in with the crowd" and would like to own a car as similar as possible to that of the neighbor. Others, on the other hand, want to stand out. In the consumption context, then, a consumer may choose to spend a great deal of money on buying and maintaining neat and professional attire, not because he or she is particularly interested in that appearance for its own sake, but rather because this will help the consumer be successful in his or her career.

Subculture often significantly influences the consumer. There are several potential ways that a society can be divided up. Some consumers are highly influenced by their ethnic origin. In some areas in Los Angeles, shopkeepers may transact all their business in a language of the predominant immigration patterns into the neighborhood-e.g., Spanish or Korean in some parts of downtown and Chinese in parts of the San Gabriel Valley. Virtual pets at first spread in the U.S. through Asian-American teenagers. Only after a while did the product diffuse into other ethnic groups. Occasionally, religious groups will influence consumers' behavior, usually because a religion may set certain standards-e.g., some religions do not allow the consumption of alcohol, while others may disapprove of charging interest. The fact that many Americans spend a great deal of time with members of their religious groups in churches, synagogues, and mosques implies that members have a great deal of influence on each other. People in similar age groups also tend to have more influence on each other. This is particularly evident in the spread of fashion. Social status may also have some influence, as people may tend to emulate others in similar occupations or neighborhoods.

One way to look at social influence is though "reference groups"-people against which one compares oneself. Thus, a consumer may notice that all his friends are wearing a special kind of jeans and may expect to be ostracized if he or she chooses to wear a different brand. Interestingly, however, one may also hold dissociative reference groups-people that one would not want to be compared to. For example, Cadillac has an image problem in being associated with older consumers, who are not considered "hip" enough by younger, upwardly mobile consumers that the firm would like to target. Thus, Cadillac ran the campaign "It's not your father's car."

Family may influence the consumer's choices a great deal. Research has shown, for example, that there is a tendency for adult children to use the same brands that their parents used over time. In many cases, these brand choices are made without much conscious thought.

In marketing jargon, a consumer problem refers to a "discrepancy" between the "ideal" situation and reality. Thus, problems can range greatly in severity. One problem, for example, is that you are hungry. The problem is easily solved by eating. Other problems can be significantly more severe-for example, a consumer is scared that he will be rejected by his wife because he is growing bald. Note that problems can be solved in more than one way. Baldness could be addressed by obtaining a wig, medical treatment, buying a fancy car (as an alternative way to achieve attractiveness), or some other creative way. One model of consumer decision making involves several steps. The first one is problem recognition-you realize that something is not as it should be. Perhaps, for example, your car is getting more difficult to start and is not accelerating well. The second step is information search-what are some alternative ways of solving the problem? You might buy a new car, buy a used car, take your car in for repair, ride the bus, ride a taxi, or ride a skateboard to work. The third step involves evaluation of alternatives. A skateboard is inexpensive, but may be ill-suited for long distances and for rainy days. Finally, we have the purchase stage, and sometimes a post-purchase stage (e.g., you return a product to the store because you did not find it satisfactory). In reality, people may go back and forth between the stages. For example, a person may resume alternative identification during while evaluating already known alternatives. Consumer involvement will tend to vary dramatically depending on the type of product. In general, consumer involvement will be higher for products that are very expensive (e.g., a home, a car) or are highly significant in the consumer's life in some other way (e.g., a word processing program or acne medication).

It is important to consider the consumer's motivation for buying products. To achieve this goal, we can use the Means-End chain, wherein we consider a logical progression of consequences of product use that eventually lead to desired end benefit. Thus, for example, a consumer may see that a car has a large engine, leading to fast acceleration, leading to a feeling of performance, leading to a feeling of power, which ultimately improves the consumer's self-esteem. A handgun may aim bullets with precision, which enables the user to kill an intruder, which means that the intruder will not be able to harm the consumer's family, which achieves the desired end-state of security. In advertising, it is important to portray the desired end-states. Focusing on the large motor will do less good than portraying a successful person driving the car.

Information search and decision making. Consumers engage in both internal and external information search. Internal search involves the consumer identifying alternatives from his or her memory. For certain low involvement products, it is very important that marketing programs achieve "top of mind" awareness. For example, few people will search the Yellow Pages for fast food restaurants; thus, the consumer must be able to retrieve one's restaurant from memory before it will be considered. For high involvement products, consumers are more likely to use an external search. Before buying a car, for example, the consumer may ask friends' opinions, read reviews in Consumer Reports, consult several web sites, and visit several dealerships. Thus, firms that make products that are selected predominantly through external search must invest in having information available to the consumer in need-e.g., through brochures, web sites, or news coverage.

A compensatory decision involves the consumer "trading off" good and bad attributes of a product. For example, a car may have a low price and good gas mileage but slow acceleration. If the price is sufficiently inexpensive and gas efficient, the consumer may then select it over a car with better acceleration that costs more and uses more gas. Occasionally, a decision will involve a non-compensatory strategy. For example, a parent may reject all soft drinks that contain artificial sweeteners. Here, other good features such as taste and low calories cannot overcome this one "non-negotiable" attribute.

The amount of effort a consumer puts into searching depends on a number of factors such as the market (how many competitors are there, and how great are differences between brands expected to be?), product characteristics (how important is this product? How complex is the product? How obvious are indications of quality?), consumer characteristics (how interested is a consumer, generally, in analyzing product characteristics and making the best possible deal?), and situational characteristics (as previously discussed).

Two interesting issues in decisions are:

- Variety seeking (where consumers seek to try new brands not because these brands are expected to be "better" in any way, but rather because the consumer wants a "change of pace," and

- "Impulse" purchases-unplanned buys. This represents a somewhat "fuzzy" group. For example, a shopper may plan to buy vegetables but only decide in the store to actually buy broccoli and corn. Alternatively, a person may buy an item which is currently on sale, or one that he or she remembers that is needed only once inside the store.

A number of factors involve consumer choices. In some cases, consumers will be more motivated.

For example, one may be more careful choosing a gift for an in-law than when buying the same thing for one self. Some consumers are also more motivated to comparison shop for the best prices, while others are more convenience oriented. Personality impacts decisions. Some like variety more than others, and some are more receptive to stimulation and excitement in trying new stores. Perception influences decisions. Some people, for example, can taste the difference between generic and name brand foods while many cannot. Selective perception occurs when a person is paying attention only to information of interest.

For example, when looking for a new car, the consumer may pay more attention to car ads than when this is not in the horizon. Some consumers are put off by perceived risk. Thus, many marketers offer a money back guarantee. Consumers will tend to change their behavior through learning-e.g., they will avoid restaurants they have found to be crowded and will settle on brands that best meet their tastes. Consumers differ in the values they hold (e.g., some people are more committed to recycling than others who will not want to go through the hassle). We will consider the issue of lifestyle under segmentation.

Attitudes. Consumer attitudes are a composite of a consumer's (1) beliefs about, (2) feelings about, (3) and behavioral intentions toward some "object"-within the context of marketing, usually a brand, product category, or retail store. These components are viewed together since they are highly interdependent and together represent forces that influence how the consumer will react to the object.

Beliefs. The first component is beliefs. A consumer may hold both positive beliefs toward an object (e.g., coffee tastes good) as well as negative beliefs (e.g., coffee is easily spilled and stains papers). In addition, some beliefs may be neutral (coffee is black), and some may be differ in valance depending on the person or the situation (e.g., coffee is hot and stimulates--good on a cold morning, but not good on a hot summer evening when one wants to sleep). Note also that the beliefs that consumers hold need not be accurate (e.g., that pork contains little fat), and some beliefs may, upon closer examination, be contradictory.

Affect. Consumers also hold certain feelings toward brands or other objects. Sometimes these feelings are based on the beliefs (e.g., a person feels nauseated when thinking about a hamburger because of the tremendous amount of fat it contains), but there may also be feelings which are relatively independent of beliefs. For example, an extreme environmentalist may believe that cutting down trees is morally wrong, but may have positive affect toward Christmas trees because he or she unconsciously associates these trees with the experience that he or she had at Christmas as a child.

Behavioral intention. The behavioral intention is what the consumer plans to do with respect to the object (e.g., buy or not buy the brand). As with affect, this is sometimes a logical consequence of beliefs (or affect), but may sometimes reflect other circumstances--e.g., although a consumer does not really like a restaurant, he or she will go there because it is a hangout for his or her friends.

Changing attitudes is generally very difficult, particularly when consumers suspect that the marketer has a self-serving "agenda" in bringing about this change (e.g., to get the consumer to buy more or to switch brands). Here are some possible methods:

- *Changing Affect:* One approach is to try to change affect, which may or may not involve getting consumers to change their beliefs. One strategy uses the approach of classical conditioning try to "pair" the product with a liked stimulus. For example, we "pair" a car with a beautiful woman. Alternatively, we can try to get people to like the advertisement and hope that this liking will "spill over" into the purchase of a product. For example, the Pillsbury Doughboy does not really emphasize the conveyance of much information to the consumer; instead, it attempts to create a warm, "fuzzy" image. Although Energizer Bunny ads try to get people to believe that their batteries last longer, the main emphasis is on the likeable bunny. Finally, products which are better known, through the mere exposure effect, tend to be better liked-that is, the more a product is advertised and seen in stores, the more it will generally be liked, even if consumers to do not develop any specific beliefs about the product.

- *Changing Behavior:* People like to believe that their behavior is rational; thus, once they use our products, chances are that they will continue unless someone is able to get them to switch. One way to get people to switch to our brand is to use temporary price discounts and coupons; however, when consumers buy a product on deal, they may justify the purchase based on that deal (i.e., the low price) and may then switch to other brands on deal later. A better way to get people to switch to our brand is to at least temporarily obtain better shelf space so that the product is more convenient. Consumers are less likely to use this availability as a rationale for their purchase and may continue to buy the product even when the product is less conveniently located.
- *Changing Beliefs:* Although attempting to change beliefs is the obvious way to attempt attitude change, particularly when consumers hold unfavorable or inaccurate ones, this is often difficult to achieve because consumers tend to resist. Several approaches to belief change exist:
  - o *Change Currently held Beliefs:* It is generally very difficult to attempt to change beliefs that people hold, particularly those that are strongly held, even if they are inaccurate. For example, the petroleum

industry advertised for a long time that its profits were lower than were commonly believed, and provided extensive factual evidence in its advertising to support this reality. Consumers were suspicious and rejected this information, however.

- o *Change the Importance of Beliefs:* Although the sugar manufacturers would undoubtedly like to decrease the importance of healthy teeth, it is usually not feasible to make beliefs less important--consumers are likely to reason, why, then, would you bother bringing them up in the first place? However, it may be possible to strengthen beliefs that favor us--e.g., a vitamin supplement manufacturer may advertise that it is extremely important for women to replace iron lost through menstruation. Most Add consumers already agree with this, but the belief can be made stronger. beliefs. Consumers are less likely to resist the addition of beliefs so long as they do not conflict with existing beliefs. Thus, the beef industry has added beliefs that beef (1) is convenient and (2) can be used to make a number of creative dishes. Vitamin manufacturers attempt to add the belief that stress causes vitamin depletion, which sounds quite plausible to most people.

- *Change the Ideal:* It usually difficult, and very risky, to attempt to change ideals, and only few firms succeed. For example, Hard Candy may have attempted to change the ideal away from traditional beauty toward more unique self expression.

One-sided vs. two-sided appeals. Attitude research has shown that consumers often tend to react more favorably to advertisements which either (1) admit something negative about the sponsoring brand (e.g., the Volvo is a clumsy car, but very safe) or (2) admits something positive about a competing brand (e.g., a competing supermarket has slightly lower prices, but offers less service and selection). Two-sided appeals must, contain overriding arguments why the sponsoring brand is ultimately superior-that is, in the above examples, the "but" part must be emphasized.

Reference Groups: A useful framework of analysis of group influence on the individual is the so called reference group-the term comes about because an individual uses a relevant group as a standard of "reference" against which oneself is compared. Reference groups come in several different forms. The aspirational reference group refers to those others against whom one would like to compare oneself. For example, many firms use athletes as spokespeople, and these represent what many people would ideally like to be. Associative reference groups include people who more realistically represent the individuals' current equals or near-equals-e.g., coworkers, neighbors, or members of churches, clubs, and organizations. Finally, the dissociative reference group includes people that the individual would not like to be like.

For example, the store literally named The Gap came about because many younger people wanted to actively dissociate from parents and other older and "uncool" people. The Quality Paperback Book specifically suggests in its advertising that its members are "a breed apart" from conventional readers of popular books.

The Family Life Cycle. Individuals and families tend to go through a "life cycle." The simple life cycle goes from:

child/teenager — young single — young couple — full nest — empty nest — widow(er).

In real life, this situation is, of course, a bit more complicated. For example, many couples undergo divorce. Then we have the scenario:

full nest — single parent

This situation can result either from divorce or from the death of one parent. Divorce usually entails a significant change in the relative wealth of spouses. In some cases, the non-custodial parent (usually the father) will not pay the required child support, and even if he or she does, that still may not leave the custodial parent and children as well off as they were during the marriage. On the other hand, in some cases, some non-custodial parents will be called on to pay a large part of their income in child support. This is particularly a problem when the non-custodial parent remarries and has additional children in the second (or subsequent marriages). In any event, divorce often results in a large demand for:

- low cost furniture and household items
- time-saving goods and services.

Divorced parents frequently remarry, or become involved in other non-marital relationships; thus, we may see

full nest — single parent — blended family

Another variation involves

young single — single parent

Here, the single parent who assumes responsibility for one or more children may not form a relationship with the other parent of the child.

Generally, there are two main themes in the Family Life Cycle, subject to significant exceptions:

- As a person gets older, he or she tends to advance in his or her career and tends to get greater income (exceptions: maternity leave, divorce, retirement).
- Unfortunately, obligations also tend to increase with time (at least until one's mortgage has been paid off). Children and paying for one's house are two of the greatest expenses.

Note that although a single person may have a lower income than a married couple, the single may be able to buy more discretionary items since he or she has fewer current obligations. This will change when a house is bought or children come along.

Family Decision Making: Individual members of families often serve different roles in decisions that ultimately draw on shared family resources. Some individuals are information gatherers/holders, who seek out information about products of relevance. These individuals often have a great deal of power because they may selectively pass on information that favors their chosen alternatives. Influencers do not ultimately have the power decide between alternatives, but they may make their wishes known by asking for specific products or causing embarrassing situations if their demands are not met. The decision maker(s) have the power to determine issues such as:

- Whether to buy;
- Which product to buy (pick-up or passenger car?);
- Which brand to buy;
- Where to buy it; and
- When to buy.

Note, however, that the role of the decision maker is separate from that of the purchaser. From the point of view of the marketer, this introduces some problems since the purchaser can be targeted by point-of-purchase (POP) marketing efforts that cannot be aimed at the decision maker. Also note that the distinction between the purchaser and decision maker may be somewhat blurred:

- The decision maker may specify what kind of product to buy, but not which brand;
- The purchaser may have to make a substitution if the desired brand is not in stock;
- The purchaser may disregard instructions (by error or deliberately).

It should be noted that family decisions are often subject to a great deal of conflict. The reality is that few families are wealthy enough to avoid a strong tension between demands on the family's resources. Conflicting pressures are especially likely in families with children and/or when only one spouse works outside the home. Note that many decisions inherently come down to values, and that there is frequently no "objective" way to arbitrate differences. One spouse may believe that it is important to save for the children's future; the other may value spending now (on private schools and computer equipment) to help prepare the children for the future. Who is right? There is no clear answer here. The situation becomes even more complex when more parties-such as children or other relatives-are involved. Culture is part of the external influences that impact the consumer. That is, culture represents influences that are imposed on the consumer by other individuals. The United States has undergone some changes in its predominant culture over the last several decades. Again, however, it should be kept in mind that there are great variations within the culture. For example, on the average, Americans have become less materialistic and have sought more leisure; on the other hand, the percentage of people working extremely long hours has also increased.

Significant changes have occurred in gender roles in American society. One of the reasons for this is that more women work outside the home than before. However, women still perform a disproportionate amount of housework, and men who participate in this activity tend to do so reluctantly. In general, commercials tend to lag somewhat behind reality-e.g., few men are seen doing housework, and few women are seen as buyers and decision makers on automobile purchases.

Regional influence, both in the United States and other areas, is significant. Many food manufacturers offer different product variations for different regions. Joel Girardeau, in his book The Nine Nations of North America, proposed nine distinct regional subcultures that cut across state lines. Although significant regional differences undoubtedly exist, research has failed to support Garreau's specific characterizations/

Consumer behavior is frequently affected by the situation. For example, people may buy different products when shopping for others than they would for themselves. We tend to make quicker but less elaborate decisions when facing time pressure. There are also influences of mood. For example, people who are unhappy tend to make more rational and more critical decisions.

The Means-End Chain: Consumers often buy products not because of their attributes per se but rather because of the ultimate benefits that these attributes provide, in turn leading to the satisfaction of ultimate values. For example, a consumer may not be particularly interested in the chemistry of plastic roses, but might reason as follows:

Highly reliable synthetic content of roses — Roses will stay in original condition for a long time — Significant other will appreciate the roses longer — Significant other will continue to love one — Self esteem.

The important thing in a means-end chain is to start with an attribute, a concrete characteristic of the product, and then logically progress to a series of consequences (which tend to become progressively more abstract) that end with a value being satisfied. Thus, each chain must start with an attribute and end with a value. An important implication of means-end chains is that it is usually most effective in advertising to focus on higher level items. For example, in the flower example above, an individual giving the flowers to the significant other might better be portrayed than the flowers alone.

Organizational Buyers: A large portion of the market for goods and services is attributable to organizational, as opposed to individual, buyers. In general, organizational buyers, who make buying decisions for their companies for a living, tend to be somewhat more sophisticated than ordinary consumers. However, these organizational buyers are also often more risk averse. There is a risk in going with a new, possibly better (lower price or higher quality) supplier whose product is unproven and may turn out to be problematic. Often the fear of running this risk is greater than the potential rewards for getting a better deal. In the old days, it used to be said that "You can't get fired for buying IBM." This attitude is beginning to soften a bit today as firms face increasing pressures to cut costs.

Organizational Buyers Come in Several Forms: Resellers involve either wholesalers or retailers that buy from one organization and resell to some other entity. For example, large grocery chains sometimes buy products directly from the manufacturer and resell them to end-consumers. Wholesalers may sell to retailers who in turn sell to consumers. Producers also buy products from sub-manufacturers to create a finished product. For example, rather than manufacturing the parts themselves, computer manufacturers often buy hard drives, motherboards, cases, monitors, keyboards, and other components from manufacturers and put them together to create a finished product. Governments buy a great deal of things. For example, the military needs an incredible amount of supplies to feed and equip troops. Finally, large institutions buy products in huge quantities. For example, UCR probably buys thousands of reams of paper every month.

Organizational buying usually involves more people than individual buying. Often, many people are involved in making decisions as to (a) whether to buy, (b) what to buy, (c) at what quantity, and (d) from whom. An engineer may make a specification as to what is needed, which may be approved by a manager, with the final purchase being made by a purchase specialist who spends all his or her time finding the best deal on the goods that the organization needs. Often, such long purchase processes can cause long delays. In the government, rules are often especially stringent-e.g., vendors of fruit cake have to meet fourteen pages of specifications put out by the General Services Administration. In many cases, government buyers are also heavily bound to go with the lowest price. Even if it is obvious that a higher priced vendor will offer a superior product, it may be difficult to accept that bid.

INTERNATIONAL MARKETING

Protectionism: Although trade generally benefits a country as a whole, powerful interests within countries frequently put obstacles-i.e., they seek to inhibit free trade. There are several ways this can be done:

- *Tariff Barriers:* A duty, or tax or fee, is put on products imported. This is usually a percentage of the cost of the good.
- *Quotas:* A country can export only a certain number of goods to the importing country. For example, Mexico can export only a certain quantity of tomatoes to the United States, and Asian countries can send only a certain quota of textiles here.
- *"Voluntary" Export Restraints:* These are not official quotas, but involve agreements made by countries to limit the amount of goods they export to an importing country. Such restraints are typically motivated by the desire to avoid more stringent restrictions if the exporters

do not agree to limit themselves. For example, Japanese car manufacturers have agreed to limit the number of automobiles they export to the United States.

- *Subsidies to Domestic Products:* If the government supports domestic producers of a product, these may end up with a cost advantage relative to foreign producers who do not get this subsidy. U.S. honey manufacturers receive such subsidies.
- Non-tariff barriers, such .as differential standards in testing foreign and domestic products for safety, disclosure of less information to foreign manufacturers needed to get products approved, slow processing of imports at ports of entry, or arbitrary laws which favor domestic manufacturers.

Cultural Lessons: We considered several cultural lessons in class; the important thing here is the big picture. For example, within the Muslim tradition, the dog is considered a "dirty" animal, so portraying it as "man's best friend" in an advertisement is counter-productive. Packaging, seen as a reflection of the quality of the "real" product, is considerably more important in Asia than in the U.S., where there is a tendency to focus on the contents which "really count." Many cultures observe significantly greater levels of formality than that typical in the U.S., and Japanese negotiator tend to observe long silent pauses as a speaker's point is considered.

Product Need Satisfaction: We often take for granted the "obvious" need that products seem to fill in our own culture; however, functions served may be very different in others-for example, while cars have a large transportation role in the U.S., they are impractical to drive in Japan, and thus cars there serve more of a role of being a status symbol or providing for individual indulgence.

In the U.S., fast food and instant drinks such as Tang are intended for convenience; elsewhere, they may represent more of a treat. Thus, it is important to examine through marketing research consumers' true motives, desires, and expectations in buying a product.

Approaches to Product Introduction: Firms face a choice of alternatives in marketing their products across markets. An extreme strategy involves customization, whereby the firm introduces a unique product in each country, usually with the belief tastes differ so much between countries that it is necessary more or less to start from "scratch" in creating a product for each market. On the other extreme, standardization involves making one global product in the belief the same product can be sold across markets without significant modification-e.g., Intel microprocessors are the same regardless of the country in which they are sold. Finally, in most cases firms will resort to some kind of adaptation, whereby a common product is modified to some extent when moved between some markets-e.g., in the United States, where fuel is relatively less expensive, many cars have larger engines than their comparable models in Europe and Asia; however, much of the design is similar or identical, so some economies are achieved. Similarly, while Kentucky Fried Chicken serves much the same chicken with the eleven herbs and spices in Japan, a lesser amount of sugar is used in the potato salad, and fries are substituted for mashed potatoes.

There are certain benefits to standardization. Firms that produce a global product can obtain economies of scale in manufacturing, and higher quantities produced also lead to a faster advancement along the experience curve. Further, it is more feasible to establish a global brand as less confusion will occur when consumers travel across countries and see the same product. On the down side, there may be significant differences in desires between cultures and physical environments-e.g., software sold in the U.S. and Europe will often utter a "beep" to alert the user when a mistake has been made; however, in Asia, where office workers are often seated closely together, this could cause embarrassment.

Adaptations Come in Several Forms: Mandatory adaptations involve changes that have to be made before the product can be used-e.g., appliances made for the U.S. and Europe must run on different voltages, and a major problem was experienced in the European Union when hoses for restaurant frying machines could not simultaneously meet the legal requirements of different countries. "Discretionary" changes are changes that do not have to be made before a product can be introduced (e.g., there is nothing to prevent an American firm from introducing an overly sweet soft drink into the Japanese market), although products may face poor sales if such changes are not made. Discretionary changes may also involve cultural adaptations-e.g., in Sesame Street, the Big Bird became the Big Camel in Saudi Arabia.

Another distinction involves physical product vs. communication adaptations. In order for gasoline to be effective in high altitude regions, its octane must be higher, but it can be promoted much the same way. On the other hand, while the same bicycle might be sold in China and the U.S., it might be positioned as a serious means of transportation in the former and as a recreational tool in the latter. In some cases, products may not need to be adapted in either way (e.g., industrial equipment), while in other cases, it might have to be adapted in both (e.g., greeting cards, where the both occasions, language, and motivations for sending differ). Finally, a market may exist abroad for a product which has no analogue at home-e.g., hand-powered washing machines. Measuring country wealth.

Economics: There are two ways to measure the wealth of a country. The nominal per capita gross domestic product (GDP) refers to the value of goods and services produced per person in a country if this value in local currency were to be exchanged into dollars. Suppose, for example, that the per capita GDP of Japan is 3,500,000 yen and the dollar exchanges for 100 yen, so that the per capita GDP is (3,500,000/100)=$35,000. However, that $35,000 will not buy as much in Japan-food and housing are much more expensive there. Therefore, we introduce the idea of purchase parity adjusted per capita GDP, which reflects what this money can buy in the country. This is typically based on the relative costs of a weighted "basket" of goods in a country (e.g., 35% of the cost of housing, 40% the cost of food, 10% the cost of clothing, and 15% cost of other items). If it turns out that this measure of cost of living is 30% higher in Japan, the purchase parity adjusted GPD in

Japan would then be ($35,000/(130%) = $26,923. (The Gross Domestic Product (GPD) and Gross National Product (GNP) are almost identical figures. The GNP, for example, includes income made by citizens working abroad, and does not include the income of foreigners working in the country. Traditionally, the GNP was more prevalent; today the GPD is more commonly used-in practice, the two measures fall within a few percent of each other.)

In general, the nominal per capita GPD is more useful for determining local consumers' ability to buy imported goods, the cost of which are determined in large measure by the costs in the home market, while the purchase parity adjusted measure is more useful when products are produced, at local costs, in the country of purchase. For example, the ability of Argentineans to purchase micro computer chips, which are produced mostly in the U.S. and Japan, is better predicted by nominal income, while the ability to purchase toothpaste made by a U.S. firm in a factory in Argentina is better predicted by purchase parity adjusted income.

It should be noted that, in some countries, income is quite unevenly distributed so that these average measures may not be very meaningful. In Brazil, for example, there is a very large underclass making significantly less than the national average, and thus, the national figure is not a good indicator of the purchase power of the mass market. Similarly, great regional differences exist within some countries-income is much higher in northern Germany than it is in the former East Germany, and income in southern Italy is much lower than in northern Italy.

Methods of Entry: With rare exceptions, products just don't emerge in foreign markets overnight-a firm has to build up a market over time. Several strategies, which differ in aggressiveness, risk, and the amount of control that the firm is able to maintain, are available:

- Exporting is a relatively low risk strategy in which few investments are made in the new country. A drawback is that, because the firm makes few if any marketing investments in the new country, market share may be below potential. Further, the firm, by not operating in the country, learns less about the market (What do consumers really want? Which kinds of advertising campaigns are most successful? What are the most effective methods of distribution?) If an importer is willing to do a good job of marketing, this arrangement may represent a "win-win" situation, but it may be more difficult for the firm to enter on its own later if it decides that larger profits can be made within the country.

- Licensing and franchising are also low exposure methods of entry-you allow someone else to use your trademarks and accumulated expertise. Your partner puts up the money and assumes the risk. Problems here involve the fact that you are training a potential competitor and that you have little control over how the business is operated. For example, American fast food restaurants have found that foreign franchisers often fail to maintain American standards of cleanliness. Similarly, a foreign manufacturer may use lower quality ingredients in manufacturing a brand based on premium contents in the home country.
- *Joint Venture:* Here, a firm partners up with a firm already in the country. Each partner contributes. Usually, the host country partner contributes expertise about the country and possibly some manufacturing facilities. The "guest" partner usually contributes technology and/or financial resources. This reduces risk and investment to some extent, but also reduces the control since agreements must now be made to satisfy the partner.
- Direct entry strategies, where the firm either acquires a firm or builds operations "from scratch" involve the highest exposure, but also the greatest opportunities for profits. The firm gains more knowledge about the local market and maintains greater control, but now has a huge investment. In some countries, the government may expropriate assets without compensation, so direct

investment entails an additional risk. A variation involves a joint venture, where a local firm puts up some of the money and knowledge about the local market.

U.S. laws of particular interest to firms doing business abroad.

- *Anti-trust:* U.S. antitrust laws are generally enforced in U.S. courts even if the alleged transgression occurred outside U.S. jurisdiction. For example, if two Japanese firms collude to limit the World supply of VCRs, they may be sued by the U.S. government (or injured third parties) in U.S. courts, and may have their U.S. assets seized.
- The Foreign Corrupt Influences Act came about as Congress was upset with U.S. firms' bribery of foreign officials. Although most if not all countries ban the payment of bribes, such laws are widely flaunted in many countries, and it is often useful to pay a bribe to get foreign government officials to act favorably. Firms engaging in this behavior, even if it takes place entirely outside the U.S., can be prosecuted in U.S. courts, and many executives have served long prison sentences for giving in to temptation. In contrast, in the past some European firms could actually deduct the cost of foreign bribes from their taxes! There are some gray areas here-it may be legal to pay certain "tips"-known as "facilitating payments"-to low level government workers in some countries who rely on such payments as part of their salary so long as these payments are intended only to speed up actions that would be taken anyway. For example, it may be acceptable to give a reasonable (not large) facilitating payment to get customs workers to process a shipment faster, but it would not be legal to pay these individuals to change the classification of a product into one that carries a lower tariff.
- *Anti-boycott Laws:* Many Arab countries maintain a boycott of Israel, and foreigners that want to do business with them may be asked to join in this boycott by stopping any deals they do with Israel and certifying

that they do not trade with that country. It is illegal for U.S. firms to make this certification even if they have not dropped any actual deals with Israel to get a deal with boycotters.

- *Trading with the Enemy:* It is illegal for U.S. firms to trade with certain countries that are viewed to be hostile to the U.S.-e.g., Libya and Iraq.

MARKETING RESEARCH

Marketing research is often needed to ensure that we produce what customers really want and not what we think they want.

Primary vs. secondary research methods. There are two main approaches to marketing. Secondary research involves using information that others have already put together. For example, if you are thinking about starting a business making clothes for tall people, you don't need to question people about how tall they are to find out how many tall people exist-that information has already been published by the U.S. Government. Primary research, in contrast, is research that you design and conduct yourself. For example, you may need to find out whether consumers would prefer that your soft drinks be sweater or tarter.

Research will often help us reduce risks associated with a new product, but it cannot take the risk away entirely. It is also important to ascertain whether the research has been complete. For example, Coca Cola did a great deal of research prior to releasing the New Coke, and consumers seemed to prefer the taste. However, consumers were not prepared to have this drink replace traditional Coke.

Several tools are available to the market researcher-e.g., mail questionnaires, phone surveys, observation, and focus groups. Please see the chart for advantages and disadvantages of each.

Surveys are useful for getting a great deal of specific information. Surveys can contain open-ended questions (e.g., "In which city and state were you born? ___________") or closed-ended, where the respondent is asked to select answers from a brief list (e.g., "__Male ___Female." Open ended questions have the advantage that the respondent is not limited to the options listed, and that the respondent is not being influenced by seeing a list of responses. However, open-ended questions are often skipped by respondents, and coding them can be quite a challenge. In general, for surveys to yield meaningful responses, sample sizes of over 100 are usually required because precision is essential. For example, if a market share of twenty percent would result in a loss while thirty percent would be profitable, a confidence interval of 20-35% is too wide to be useful.

Surveys come in several different forms. Mail surveys are relatively inexpensive, but response rates are typically quite low-typically from 5-20%. Phone-surveys get somewhat higher response rates, but not many questions can be asked because many answer options have to be repeated and few people are willing to stay on the phone for more than five minutes. Mall intercepts are a convenient way to reach consumers, but respondents may be reluctant to discuss anything sensitive face-to-face with an interviewer.

Surveys, as any kind of research, are vulnerable to bias. The wording of a question can influence the outcome a great deal. For example, more people answered no to the question "Should speeches against democracy be allowed?" than answered yes to "Should speeches against democracy be forbidden?" For face-to-face interviews, interviewer bias is a danger, too. Interviewer bias occurs when the interviewer influences the way the respondent answers. For example, unconsciously an interviewer that works for the firm manufacturing the product in question may smile a little when something good is being said about the product and frown a little when something negative is being said.

The respondent may catch on and say something more positive than his or her real opinion. Finally, a response bias may occur-if only part of the sample responds to a survey, the respondents' answers may not be representative of the population.

Focus groups are useful when the marketer wants to launch a new product or modify an existing one. A focus group usually involves having some 8-12 people come together in a room to discuss their consumption preferences and experiences. The group is usually led by a moderator, who will start out talking broadly about topics related broadly to the product without mentioning the product itself. For example, a focus group aimed at sugar-free cookies might first address consumers' snacking preferences, only gradually moving toward the specific product of sugar-free cookies. By not mentioning the product up front, we avoid biasing the participants into thinking only in terms of the specific product brought out. Thus, instead of having consumers think primarily in terms of what might be good or bad about the product, we can ask them to discuss more broadly the ultimate benefits they really seek.

For example, instead of having consumers merely discuss what they think about some sugar-free cookies that we are considering releasing to the market, we can have consumers speak about their motivations for using snacks and what general kinds of benefits they seek. Such a discussion might reveal a concern about healthfulness and a desire for wholesome foods. Probing on the meaning of wholesomeness, consumers might indicate a desire to avoid artificial ingredients. This would be an important concern in the marketing of sugar-free cookies, but might not have come up if consumers were asked to comment directly on the product where the use of artificial ingredients is, by virtue of the nature of the product, necessary.

Focus groups are well suited for some purposes, but poorly suited for others. In general, focus groups are very good for getting breadth-i.e., finding out what kinds of issues are important for consumers in a given product category. Here, it is helpful that focus groups are completely "open-ended:" The consumer mentions his or her preferences and opinions, and the focus group moderator can ask the consumer to elaborate. In a questionnaire, if one did not think to ask about something, chances are that few consumers would take the time to write out an elaborate answer. Focus groups also have some drawbacks, for example: They represent small sample sizes.

Because of the cost of running focus groups, only a few groups can be run. Suppose you run four focus groups with ten members each. This will result in an n of 4(10)=40, which is too small to generalize from. Therefore, focus groups cannot give us a good idea of: What proportion of the population is likely to buy the product. What price consumers are willing to pay. The groups are inherently social. This means that: Consumers will often say things that may make them look good (i.e., they watch public television rather than soap operas or cook fresh meals for their families daily) even if that is not true. Consumers may be reluctant to speak about embarrassing issues (e.g., weight control, birth control).

Personal interviews involve in-depth questioning of an individual about his or her interest in or experiences with a product. The benefit here is that we can get really into depth (when the respondent says something interesting, we can ask him or her to elaborate), but this method of research is costly and can be extremely vulnerable to interviewer bias.

Projective techniques are used when a consumer may feel embarrassed to admit to certain opinions, feelings, or preferences. For example, many older executives may not be comfortable admitting to being intimidated by computers. It has been found that in such cases, people will tend to respond more openly about "someone else." Thus, we may ask them to explain reasons why a friend has not yet bought a computer, or to tell a story about a person in a picture who is or is not using a product. The main problem with this method is that it is difficult to analyze responses.

Observation of consumers is often a powerful tool. Looking at how consumers select products may yield insights into how they make decisions and what they look for. For example, some American manufacturers were concerned about low sales of their products in Japan. Observing Japanese consumers, it was found that many of these Japanese consumers scrutinized packages looking for a name of a major manufacturer-the product specific-brands that are common in the U.S. (e.g., Tide) were not impressive to the Japanese, who wanted a name of a major firm like Mitsubishi or Proctor & Gamble. Observation may help us determine how much time consumers spend comparing prices, or whether nutritional labels are being consulted.

Physiological measures are occasionally used to examine consumer response. For example, advertisers may want to measure a consumer's level of arousal during various parts of an advertisement.

Some cautions should be heeded in marketing research. First, in general, research should only be commissioned when it is worth the cost. Thus, research should normally be useful in making specific decisions (what size should the product be? Should the product be launched? Should we charge $1.75 or $2.25?)

Secondly, marketing research can be, and often is, abused. Managers frequently have their own "agendas" (e.g., they either would like a product to be launched or would prefer that it not be launched so that the firm will have more resources left over to tackle their favorite products). Often, a way to get your way is to demonstrate through "objective" research that your opinions make economic sense. One example of misleading research, which was reported nationwide in the media, involved the case of "The Pentagon Declares War on Rush Limbaugh." The Pentagon, within a year of the election of Democrat Bill Clinton, reported that only 4.2% of soldiers listening to the Armed Forces Network wanted to hear Rush Limbaugh. However, although this finding was reported without question in the media, it was later found that the conclusion was based on the question "What single thing can we do to improve programming?" If you did not write in something like "Carry Rush Limbaugh," you were counted as not wanting to hear him.

Segmentation, Targeting and Positioning

Segmentation, targeting, and positioning together comprise a three stage process. We first (1) determine which kinds of customers exist, then (2) select which ones we are best off trying to serve and, finally, (3) implement our segmentation by optimizing our products/services for that segment and communicating that we have made the choice to distinguish ourselves that way. Segmentation involves finding out what kinds of consumers with different needs exist. In the auto market, for example, some consumers demand speed and performance, while others are much more concerned about roominess and safety. In general, it holds true that "You can't be all things to all people," and experience has demonstrated that firms that specialize in meeting the needs of one group of consumers over another tend to be more profitable.

Generally, there are three approaches to marketing:

- In the undifferentiated strategy, all consumers are treated as the same, with firms not making any specific efforts to satisfy particular groups. This may work when the product is a standard one where one competitor really can't offer much that another one can't. Usually, this is the case only for commodities.
- In the concentrated strategy, one firm chooses to focus on one of several segments that exist while leaving other segments to competitors. For example, Southwest Airlines focuses on price sensitive consumers who will forego meals and assigned seating for low prices.
- In contrast, most airlines follow the differentiated strategy: They offer high priced tickets to those who are inflexible in that they cannot tell in advance when they need to fly and find it impractical to stay over a Saturday. These travelers-usually business travelers-pay high fares but can only fill the planes up partially. The same airlines then sell some of the remaining seats to more price sensitive customers who can buy two weeks in advance and stay over.

Note that segmentation calls for some tough choices. There may be a large number of variables that can be used to differentiate consumers of a given product category; yet, in practice, it becomes impossibly cumbersome to work with more than a few at a time. Thus, we need to determine which variables will be most useful in distinguishing different groups of consumers. We might thus decide, for example, that the variables that are most relevant in separating different kinds of soft drink consumers are (1) preference for taste vs. low calories, (2) preference for Cola vs. non-cola taste, (3) price sensitivity-willingness to pay for brand names; and (4) heavy vs. light consumers. We now put these variables together to arrive at various combinations. Several different kinds of variables can be used for segmentation. Demographic variables essentially refer to personal statistics such as income, gender, education, location (rural vs. urban, East vs. West), ethnicity, and family size. Campbell's soup, for instance, has found that Western U.S. consumers on the average prefer spicier soups-thus, you get a different product in the same cans at the East and West coasts. Facing flat sales of guns in the traditional male dominated market, a manufacturer came out with the Lady Remmington, a more compact, handier gun more attractive to women.

Taking this a step farther, it is also possible to segment on lifestyle and values. Some consumers want to be seen as similar to others, while a different segment wants to stand apart from the crowd. Another basis for segmentation is behavior. Some consumers are "brand loyal"-i.e., they tend to stick with their preferred brands even when a competing one is on sale. Some consumers are "heavy" users while others are "light" users. For example, research conducted by the wine industry shows that some 80% of the product is consumed by 20% of the consumers-presumably a rather intoxicated group.

One can also segment on benefits sought, essentially bypassing demographic explanatory variables. Some consumers, for example, like scented soap (a segment likely to be attracted to brands such as Irish Spring), while others prefer the "clean" feeling of unscented soap (the "Ivory" segment). Some consumers use toothpaste primarily to promote oral health, while another segment is more interested in breath freshening. In the next step, we decide to target one or more segments. Our choice should generally depend on several factors.

First, how well are existing segments served by other manufacturers? It will be more difficult to appeal to a segment that is already well served than to one whose needs are not currently being served well.

Secondly, how large is the segment, and how can we expect it to grow? (Note that a downside to a large, rapidly growing segment is that it tends to attract competition).

Thirdly, do we have strengths as a company that will help us appeal particularly to one group of consumers? Firms may already have an established reputation. While McDonald's has a great reputation for fast, consistent quality, family friendly food, it would be difficult to convince consumers that McDonald's now offers gourmet food. Thus, McD's would probably be better off targeting families in search of consistent quality food in nice, clean restaurants.

Positioning involves implementing our targeting. For example, Apple Computer has chosen to position itself as a maker of user-friendly computers. Thus, Apple has done a lot through its advertising to promote itself, through its unintimidating icons, as a computer for "non-geeks." The Visual C software programming language, in contrast, is aimed a "techies."

Repositioning involves an attempt to change consumer perceptions of a brand, usually because the existing position that the brand holds has become less attractive. Sears, for example, attempted to reposition itself from a place that offered great sales but unattractive prices the rest of the time to a store that consistently offered "everyday low prices." Repositioning in practice is very difficult to accomplish. A great deal of money is often needed for advertising and other promotional efforts, and in many cases, the repositioning fails.

Product Mix

Products come in several forms. Consumer products can be categorized as convenience goods, for which consumers are willing to invest very limited shopping efforts. Thus, it is essential to have these products readily available and have the brand name well known. Shopping goods, in contrast, are goods in which the consumer is willing to invest a great deal of time and effort. For example, consumers will spend a great deal of time looking for a new car or a medical procedure. Speciality goods are those that are of interest only to a narrow segment of the population-e.g., drilling machines. Industrial goods can also be broken down into subgroups, depending on their uses. It should also be noted that, within the context of marketing decisions, the term product refers to more than tangible goods-a service can be a product, too.

A firm's product line or lines refers to the assortment of similar things that the firm holds. Brother, for example, has both a line of laser printers and one of typewriters. In contrast, the firm's product mix describes the combination of different product lines that the firm holds. Boeing, for example, has both a commercial aircraft and a defense line of products that each take advantage of some of the same core competencies and technologies of the firm. Some firms have one very focused or narrow product line (e.g., KFC does only chicken right) while others maintain numerous lines that hopefully all have some common theme. This represents a wide product mix 3M, for example, makes a large assortment of goods that are thought to be related in the sense that they use the firm's ability to bond surfaces together. Depth refers to the variety that is offered within each product line. Maybeline offers a great deal of depth in lipsticks with subtle differences in shades while Morton Salt offers few varieties of its product.

Products may be differentiated in several ways. Some may be represented as being of superior quality (e.g., Maytag), or they may differ in more arbitrary ways in terms of styles-some people like one style better than another, while there is no real consensus on which one is the superior one. Finally, products can be differentiated in terms of offering different levels of service-for example, Volvo offers a guarantee of free, reliable towing anywhere should the vehicle break down. American Express offers services not offered by many other charge cards.

New product development tends to happen in stages. Although firms often go back and forth between these idealized stages, the following sequence is illustrative of the development of a new product:

- *New Product Strategy Development:* Different firms will have different strategies on how to approach new products. Some firms have stockholders who want to minimize risk and avoid investing in too many new innovations. Some firms can only survive if they innovate frequently and have stockholders who are willing to take this risk. For example, Hewlett-Packard has to constantly invent new products since competitors learn to work around its patents and will be able to manufacture the products at a lower cost.

- *Idea Generation:* Firms solicit ideas as to new products it can make. Ideas might come from customers, employees, consultants, or engineers. Many firms receive a large number of ideas each year and can only invest in some of them.
- *Screening and Evaluation:* Some products that after some analysis are clearly not feasible or are not consistent with the core competencies of the firm are eliminated.
- *Business Analysis:* Ideas are now exposed to more rigorous analysis. Profit projections, risks, market size, and competitive response are considered. If promising, market research may be done.
- *Development:* The product is designed and manufacturing facilities are planned.
- *Market Testing:* Frequently, firms will try to "test" a product in one region to see if it will sell in reality before it is released nationally and internationally. There is a lesser risk if the firm only commits money to advertising and other marketing efforts in one region. Retailers will also be more receptive in other parts of the country and world if it has been demonstrated that the product sold well in one region. The firm may also experiment with different prices for the product.
- *Commercialization:* Facilities to manufacture the product on a larger scale are now put into operation and the firm starts a national marketing campaign and distribution effort.

Products often go through a life cycle. Initially, a product is introduced. Since the product is not well known and is usually expensive (e.g., as microwave ovens were in the late 1970s), sales are usually limited. Eventually, however, many products reach a growth phase-sales increase dramatically. More firms enter with their models of the product. Frequently, unfortunately, the product will reach a maturity stage where little growth will be seen. For example, in the United States, almost every household has at least one color TV set. Some products may also reach a decline stage, usually because the product category is being replaced by something better. For example, typewriters experienced declining sales as more consumers switched to computers or other word processing equipment. The product life cycle is tied to the phenomenon of diffusion of innovation. When a new product comes out, it is likely to first be adopted by consumers who are more innovative than others-they are willing to pay a premium price for the new product and take a risk on unproven technology. It is important to be on the good side of innovators since many other later adopters will tend to rely for advice on the innovators who are thought to be more knowledgeable about new products for advice.

At later phases of the PLC, the firm may need to modify its market strategy. For example, facing a saturated market for baking soda in its traditional use, Arm & Hammer launched a major campaign to get consumers to use the product to deodorize refrigerators. Deodorizing powders to be used before vacuuming were also created.

It is sometimes useful to think of products as being either new or existing. Many firms today rely increasingly on new products for a large part of their sales. New products can be new in several ways. They can be new to the market-no one else ever made a product like this before. For example, Chrysler invented the minivan. Products can also be new to the firm-another firm invented the product, but the firm is now making its own version. For example, IBM did not invent the personal computer, but entered after other firms showed the market to have a high potential. Products can be new to the segment-e.g., cellular phones and pagers were first aimed at physicians and other price-insensitive segments. Later, firms decided to target the more price-sensitive mass market. A product can be new for legal purposes. Because consumers tend to be attracted to "new and improved" products, the Federal Trade Commission (FTC) only allows firms to put that label on reformulated products for six months after a significant change has been made.

The diffusion of innovation refers to the tendency of new products, practices, or ideas to spread among people. Usually, when new products or ideas come about, they are initially only adopted by a small group of people. Later, many innovations spread to other people. The bell shaped curve frequently illustrates the rate of adoption of a new product. Cumulative adoptions are reflected by the S-shaped curve. The saturation point is the maximum proportion of consumers likely to adopt a product. In the case of refrigerators in the U.S., the saturation level is nearly one hundred percent of households. The figure will almost certainly be well below that for video games that, even when spread out to a large part of the population, will be of interest to far from everyone.

Several specific product categories have case histories that illustrate important issues in adoption. Until some time in the 1800s, few physicians bothered to scrub prior to surgery, even though new scientific theories predicted that small microbes not visible to the naked eye could cause infection. Younger and more progressive physicians began scrubbing early on, but they lacked the stature to make their older colleagues follow.

ATM cards spread relatively quickly. Since the cards were used in public, others who did not yet hold the cards could see how convenient they were. Although some people were concerned about security, the convenience factors seemed to be a decisive factor in the "tug-of-war" for and against adoption.

The case of credit cards was a bit more complicated and involved a "chicken-and-egg" paradox. Accepting credit cards was not a particularly attractive option for retailers until they were carried by a large enough number of consumers. Consumers, in contrast, were not particularly interested in cards that were not accepted by a large number of retailers. Thus, it was necessary to "jump start" the process, signing up large corporate accounts, under favorable terms, early in the cycle, after which the cards became worthwhile for retailers to accept.

Rap music initially spread quickly among urban youths in large part because of the low costs of recording. Later, rap music became popular among a very different segment, suburban youths, because of its apparently authentic depiction of an exotic urban lifestyle.

Hybrid corn was adopted only slowly among many farmers. Although hybrid corn provided yields of about 20% more than traditional corn, many farmers had difficulty believing that this smaller seed could provide a superior harvest. They were usually reluctant to try it because a failed harvest could have serious economic consequences, including a possible loss of the farm. Agricultural extension agents then sought out the most progressive farmers to try hybrid corn, also aiming for farmers who were most respected and most likely to be imitated by others. Few farmers switched to hybrid corn outright from year to year. Instead, many started out with a fraction of their land, and gradually switched to 100% hybrid corn when this innovation had proven itself useful.

Several forces often work against innovation. One is risk, which can be either social or financial. For example, early buyers of the CD player risked that few CDs would be recorded before the CD player went the way of the 8 track player. Another risk is being perceived by others as being weird for trying a "fringe" product or idea. For example, Barbara Mandrell sings the song "I Was Country When Country Wasn't Cool."

Other sources of resistance include the initial effort needed to learn to use new products (e.g., it takes time to learn to meditate or to learn how to use a computer) and concerns about compatibility with the existing culture or technology. For example, birth control is incompatible with religious beliefs that predominate in some areas, and a computer database is incompatible with a large, established card file.

Innovations come in different degrees. A continuous innovation includes slight improvements over time. Very little usually changes from year to year in automobiles, and even automobiles of the 1990s are driven much the same way that automobiles of the 1950 were driven. A dynamically continuous innovation involves some change in technology, although the product is used much the same way that its predecessors were used-e.g., jet vs. propeller aircraft. A discontinous innovation involves a product that fundamentally changes the way that things are done-e.g., the fax and photocopiers. In general, discontinuous innovations are more difficult to market since greater changes are required in the way things are done, but the rewards are also often significant.

Several factors influence the speed with which an innovation spreads. One issue is relative advantage (i.e., the ratio of risk or cost to benefits). Some products, such as cellular phones, fax machines, and ATM cards, have a strong relative advantage. Other products, such as automobile satellite navigation systems, entail some advantages, but the cost ratio is high. Lower priced products often spread more quickly, and the extent to which the product is trialable (farmers did not have to plant all their land with hybrid corn at once, while one usually has to buy a cellular phone to try it out) influence the speed of diffusion. Finally, the extent of switching difficulties influences speed-many offices were slow to adopt computers because users had to learn how to use them.

Some cultures tend to adopt new products more Modernity: The extent to which quickly than others, based on several factors: the culture is receptive to new things. In some countries, such as Britain and Saudi Arabia, tradition is greatly valued-thus, new products often don't fare Homophily: too well. The United States, in contrast, tends to value progress. The more similar to each other that members of a culture are, the more likely an innovation is to spread-people are more likely to imitate similar than different models. The two most rapidly adopting countries in the World are the U.S. and Japan. While the U.S. interestingly scores very low, Japan scores high. Physical distance: The greater the distance between people, the less likely Opinion leadership: The more opinion leaders are innovation is to spread valued and respected, the more likely an innovation is to spread. The style of opinion leaders moderates this influence, however. In less innovative countries, opinion leaders tend to be more conservative, i.e., to reflect the local norms of resistance.

It should be noted that innovation is not always an unqualifiedly good thing. Some innovations, such as infant formula adopted in developing countries, may do more harm than good. Individuals may also become dependent on the innovations. For example, travel agents who get used to booking online may be unable to process manual reservations.

Sometimes innovations are disadopted. For example, many individuals disadopt cellular phones if they find out that they don't end up using them much.

Branding: An essential issue in product management is branding. Different firms have different policies on the branding on their products. While 3M puts its brand name on a great diversity of products, Proctor & Gamble, on the opposite extreme, maintains a separate brand name for each product. In general, the use of brand extensions should be evaluated on the basis of the compatibility of various products-can the same brand name represent different products without conflict or confusion? Coca Cola for many years resisted putting its coveted brand name on a diet soft drink. In the old days, available sweeteners such as saccharin added an undesirable aftertaste, implying a clear sacrifice in taste for the reduction in calories. Thus, to avoid damaging the brand name Coca Cola, Coke instead named its diet cola Tab. Only after Nutrasweet was introduced was the brand extension allowed. Research shows that consumers are more receptive to brand extensions when (1) the company appears to have the expertise to make the product [McDonald's was not thought as credible as a photo-finishing service], (2) the products are congruent (compatible), and (3) the brand extension is not seen as being exploitative of a high quality brand name [e.g., one should not use a premium brand name like Heineken to make a trivially easy product like popcorn].

Co-branding involves firms using two or more brands together to maximize appeal to consumers. Some ice cream makers, for example, use their own brand name in addition to naming the brands of ingredients contained. Sometimes, this strategy may help one brand at the expense of the other. It is widely believed, for example, that the "Intel inside" messages, which Intel paid computer makers to put on their products and packaging, reduced the value of the computer makers' brand names because the emphasis was now put on the Intel component. Certain "peripheral" characteristics of products may "signal" quality or other value to consumers. For some products, packaging accounts for a large part of the total product manufacturing cost. Long warranties often signal to consumers that the product is of good quality since the manufacturer is willing to take responsibility for its functioning.

There is no clear distinction between a "pure" tangible product and a service. Most products contain some of both. A computer, for example, is a tangible product, but it often comes with a warranty and software updates.

Distribution System of Products

Distribution (also known as the place variable in the marketing mix, or the 4 Ps) involves getting the product from the manufacturer to the ultimate consumer. Distribution is often a much underestimated factor in marketing. Many marketers fall for the trap that if you make a better product, consumers will buy it. The problem is that retailers may not be willing to devote shelf-space to new products. Retailers would often rather use that shelf-space for existing products have that proven records of selling. Although many firms advertise that they save the consumer money by selling direct and "eliminating the middleman," this is a dubious claim. The truth is that intermediaries, such as retailers and wholesalers, tend to add efficiency because they can do specialized tasks better than the consumer or the manufacturer. Because wholesalers and retailers exist, the consumer can buy one pen at a time in a store located conveniently rather than having to order it from a distant factory. Thus, distributors add efficiency by:

- Breaking bulk-the consumer can buy small quantities at a time. Modest scale retailers (e.g., a college bookstore) can buy modest quantities.

- Distributing. The consumers can buy at a neighborhood store, which in turn can buy from a regional warehouse.
- Carrying inventory
- Financing

Channel structures vary somewhat by the nature of the product. Jet aircraft are custom made and shipped directly to the airline. Automobiles, because they are difficult to move, are shipped directly to a dealer. Other products are shipped through a wholesaler who can more efficiently handle, and combine, products from many different suppliers. Several layers of wholesalers may exist, depending on the product. Occasionally, agents may also be involved. Agents usually do not handle products, but instead take care of the business aspect of negotiating with distributors, which manufacturers may feel uncomfortable or ill prepared for doing themselves.

Manufacturers of different kinds of products have different interests with respect to the availability of their products. For convenience products such as soft drinks, it is essential that your product be available widely. Chances are that if a store does not have a consumer's preferred brand of soft drinks, the consumer will settle for another brand rather than taking the trouble to go to another store. Occasionally, however, manufacturers will prefer selective distribution since they prefer to have their products available only in upscale stores.

Parallel distribution structures refer to the fact that products may reach consumers in different ways. Most products flow through the traditional manufacturer--> retailer--> consumer channel. Certain large chains may, however, demand to buy directly from the manufacturer since they believe they can provide the distribution services at a lower cost themselves. In turn, of course, they want lower prices, which may anger the traditional retailers who feel that this represents unfair competition. Firms may also choose to utilize factory outlet stores. To allay concerns held by conventional stores, however, these factory outlet stores are usually located in areas where they are not easily accessible. We must consider what is realistically available to each firm. A small manufacturer of potato chips would like to be available in grocery stores nationally, but this may not be realistic. We need to consider, then, both who will be willing to carry our products and whom we would actually like to carry them. In general, for convenience products, intense distribution is desirable, but only brands that have a certain amount of power-e.g., an established brand name-can hope to gain national intense distribution.

Note that for convenience goods, intense distribution is less likely to harm the brand image-it is not a problem, for example, for Haagen Dazs to be available in a convenience store along with bargain brands-it is expected that people will not travel much for these products, so they should be available anywhere the consumer demands them. However, in the category of shopping goods, having Rolex watches sold in discount stores would be undesirable-here, consumers do travel, and goods are evaluated by customers to some extent based on the surrounding merchandise.

In general, a brand can expect lesser distribution in its early stages-fewer retailers are motivated to carry it. Similarly, when a product category is new, it will be available in fewer stores-e.g., in the early days, computer disks were available only in specialty stores, but now they can be found in supermarkets and convenience stores as well. Certain products that are not well established may have to get their start on "infomercials," only slowly getting entry into other types out outlets. Different parties involved in the marketing of products tend to have different, and often conflicting, interests:

- Full service retailers tend dislike intensive distribution.
- Low service channel members can "free ride" on full service sellers.
- Manufacturers may be tempted toward intensive distribution-appropriate only for some; may be profitable in the short run.

Market balance suggests a need for diversity in product categories where intensive distribution is appropriate. Service requirements also differ by product category. Diversion occurs when merchandise intended for one market is bought up by a distributor that then ships it to a different market. Sometimes, a manufacturer will run a promotion in one region but not in another, and speculators will then buy extra quantity in the promoted area and ship it another area. The speculator will then sell it to local retailers or distributors for a price slightly lower than what is being charged through the regular channel but at a price that still allows a nice profit. Certain products sell for different prices in different countries. As we discussed in the unit of international marketing, a gray market occurs when a product is bought in one country and exported to another where the price is generally higher. Both Luis Vuitton suitcases and golf clubs were imported to Japan, depressing prices there.

Integrated Marketing: Communication and Promotion

Integrated Marketing Communication (IMC) involves the idea that a firm's promotional efforts should be coordinated to achieve the best combined effects of the firm's efforts. Resources are allocated to achieve those outcomes that the firm values the most. Promotion involves a number of tools we can use to increase demand for our products.

The most well known component of promotion is advertising, but we can also use tools such as the following:

- Public relations (the firm's staff provides information to the media in the hopes of getting coverage). This strategy has benefits (it is often less expensive and media coverage is usually more credible than advertising) but it also entails a risk in that we can't control what the media will say. Note that this is particularly a useful tool for small and growing businesses-especially those that make a product which is inherently interesting to the audience.
- *Trade Promotion:* Here, the firm offers retailers and wholesalers temporary discounts, which may or may not be passed on to the consumer, to stimulate sales.
- *Sales Promotion:* Consumers are given either price discounts, coupons, or rebates.
- *Personal Selling:* Sales people either make "cold" calls on potential customers and/or respond to inquiries.

- *In-store Displays:* Firms often pay a great deal of money to have their goods displayed prominently in the store. More desirable display spaces include: end of an aisle, free-standing displays, and near the check-out counter. Occasionally, a representative may display the product.
- Samples.

Generally, a sequence of events is needed before a consumer will buy a product. This is known as a "hierarchy of effects." The consumer must first be aware that the product exists. He or she must then be motivated to give some attention to the product and what it may provide. In the next stage, the need is for the consumer to evaluate the merits of the product, hopefully giving the product a try. A good experience may lead to continued use. Note that the consumer must go through the earlier phases before the later ones can be accomplished.

Promotional objectives that are appropriate differ across the Product Life Cycle (PLC). Early in the PLC-during the introduction stage-the most important objective is creating awareness among consumers. For example, many consumers currently do not know the Garmin is making auto navigation devices based on the global position satellite (GPS) system and what this system can do for them. A second step is to induce trial-to get consumers to buy the product for the first time. During the growth stage, important needs are persuading the consumer to buy the product and prefer the brand over competing ones. Here, it is also important to persuade retailers to carry the brand, and thus, a large proportion of promotional resources may need to be devoted to retailer incentives. During the maturity stage, the firm may need to focus on maintaining shelf space, distribution channels, and sales.

Different promotional approaches will be appropriate depending on the stage of the consumer's decision process that the marketer wishes to influence. Prior to the purchase, the marketer will want to establish a decision to purchase the product and the specific brand. Here, samples might be used to induce trial. During the purchase stage, when the consumer is in the retail store, efforts may be made to ensure that the consumer will choose one's specific brands. Paying retailers for preferred shelf space as well as point of purchase (POP) displays and coupons may be appropriate. After the purchase, an appropriate objective may be to induce a repurchase or to influence the consumer to choose the same brand again. Thus, the package may contain a coupon for future purchase.

There are two main approaches to promoting products

- The "push" strategy is closely related to the "selling concept" and involves "hard" sell and aggressive price promotions to sell at this specific purchase occasion.
- In contrast, the "pull" strategy emphasizes creating demand for the brand so that consumers will come to the store with the intention of buying the product. Hallmark, for example, has invested a great deal in creating a preference for its greeting cards among consumers.

There are several ways that a firm can budget for advertising. The strategy used depends on the firm's policy and internal politics. Some of the methods commonly used are:

- *Percentage of Sales:* Here, the firm decides to base its advertising budget on how much has been sold. This appears to be an "objective" way to make the budget decision and to "reward" performing brands and products with resources. However, this method is quite arbitrary. A firm may find it worthwhile to invest heavily in advertising up-front-before the product has begun to sell significantly-so that a promising product can achieve its potential. When a product is performing well, staying with a fixed percentage may also result in spending more than is cost-effective.
- *Percentage of Profits:* This is similar to the above, but takes into consideration that some products may have larger margins than others. Thus, a product with lesser sales but high margins may be a better investment than one with high sales but low margins. Still, however, this method is arbitrary and questionable because of the factors listed above.

- *Competitive Parity:* This entails setting the budget to match competitors. Note, however, that different brands may have different needs. Coke and Pepsi may be competing "head-on," and competitive parity may be appropriate. In contrast, some firms may be targeting customers who are relatively brand loyal while others target "switchers." The firm that targets loyal customers may be better off spending money on product quality than on promotion.
- *Affordability:* This entails budgeting based on the resources that the firm has available. Smaller firms obviously do not have the same resources as larger ones. However, the firm should still evaluate how effective such a budget will be in meeting the brand's needs. A firm may be able to afford to spend more than is appropriate. In contrast, other firms may not be able to spend what is needed to adequately influence consumers. In such cases, it may be more appropriate for the firm to try to sell of this brand rather than fighting a losing battle.
- *Objective and Task:* This method sets the budget based on what is needed to achieve what the firm has set out to accomplish. The ultimate budget may then have little relation to the factors discussed above.

There are several types of advertising. In terms of product advertising, the "pioneering" ad seeks to create awareness of a product and brand and to instill an appreciation among consumers for its possibilities.

The competitive or persuasive ad attempts to convince the consumer either of the performance of the product and/or how it is superior in some way to that of others. Comparative advertisements are a prime example of this. For instance, note the ads that show that some trash bags are more durable than others. Reminder advertising seeks to keep the consumer believing what other ads have already established. For example, Coca Cola ads tend not to provide new information but keep reinforcing what a great drink it is.

Developing an advertising program entails several steps:

- Identifying the target audience. Market reports can be bought that investigate the media habits of consumers of different products and/or the segments that the firm has chosen to target.
- Determining appropriate advertising objectives. As discussed, these objectives might include awareness, trial, repurchase, inducing consumers to switch from another brand, or developing a preference for the brand.
- Settling on an advertising budget.
- Designing the advertisements. Some commonly used approaches:
    - o Information/persuasion. Comparative ads attempt to get consumers to believe that the sponsoring product is better. Although these are frequently disliked by Americans, they tend to be among the most effective ads in the U.S. Comparative advertising is illegal in some countries and is considered very inappropriate culturally in some societies, especially in Asia.
    - o Fear appeals try to motivate consumers by telling them the consequences of not using a product. Mouthwash ads, for example, talk about the how gingivitis and tooth loss can result from poor oral hygiene. It is important, however, that a specific way to avoid the feared stimulus be suggested directly in the ad. Thus, simply by using the mouthwash advertised, these terrible things can be avoided.
    - o Sex appeals are more common-and more explicit-in some cultures than in others. Their effectiveness depends a great deal on how well such ads are designed for the specific product category. In many cases, sex appeal is used more to get the consumer's attention than for actual persuasion. o Humor appeal. The use of humor in advertisements is quite common. This method tends not to be particularly

> useful in persuading the consumer. However, more and more advertisers find themselves using humor in order to compete for the consumer's attention. Often, the humor actually draws attention away from the product-people will remember what was funny in the ad but not the product that was advertised. Thus, for ads to be effective, the product advertised should be an integral part of what is funny.

Numerous media are available for the advertiser to choose from. Each medium tends to have advantages and disadvantages.

It is essential to pretest advertisements to see how effective they actually are in influencing consumers. An ad may have to be redesigned if it is found not be to be as effective as targeted. Note that selecting advertisements is often a "numbers game" where a lot of advertisements are created and the ones that "test" best are selected.

The effectiveness of advertising is a highly controversial topic. Research suggests that in many cases advertising leads to a relatively modest increase in sales. One study suggests, for example, that when a firm increases its advertising spending by 1%, sales go up by 0.05%. (The same research found that, in contrast, if prices are lowered by 1%, sales tend to increase by 2%). In general, it appears that advertising is more effective in selling durable goods (e.g., stereo systems, cars, refrigerators, and furniture) than for non-durable goods (e.g., restaurant meals, candy bars, toilet paper, and bottled water). Also, advertising appears to be more effective for new products. This suggests that advertising is probably most effective for providing information (rather than persuading people). Note that many advertising agencies make a large part of their money on commissions on advertising sold. Thus, they have a vested interest in selling as much advertising as possible, and may strongly advise clients to spend excessive amounts on advertising.

Research suggests that advertising effectiveness follows a sort of "S-" shaped curve. Very small amounts of advertising are too small to truly register with consumers. At the medium level, advertising may be effective. However, above a certain level (labeled "saturation point" on the chart), additional adverting appears to have a limited effect. (This is comparable to the notion of "diminishing returns to scale" encountered in economics). There are several potential ways to measure advertising effectiveness. Two main categories include:

- "Field" based studies. These studies look at what happens with real consumers in real life. Thus, for example, we can examine what happens to sales of a company's products when the firm increases advertising. Unfortunately, this is often a misleading way to measure advertising impact because we live in a "messy" world where other factors influence sales as well. For example, a soft drink firm could conclude that there is very little correlation between advertising and sales because another, much more powerful factor is at work: temperature. That is, the firm may find that although a great deal of advertising is done in the winter, sales are greater in summer months because people drink more soft drinks in hot weather. Note that the choice of brand of soft drink purchased in the summer may very well be influenced by advertising heard at other times.
- Laboratory studies. To get around the confounds imposed by nature, advertising reseachers often use artificial situations to evaluate advertising. This sacrifices the use of real consumers in real settings, but allows the marketer to control sources of influence. An advertising firm may hire people to come in and participate in research. The consumers may come in and be asked to view some television and respond to a questionnaire about the programming later. Half of the subjects can then see a version which includes an ad to be tested (the other half is known as the "control" group, which will serve as a basis for comparison). We can now compare the two groups on factors such as attitude toward the brand, purchase intention, and preference.

A significant objective of advertising is attitude change. A consumer's attitude toward a product refers to his or her beliefs about, feeling toward, and purchase intentions for the product. Beliefs can be both positive (e.g., for McDonald's food: tastes good, is convenient) and negative (is high in fat). In general, it is usually very difficult to change deeply held beliefs. Thus, in most cases, the advertiser may better off trying to add a belief (e.g., beef is convenient) rather than trying to change one (beef is really not very fatty). Consumer receptivity to messages aimed at altering their beliefs will tend to vary a great deal depending on the nature of the product. For unimportant products such as soft drinks, research suggests that consumers are often persuaded by having a large number of arguments with little merit presented (e.g., the soda comes in a neat bottle, the bottle contains five percent more soda than competing ones). In contrast, for high involvement, more important products, consumers tend to scrutinize arguments more closely, and will tend to be persuaded more by high quality arguments.

Celebrity endorsements are believed to follow a similar pattern of effectiveness. For trivial products, a popular endorser is often effective regardless of his or her qualifications to endorse (e.g, Bill Cosby endorses Coca Cola and Jell-O without having particular credentials to do so). On the other hand, for more important products, consumers will often scrutinize the endorser's credentials. For example, a basket ball player may be perceived as knowledgeable about athletic shoes, but not particularly so about life insurance.

DIRECT MARKETING

Direct marketing involves bypassing the retailer in reaching the consumer. Generally, this is not cost-effective, but exceptional situations may make it so. For example, certain customers may buy in very large quantities. Others may be spread over large geographic areas and require specialized products (e.g., beekeepers).

Direct marketing provides exceptional opportunities for segmentation. An excellent tool is the so called "merge-purge" technique. Marketers can buy lists of names and addresses of consumers from numerous sources (e.g., vehicle registrations, college enrollment, magazine subscriptions, catalog purchases). One can then combine different sources (e.g., surfers are likely to live in areas indicated by coastal zip codes, may subscribe to surfing magazines, and may have made purchases from surfing goods catalogs) and eliminate the overlaps (those people who appear on more than one list). Thus, we can target our potential buyers more closely than we could by advertising in newspapers (which are not read by many surfers and also reach a large number of non-surfers who are not interested in our products). A great deal of interest has arisen in recent years on the potential for marketing on the Internet. While the jury is still out on this medium's ultimate potential, sales so far have been limited, although a large potential may exist. It should be noted that a large segment of the population in the U.S. is still not "connected," with numbers being even lower in even many developed countries. Many consumers are also reluctant to provide credit cards and other personal information on the Net, although attitudes in this area may change with. Note that the Internet may serve purposes other than direct sales. For example, the Internet is a good way to provide information to consumers, and this can be done at a relatively low cost.

ELECTRONIC COMMERCE

Online marketing can serve several purposes:

- *Promotion/advertising:* Customers can be quite effectively targeted in many situations because of the context that they, themselves, have sought out. For example, when a consumer searches for a specific term in a search engine, a "banner" or link to a firm selling products in that area can be displayed. Print and television advertisements can also feature the firm's web address, thus inexpensively drawing in those who would like additional information.
- *Customer Service:* The site may contain information for those who no longer have their manuals handy and, for electronic products, provide updated drivers and software patches.

- *Market Research:* Data can be collected relatively inexpensively on the Net. However, the response rates are likely to be very unrepresentative and recent research shows that it is very difficult to get consumers to read instructions. This is one of the reasons why the quality of data collected online is often suspect.

There are many obstacles to the growth of e-commerce:

- *Reach:* Although the majority of U.S. households now have computers connected to the Internet, a very large minority does not, and penetration rates are considerably lower in some countries. In foreign countries, even those households that have computers may be reluctant to spend time online due to the per minute charges, which discourage the more leisurely "browsing" American style.
- *Concerns about Privacy:* A number of consumers are concerned about giving up information to marketers that can easily be collected electronically. Naturally, few consumers would like information about their medical status widely collected by firms, but many consumers are even reluctant to have marketers know the ages of their children and past book purchase records.
- *Reputational Issues:* Although not as much of a problem as before, firms operating online or through direct mail have often been viewed with suspicion since consumers may question whether they will be around if they do not deliver satisfactorily.
- *Costs:* During the "boom," Internet firms were not expected to be efficient and thus developed bad habits. Although shipping and handling charges can help cover costs of shipping and administration, these often take away the attractiveness of Internet shopping. The most successful e-commerce firms turn out to be the ones that have been successful doing other kinds of direct marketing (e.g., catalog sales) before and have developed the discipline and efficiency required there. For products that have relatively high absolute margins-e.g., computers-there is more money to cover administrative costs.

- *Language:* Since the Internet reaches around the world, it is often difficult to match viewers with their preferred languages. Because U.S. firms and individuals tended to predominate among those first to occupy the Web, most sites are in U.S. English. British speakers of English generally do not perceive American English as American- they tend to perceive spelling such as "color" rather than their "colour" as misspellings. French consumers do not like to have to click to get from an English language to a French language site. It is estimated that by the year 2007, the majority of web surfers will not be comfortable in English and will want sites in their own languages.
- *Government Regulations:* In the U.S., the government has tried to keep its hands off the Net as much as possible to foster its growth as a trade area, and a recently expired moratorium on new sales taxes was even instituted to make Internet shopping more attractive. However, governments in many other countries are more forceful in their regulations. In countries such as China, where sites can be used to spread "subversive" ideas, there is a great deal of government scrutiny and suspicion.
- *Cultural Obstacles:* The whole purpose of the web is to make information readily available. In countries where information is closely guarded, that is a frightening idea. There is often also a desire for personal interaction, which may be required to establish the trust needed to secure a deal.
- *Payment Issues:* U.S. consumers exposed to credit card fraud have very limited liabilities, but these protections do not exist to the same extent in Europe or Asia. In China, much of the purpose of the Internet is defeated with some 80% of transactions being completed off-line, usually with funding instruments other than credit cards.

There are a number of problems in running and developing web sites. First of all, the desired domain name may not be available-e.g., American Airlines could not get "American.com" and had to settle for "AmericanAir.com." There is also a question having your site identified to potential users. Research has found that most search engines have a great deal of "false hits" (sites irrelevant that are identified in a search-e.g., information about computer languages when the user searches for foreign language instruction) and "misses" (sites that would have been relevant but are not identified). It is crucial for a firm to have its site indexed favorably in major search engines such as Yahoo, AOLFind, and Google.

However, there is often a constant struggle between web site operators and the search engines to outguess each other, with the web promoters trying to "spam" the search engines with repeated usage of terms and "meta tags." The fact that many computer users employ different web browsers raises questions about compatibility.

A major problem is that many of the more recent, fancier web sites rely on "java script" to provide animation and various other impressive features. These animations have proven very unreliable. Sites may "crash" on the user or prove unreliable, and many consumers have found themselves unable to complete their transactions.

There are a number of legal issues associated with the Internet:

- *Reach Across Borders:* Web sites transcend country lines and thus, a firm may be subjected to legal standards of different countries. It may be difficult to create advertising that simultaneously complies with rules for each country.
- *Taxation:* There is a great deal of ambiguity as to which state and local governments may collect taxes on merchandise sold on the Internet. There is also a question as to who has the responsibility for making the payment-the seller or the buyer?
- *Privacy Issues:* Many foreign governments prohibit the collection of personal information of consumers (as Amazon.com does), which greatly reduces the customization opportunities online.

Web Site Design: The web designer must make various issues into consideration:

- *Speed vs. Aesthetics:* As we saw, some of the fancier sites have serious problems functioning practically. Consumers may be impressed by a fancy site, or may lack confidence in a firm that offers a simple one. Yet, fancier sites with extensive graphics take time to download-particularly for users dialing in with a modem as opposed to being "hard" wired-and may result in site crashes.
- *Keeping users on the Site:* A large number of "baskets" are abandoned online as consumers fail to complete the "check-out" process for the products they have selected. One problem here is that many consumers are drawn away from a site and then are unlikely to come back. A large number of links may be desirable to consumers, but they tend to draw people away. Taking banner advertisers on your site from other sites may be profitable, but it may result in customers lost.
- *Information Collection:* An increasing number of consumers resist collection of information about them, and a number of consumers have set up their browsers to disallow "cookies," files that contain information about their computers and shopping habits.

TOURISM & DESTINATION MANAGEMENT

Managing tourism destinations is an important part of controlling tourism's environmental impacts. Destination management can include land use planning, business permits and zoning controls, environmental and other regulations, business association initiatives, and a host of other techniques to shape the development and daily operation of tourism-related activities.

The term "destination" refers broadly to an area where tourism is a relatively important activity and where the economy may be significantly influenced by tourism revenues. Destination management is complicated by the fact that a single, recognizable destination may include several municipalities, provinces, or other government entities-in island environments it may be the entire country.

Participating governance structures led by local authorities, with the involvement of local NGOs, community and indigenous representatives, academia, and local chambers of commerce, make up what are known as "Destination Management Organizations" (DMOs). Often DMOs take the form of local tourism boards, councils, or development organizations. The network of local tourism businesses (hotels, attractions, transportation services, service providers such as guides and equipment rentals, restaurants, etc.) are also a significant part of a destination.

Destination Management Approach

The needs, expectations and anticipated benefits of tourism vary greatly from one destination to the next, and there is certainly no "one size fits all" approach to destination management. As local communities living in regions with tourism potential develop a vision for what kind of tourism they want to facilitate, a comprehensive planning framework such as Local Agenda 21 has proved useful and is being used more and more often. Promoting sustainable tourism within Local Agenda 21 processes is a way to strengthen local stewardship of the environment.

Cities and Tourism

Cities to Absorb Growth in World Tourism: International tourist arrivals in 1995 were 563 million and are expected to reach 1.6 billion by the year 2020. These forecasts use a conservative growth rate of 4.3% and 6.7% respectively; less than the current growth rate. They do not include any domestic tourism which can readily be anticipated to equal the international. It is obvious that most of this increase will have to be absorbed by cities.

World Tourism Organisation: The most recent trends and forecasting studies by the World Tourism Organisation indicate that cities will continue to be in high demand by tourists of all sorts, and the problems associated with the handling of these tourists will have to be more systematically tackled by all parties concerned.

Cities face, therefore, a double challenge.

Firstly, they have to be able to respond to the expectations and needs of the growing numbers of tourists who are attracted to their rich and varied array of cultural, business, entertainment, shopping, sports and other attractions; furthermore, they need to continuously renovate and improve such facilities in order to maintain their share in the competitive tourism market and the benefits resulting from it.

Secondly, cities have to ensure that tourism is developed and managed in such a way that it benefits the resident population, does not contribute to the deterioration of the urban environment but rather to its enhancement, and does not become a financial burden to the local authority. Some of the key stakeholders in urban tourism include: Private Sector i.e. airlines, hotel chain operators and owners, tour operators, credit card companies, tourist attraction operators (theme parks, events etc.), real estate agencies;

- Public Sector i.e. city managers (from the historic city to the seaside resort), transportation planners, bus and train operators, information departments, economic development agencies, national parks, national tourist organisations;
- Touristic Institutions i.e. museums, art galleries, historic facilities (e.g. the national trust) and educational organisations.

There are three key dimensions of tourism in cities and urban areas:

- Products-the anticipated changes necessary from tourist attraction providers; theme parks, operators of events (sports, shows, fairs), museums and hotels. What are their plans, how do they respond to the anticipated growth?
- Information-How does a city make itself more tourist friendly? What are the information systems available to tourists? How do tour operators deal with this growing

demand? How to accumulate information on customer preferences and requirement, seasonal changes, age groups etc.? How to develop enduring attractions which will provide sustainable development? What information does the city provide in order to attract tourist attraction providers?

- Impacts-economic and development opportunities as well as the impact of tourism growth on sustainable development, transportation, cultural and environmental, social and economic aspects.

Environmental Management System and Eco-Tourism

Since the introduction of Agenda 21, the hospitality sector has adopted numerous strategies, approaches and measures in response to the challenge of sustainable development. These include:

- Environmental management systems and tools
- Education, awareness creation, training and information dissemination
- Voluntary initiatives
- Multi-stakeholder communication and consultation
- Environmental reporting
- Implementation of the Rio principles

The sector has particularly used environmental management systems and tools to demonstrate committment to an environmentally friendly work ethic. Many multinational and independent hotel companies have introduced environmental management practices at the property level. Ideally, the framework for this involves defining an environmental policy and building a management system to measure environmental impacts and compliance with the policy and local regulations, as well as documenting the system's performance for inspection and auditing purposes. Such environmental management systems (EMS) help businesses to evaluate, manage and reduce their negative environmental impacts by providing a methodology to integrate environment management into business operations in a systematic manner.

6

A NEW ARENA FOR CAREER BUILDING

Tourism and its related business activities belong to the most important sectors of the economies worldwide. Surprisingly this is widely underestimated because the complexity of tourism does not allow its quantitative perception and its real economic relevance. For this reason it has not been realized thoroughly that the tourism industry is the biggest employer in the world, and will continue to be despite the actual recession due to terrorism and other turbulences that have disturbed the peaceful environment of travellers.

Universities and training institutions recognized the needs of the prosperous tourism industry and have been developing qualification programmes on different levels and differentiations of focus. But they have been followers of the industry's demand rather than strategic planners aiming at an anticipated goal of management competence.

How to Support the Industry

Today it is necessary for universities and other institutions involved to be more entrepreneurial and more strategy orientated. They have to assess the actual tourism industry with its needs and demands for management excellence to enable themselves to design and implement curricula for programmes which guarantee the output of appropriate graduates.

The Growing Needs: In cooperation with the industry, universities must look ahead and try to get an imagination of the prospective development. Management skills are changing permanently, refreshing them is a continuous necessity. Tourism management is no exception. The industry is becoming more and more global. Global players are dominating the market while local partners depend on them, on their strategies and preferences. Management and operations for all people involved have become more sophisticated and challenging over the years.

Competition between tour operators, hotel chains, destinations, airlines, agencies etc. is fierce. At this stage industry needs excellent management competence, but where to recruit this excellence?

Negligence and Ignorance of Academics: The underestimation of the tourism business has been shared by universities for long. Similar to the century-long fight of business administration and management for recognition by the academic community, tourism management in many cases is not recognized as a serious subject. This irrational perception of tourism business with its relation to leisure and travel is still influencing the choice made by students today in the programmes provided by universities and other institutes.

Such programmes don´t appeal to male students because they don´t consider tourism as a reasonable career opportunity. They prefer courses in general business administration and management, however for the tight labour market they cannot avoid the tourism industry as an employer later on. What they lack in this case is a sound qualification in tourism management. This can only partly be compensated by learning on the job, what does not fulfill the career expectations of young managers and does not meet the requirements for differentiation of human resource departments as well. Additional qualification is a must. Is this qualification provided by an MBA?

Additional Qualification

An MBA is not an appropriate means for compensating the lack of compentence as long as the MBA is merely seen as an introduction to general management. Graduates of business studies got this introduction and much more in their four years degree course. Such an introduction is appropriate for those whose first academic degree was engineering, informatics, architecture etc., but not for graduates of business studies. For them the core subject of an additional qualification must be related to the specific industry or to the management function they are in respectively they want to acquire.

An elective focused on their speciality, as it is offered in many MBA programmes, does in no way fulfill the requirements. They must get the opportunity to dig deeper into their core skills (e.g. marketing or HRM) but now related to their business (e.g. global marketing in tourism) respectively to their function (e.g. staffing of subsidiaries abroad). A master of science is not the right answer to the respective demand because it is not regarded as an award of excellence in management but rather as a sign of academic excellence and a step to the PhD.

The Specialist MBA: Only a Specialist MBA is the adequate solution, an MBA in tourism or in international tourism management. Such a specialized programme would overcome the problem and results in multiple demand. Are there constraints to the implementation of a specialist tourism MBA?

A Contradiction in Terms?: In the traditional academic perspective, the MBA is by definition a broad qualification in general management. Specialities can only be electives, which should never dodge the breadth of business orientation intended. From this point of view the Specialist MBA is a contradiction in terms. But this traditional perspective to an MBA is being pushed back by the market forces. And it is not reasonable to withstand this development. Further specialisation has to be achieved by Specialist MBA programmes.

Higher Management Career: Since the MBA became the brand of highest academic award of managers it cannot be denied that this award is appreciated not only by managers whose first academic education was different to business administration and management. Should the MBA shop be closed for those who got their first degree in business administration and management and who covered almost all the subjects of the MBA syllabus so that they cannot be motivated to get an MBA in terms of a mere general introduction to business and management? Should they waive on an MBA degree, the highest appropriate practice orientated academic award for their career?

The MBA became a mark of distinction for academics in business. Therefore it must be accessible for all who want to add a specialized qualification to their first academic degree. For graduates in business administration this can only be something apart from general business management: it has to be a Specialist MBA. In such a case the entry requirement for all should be equal, a degree in a business related subject.

A Pragmatic Solution: It has to be acknowledged that the additional skills which an engineer gains by an MBA course (Type 1) deserves the same award like the additional qualification of a business graduate who gets an MBA with the specialization in international marketing or information systems (Type 2). The quality and the rating of the two types of MBAs achieve the same levels, only the qualifications differ.

Universities should not assume that the business world would not be able to identify the difference between the variety of MBAs. The Specialist MBA is improving the possibility to differentiate and to select the candidates who are fitting best into the needs of the employers.

Specialist MBA in Tourism Management

Taking all those factors into account it is only a logical consequence to create Specialist MBAs focusing on tourism management, to equip the tourism industry with highly skilled management staff. But how to dot hat? The tourism business is known for its complexity and its international dimension. An MBA specialised on tourism or international tourism cannot cover everything. Therefore even the design of this industry related Specialist MBA remains general, covering the most important basic skills required by the tourism industry.

What Tourism Management Means: The touristic product is a bundle of offered components. Many industries are brought together in a system of relationships. Their capability of interaction and cooperation in the respective environments determines the economic success of each of them. Management of the different elements in various scopes of tourism needs highly developed skills to cope with the challenges of a business which is volatile and constantly influenced by the changes of travel motivations of tourists and the trends in society or by natural disasters and political developments. Managers in the tourism business need-more than in other scopes of business-the awareness of the complexity of interrelationships of the players and a sensibility for changes in demands and environments. They need the skills to adjust the business to these respective changes. That requires strategic thinking, creativity, intercultural competence, skills of communication and leadership, the capability of self-learning and the stimulation of organizational learning as well as knowledge management.

Specialist MBA in International Tourism Management: An MBA in international tourism management with about 600 hours of class presence therefore should include the following subjects of different weight:

- The phenomenon of tourism and its systems
- Economics of tourism and its industries
- Environments of tourism
- Tourism demand
- International and global tourism management
- Culture and cross-cultural management
- Tourism marketing
- Marketing research in tourism
- Strategic planning in tourism
- Business policy and ethics
- Specific management functions in tourism (e.g. HRM, financial management, operations management, strategic quality management)
- Management of international projects
- E-tourism
- Communication and negotiation

An MBA in international tourism management is inevitably a real necessity. This need is pushed by the industry that is constantly affected not only by the economic changes but also by other phenomena surrounding them. It is therefore a rational move to be taken by the learning institutions to develop such a programme to accommodate this need-rather than to reject this demand.

The market requires Specialist MBAs. It is the logic of the general trends of more specialization driven by the concentration process in particular. Universities have to design qualification programmes which support these requirements as far as academic responsibility allows. By offering Specialist MBAs universities don´t loose their virtues. Their interest should only be to secure transparency of what is offered and which award is delivered. It is possible to avoid confusion by clear information on the respective type of MBA. So universities are contributing to the needs of employers and ambitious young managers by the differentiation of awards, which are not differing in quality but only in its specific qualification.

The Specialist MBA in international tourism management will provide the prospective candidates with the competitive advantage of securing a career in the respective industry.

7

SUPPORT IN FINANCIAL ECONOMY

The tourism industry generates substantial economic benefits to both host countries and tourists' home countries. Especially in developing countries, one of the primary motivations for a region to promote itself as a tourism destination is the expected economic improvement. As with other impacts, this massive economic development brings along both positive and negative consequences.

In this chapter we would talk about

* Negative economic impacts from tourism
* How tourism can contribute to economic development

According to the World Tourism Organization, 698 million people traveled to a foreign country in 2000, spending more US$ 478 billion. International tourism receipts combined with passenger transport currently total more than US$ 575 billion-making tourism the world's number one export earner, ahead of automotive products, chemicals, petroleum and food.

NEGATIVE IMPACTS

There are many hidden costs to tourism, which can have unfavorable economic effects on the host community. Often rich countries are better able to profit from tourism than poor ones. Whereas the least developed countries have the most urgent need for income, employment and general rise of the standard of living by means of tourism, they are least able to realize these benefits. Among the reasons for this are large-scale transfer of tourism revenues out of the host country and exclusion of local businesses and products.

Leakage

The direct income for an area is the amount of tourist expenditure that remains locally after taxes, profits, and wages are paid outside the area and after imports are purchased; these subtracted amounts are called leakage. In most all-inclusive package tours, about 80% of travelers' expenditures go to the airlines, hotels and other international companies (who often have their headquarters in the travelers' home countries), and not to local businesses or workers. In addition, significant amounts of income actually retained at destination level can leave again through leakage.

A study of tourism 'leakage' in Thailand estimated that 70% of all money spent by tourists ended up leaving Thailand (via foreign-owned tour operators, airlines, hotels, imported drinks and food, etc.). Estimates for other Third World countries range from 80% in the Caribbean to 40% in India.

Of each US$ 100 spent on a vacation tour by a tourist from a developed country, only around US$ 5 actually stays in a developing-country destination's economy. The figure below shows how the leakage happens.

There are two main ways that leakage occurs:

Import Leakage: This commonly occurs when tourists demand standards of equipment, food, and other products that the host country cannot supply. Especially in less-developed countries, food and drinks must often be imported, since local products are not up to the hotel's (i.e. tourist's) standards or the country simply doesn't have a supplying industry. Much of the income from tourism expenditures leaves the country again to pay for these imports.

The average import-related leakage for most developing countries today is between 40% and 50% of gross tourism earnings for small economies and between 10% and 20% for most advanced and diversified economies, according to UNCTAD.

Even in developed regions, local producers are often unable to supply the tourism industry appropriately even if good will is present: the 64-room hotel "Kaiser im Tirol" in Austria, an award-winning leader in sustainable practices, cannot find organic food suppliers in the local farming networks in the appropriate quantity, quality and reliability, as production cycles and processes are not compatible with its needs.

Export Leakage: Multinational corporations and large foreign businesses have a substantial share in the import leakage. Often, especially in poor developing destinations, they are the only ones that possess the necessary capital to invest in the construction of tourism infrastructure and facilities. As a consequence of this, an export leakage arises when overseas investors who finance the resorts and hotels take their profits back to their country of origin.

A 1996 UN report evaluating the contribution of tourism to national income, gross levels of incomes or gross foreign exchange, found that net earnings of tourism, after deductions were made for all necessary foreign exchange expenditures, were much more significant for the industry. This report found significant leakage associated with: (a) imports of materials and equipment for construction; (b) imports of consumer goods, particularly food and drinks; (c) repatriation of profits earned by foreign investors; (d) overseas promotional expenditures and (e) amortization of external debt incurred in the development of hotels and resorts. The impact of the leakage varied greatly across countries, depending on the structure of the economy and the tourism industry. From the data presented in this study on the Caribbean, St. Lucia had a foreign exchange leakage rate of 56% from its gross tourism receipts, Aruba had 41%, Antigua and Barbuda 25% and Jamaica 40%.

Economic Enclave Tourism

Local businesses often see their chances to earn income from tourists severely reduced by the creation of "all-inclusive" vacation packages. When tourists remain for their entire stay at the same cruise ship or resort, which provides everything they need and where they will make all their expenditures, not much opportunity is left for local people to profit from tourism. The Organization of American States (OAS) carried out a survey of Jamaica's tourist industry that looked at the role of the all-inclusives compared to other types of accommodation. It found that 'All-inclusive hotels generate the largest amount of revenue but their impact on the economy is smaller per dollar of revenue than other accommodation subsectors.'

It also concluded that all-inclusives imported more, and employed fewer people per dollar of revenue than other hotels. This information confirms the concern of those who have argued that all-inclusives have a smaller trickle-down effect on local economies.

The cruise ship industry provides another example of economic enclave tourism. Non-river cruises carried some 8.7 million international passengers in 1999. On many ships, especially in the Caribbean (the world's most popular cruise destination with 44.5% of cruise passengers), guests are encouraged to spend most of their time and money on board, and opportunities to spend in some ports are closely managed and restricted.

Other Negative Impacts

Infrastructure Cost

Tourism development can cost the local government and local taxpayers a great deal of money. Developers may want the government to improve the airport, roads and other infrastructure, and possibly to provide tax breaks and other financial advantages, which are costly activities for the government. Public resources spent on subsidized infrastructure or tax breaks may reduce government investment in other critical areas such as education and health.

Price Hikes

Increasing demand for basic services and goods from tourists will often cause price hikes that negatively affect local residents whose income does not increase proportionately. A San Francisco State University study of Belize found that, as a consequence of tourism development, the prices for locals increased by 8%. Tourism development and the related rise in real estate demand may dramatically increase building costs and land values. Not only does this make it more difficult for local people, especially in developing countries, to meet their basic daily needs, it can also result in a dominance by outsiders in land markets and in-migration that erodes economic opportunities for the locals, eventually disempowering residents. In Costa Rica, close to 65% of the hotels belong to foreigners. Long-term tourists living in second homes, and the so-called amenity migrants (wealthy or retired people and liberal professionals moving to attractive destinations in order to enjoy the atmosphere and peaceful rhythms of life) cause price hikes in their new homes if their numbers attain a certain critical mass.

Economic Dependence of the Local Community on Tourism

Diversification in an economy is a sign of health, however if a country or region becomes dependent for its economic survival upon one industry, it can put major stress upon this industry as well as the people involved to perform well. Many countries, especially developing countries with little ability to explore other resources, have embraced tourism as a way to boost the economy. In the Gambia, for instance, 30% of the workforce depends directly or indirectly on tourism. In small island developing states, percentages can range from 83% in the Maldives to 21% in the Seychelles and 34% in Jamaica, according to the WTO. Over-reliance on tourism, especially mass tourism, carries significant risks to tourism-dependent economies. Economic recession and the impacts of natural disasters such as tropical storms and cyclones as well as changing tourism patterns can have a devastating effect on the local tourism sector. Malta has only 380,000 residents, but received 1.2 million tourists in 1999. As 25% of GDP (and indirectly 40%), tourism generated more than $650 million in foreign exchange earnings. Malta's high dependence on tourism and a limited number of export products makes its trade performance vulnerable to shifts in international demand.

Seasonal Character of Jobs

The seasonal character of the tourism industry creates economic problems for destinations that are heavily dependent on it. Problems that seasonal workers face include job (and therefore income) insecurity, usually with no guarantee of employment from one season to the next, difficulties in getting training, employment-related medical benefits, and recognition of their experience, and unsatisfactory housing and working conditions.

Other Industrial Impacts

Economic crises, like the Asian crisis that hit Thailand, Malaysia and Indonesia a few years ago, can be devastating to inbound tourism flows. The financial turmoil triggered a sharp fall in tourism flows to affected countries during 1997 and 1998. In the Philippines, the crisis and the temporary closure of Philippine Airlines affected inbound arrivals significantly as there was a decline of almost 3.3% in 1998.

CONTRIBUTION OF TOURISM IN ECONOMIC CONSERVATION

The main positive economic impacts of tourism relate to foreign exchange earnings, contributions to government revenues, and generation of employment and business opportunities.

Foreign Exchange Earnings

Tourism expenditures and the export and import of related goods and services generate income to the host economy and can stimulate the investment necessary to finance growth in other economic sectors. Some countries seek to accelerate this growth by requiring visitors to bring in a certain amount of foreign currency for each day of their stay and do not allow them to take it out of the country again at the end of the trip. An important indicator of the role of international tourism is its generation of foreign exchange earnings. Tourism is one of the top five export categories for as many as 83% of countries and is a main source of foreign exchange earnings for at least 38% of countries.

Contribution to Government Revenues

Government revenues from the tourism sector can be categorized as direct and indirect contributions. Direct contributions are generated by taxes on incomes from tourism employment and tourism businesses, and by direct levies on tourists such as departure taxes. Indirect contributions are those originated from taxes and duties levied on goods and services supplied to tourists.

The United States National Park Service estimates that the 273 million visits to American national parks in 1993 generated direct and indirect expenditures of US$ 10 billion and 200,000 jobs. When visits to land managed by other agencies, and to state, local, and privately-managed parks, are added, parks were estimated to bring around US$ 22 billion annually to the US economy. These expenditures also generate significant tax revenues for the government.

The World Travel and Tourism Council estimates that travel and tourism's direct, indirect, and personal tax contribution worldwide was over US$ 800 billion in 1998-a figure it expects to double by 2010.

Employment Opportunities

The rapid expansion of international tourism has led to significant employment creation. For example, the hotel accommodation sector alone provided around 11.3 million jobs worldwide in 1995. Tourism can generate jobs directly through hotels, restaurants, nightclubs, taxis, and souvenir sales, and indirectly through the supply of goods and services needed by tourism-related businesses. According to the WTO, tourism supports some 7% of the world's workers.

Infrastructural Stimulation

Tourism can induce the local government to make infrastructure improvements such as better water and sewage systems, roads, electricity, telephone and public transport networks, all of which can improve the quality of life for residents as well as facilitate tourism.

Contribution to Local Economies

Tourism can be a significant, even essential, part of the local economy. As the environment is a basic component of the tourism industry's assets, tourism revenues are often used to measure the economic value of protected areas. For example, Dorrigo National Park in New South Wales, Australia, has been estimated to contribute 7% of gross regional output and 8.4% of regional employment. The importance of tourism to local economies can also be illustrated by the impacts when it is disrupted: the catastrophic 1997 floods that closed Yosemite National Park in California cause locally severe economic losses to the areas around the park. In the most heavily impacted county, Mariposa County, 1997 personal income was reduced by an estimated US$1,159 per capita (US$18 million for the entire county)-a 6.6% decline. The county was also estimated to have lost US$1.67 million in county occupancy and sales tax revenues, and 956 jobs, a significant number in a county of fewer than 16,000 residents.

There are other local revenues that are not easily quantified, as not all tourist expenditures are formally registered in the macro-economic statistics. Money is earned from tourism through informal employment such as street vendors, informal guides, rickshaw drivers, etc. The positive side of informal or unreported employment is that the money is returned to the local economy, and has a great multiplier effect as it is spent over and over again. The World Travel and Tourism Council estimates that tourism generates an indirect contribution equal to 100% of direct tourism expenditures.

8

NEW TRENDS IN TOURISM MANAGEMENT

Hospitality and Tourism Management (HTM) is a major in a Bachelors of Science in Business Administration. Graduate students graduate with a Masters of Business Administration, a Masters or Science, or a Doctorate of Philosophy in Hospitality and Tourism Management. It is a focus that is studied by individuals that are intending to work in the Hospitality Industry, examples of which are; Hotels, Resorts, Casinos, and Restaurants. Within the HTM concentration there is generally:

- Food Management and Operations (Examples: Food Science, Food Selection and Preparation, Food and Beverage Operations)
- Lodging Operations (Examples: Hotel Operations, Lodging Management, Financial Management and Cost Control for Hospitality Organizations)
- Global Tourism (Examples: Travel and Tourism Management, Tourism Analysis, Hospitality and Research Methods)
- Event Management (Examples: Hospitality Sales, Catering Management, Hospitality Marketing Management)

Several large corporations such as Marriot, Hyatt, Wyndham and Hilton Hotels have summer internships/manager in training programs for students majoring in Hospitality and Tourism Management, to help students get valuable work experience.

National University of Management

N.U.M. is the leading university in providing educational training to all people in the areas of Management, Economics, Commerce, IT, Business Law, Tourism, and Foreign languages accompanied by research and development in response to the needs of job market today.

Mission: The mission of N.U.M. is to serve the country through educational training by providing graduates with academic excellence, wisdom, morality, and good responsibility in the society. With the vision above, NUM is trying its best to:

- Train students with their day-to-day work for their job satisfaction.
- Illustrate the reality of conflicts and resolutions in terms of managers entrepreneurs.
- Provide opportunities for all levels of people to improve their knowledge and ability through part-time training.

History: The National University of Management (NUM) was founded in 1983 as the Economics Science Institute (ESI), and until 1991 received assistance from the National Economics University in Hanoi, Vietnam. During this period, students were enrolled in a five-year undergraduate program with the Vietnamese language serving as the main language of instruction. The curriculum, set by the visiting faculty from Hanoi, included major fields in Finance, Commerce, Agriculture, Industry, and Socialist Planning.

With the opening up of Cambodia to the international community during the early 1990's. The ESI was renamed the Faculty of Business (FOB). Initial support for the FOB was provided by the Asia Foundation and later through a three years USAID grant (1994 to 1997) by the Georgetown University and the University of Sanfrancisco.

This support provided teacher training, institutional development, and encouraged transformation of the curriculum along the lines of an international or American style business school. Marketing and Accounting majors were introduced during this period, and the length of the undergraduate program was reduced from five to four years of study. Commercial law course were also added to the curriculum by the University of San Francisco Law school.

This support provided teacher training, institutional development, and encouraged transformation of the curriculum along the lines of an international or American style business school. Marketing and Accounting majors were introduced during this period, and the length of the undergraduate program was reduced from five to four years of study. Commercial law course were also added to the curriculum by the University of San Francisco Law school.

In 2004, the FOB was transformed into the National University of Management (NIM) and program offerings were expanded to include the fields of Tourism and Hospitality Management, Finance & Banking and MIS. NUM also opened the first MBA program in Cambodia in cooperation with the University Utara Malaysia (UUM), which is s State sponsored university located in Northern Malaysia. NUM also maintains a five year faculty exchange and research program with the University of Antwerp. Belgium and has just recently opened a Center for Entrepreneurship and Development in partnership with Fisk University (Nashville,U.S) and Tennessee State University, sponsored by UNCF/USAID.

Currently, more than 10,000 students attend courses at NUM's main campus in Phnom Penh. NUM also operates a full Bachelor of Business Administration degree program in Battambang with more than 700 students attending courses at NUM 's provincial campus.

According to the World Travel and Tourism Council (1997), the economics of the 21st century will be dominated by three industries: telecommunications, information technology and tourism. The travel and tourism industries have grown by 500% in the last 25 years and it is estimated that by the year 2007 tourists will spend US$884 billion in foreign countries on tourism related activities. Travel and tourism represents a broad range of related industries. The growth of these industries has opened up many new job opportunities for graduates in areas such as:

- hotels
- restaurants
- retailing
- transportation
- travel agencies
- tour companies
- tourist attractions
- leisure, recreation and sport
- cultural industries

It is interesting to realise that in 1997 travel and tourism provides 10.5% of the total world employment, with up to 25% of all employment, in some areas, such as the Caribbean. It has been estimated that, by 2007, more than 100 million people worldwide will be employed in this sector. Because of this, tourism is now seen to be of importance to most countries of the world.

During this time, the nature of tourism has developed in scope and direction, away from traditional activities, such as the sunshine sand and sea holidays to a wide range of new activities such as cultural tourism, adventure tourism, sports and leisure activities and eco-tourism.

Careers in Hospitality and Tourism Management

Given the potential for interesting and rewarding careers in these industries many young people are looking for suitable courses which will help prepare them for careers in management within the tourism and hospitality industries.

The UK higher education system has a well developed range of courses, at all levels from Higher National Diploma, BA or BSc degrees and MA/MSc/MBA Masters courses and using alternative methods of studying, (including full-time, part-time and distance learning).

When looking at courses in hospitality and tourism, there can seem to be a bewildering variety of course titles covering the main employment areas of travel, tourism, hotels and restaurants. Typical titles include:

For hotels and restaurant management:

- hospitality management
- international hospitality management
- hotel and catering management

For travel and tourism:

- tourism management
- tourism studies
- travel and tourism

There are also joint degrees where it is possible to study combinations of subjects, such as tourism and hospitality, tourism and leisure, hospitality and marketing. Most undergraduate courses (HND/BSc/BA) will include a period of work experience as part of the course, varying in length from 6 months to one year.

This work experience is seen to be a central part of the course, where the student gets the opportunity to practise what they have learned in college or university. Employers also see great value in this work experience when considering the employment of graduates. Given the international nature of these industries, another valuable part of any course is the study of languages.

Most courses in hospitality and tourism provide access to language courses, either as core components or as options. Courses at Masters level are becoming increasingly important in tourism and hospitality. These Masters level courses are useful to two groups of people:

- those who have completed a degree course in a subject other than hospitality or tourism but who are looking at ways of getting employment in the industry;
- those who have a degree or sub-degree qualification in hospitality or tourism together with significant management experience within the hospitality or tourism industries and who wish to develop themselves to a higher level or to seek a more senior position in industry. There are many Masters courses in Hospitality

Management, Hotel and Catering Management and Tourism Management in universities and colleges in the UK.

In addition to the above courses, there are also more specialised Masters courses in Tourism covering areas such as Cultural Tourism, Tourism Marketing, Tourism Planning, Museum Management, Heritage Management, Cultural Tourism and Sustainable Tourism: these are suitable for people who have an interest in employment in a specific sector of the industry.

Within the UK there are many university and college courses to choose from, but each course will have its own unique characteristics. Before applying, you should think carefully about the type of career you want: if it is in a hotel are you interested in restaurant management or rooms division management? Do you see yourself as a practical hands-on person or someone who is happier to work behind the scenes in a desk based job? Do you aspire to become a general manager of a hotel which is part of one of the major worldwide groups, or do you want to manage your own operation? Are you more interested in one of the functional management areas, such as marketing, human resources, conferences.

9

FUTURE TRENDS

INTRODUCTION

The substantial growth of the tourism activity clearly marks tourism as one of the most remarkable economic and social phenomena of the past century. The number of international arrivals shows an evolution from a mere 25 million international arrivals in 1950 to an estimated 806 million in 2005, corresponding to an average annual growth rate of 6.5%. During this period, development was particularly strong in Asia and the Pacific (13% on average a year) and in the Middle East (10%) while the Americas (5%) and Europe (6%), grew at a slower pace and slightly below the world's average growth. New destinations are steadily increasing their market share while more mature regions such as Europe and the Americas tend to have less dynamic growth. Europe's world share declined by over 10 percentage points since 1950 whereas the Americas lost 13 percentage points. Though the Americas' performance has been most affected by the declines suffered in the past years, the fact is that its annual average growth rate for the period 1950-2000 was 5.8%, also bellow the average for the world (6.8%). Europe and the Americas were the main tourist-receiving regions between 1950 and 2000. Both regions represented a joint market share of over 95 per cent in 1950, 82% forty years later and 76% in 2000.

THIRD WORLD TOURISM CRITIQUE

Tourism has become one of the most prominent and influential global industries. It directly or indirectly employs one in every 10 employed people on earth, and maintains 3.6 trillion dollars worth of goods and services which is 10.6 percent of the gross global product. (Brown, 24.)

Tourism has become the mainstay of countless countries worldwide and is one of the greatest sources of entrepreneurial activity. Yet, despite these impressive statistics, and contrary to what most tourists, myself included, have been taught, tourism, especially in the third world, is far from the benign panacea of benefits for 'host' countries it is regularly portrayed to be.

Tourism bears a nearly direct lineage to perhaps the first arbiter of the first/third world dynamic globalization: colonialism. This is most obvious in that nearly all tourists come from the first world, notably Europe and the United States, and are also the primary owners of the tourist infrastructure. Professor McCall's observation that whites are "living it up" in South Africa is true, to a large extent, throughout the world, with tourism among the central modes of their enjoyment. Tourism, like colonialism, involves an occupation and domination of space, in this instance by the tourist structure and tourists themselves. It is also an industry that, like colonialism, is enabled by expansions of power.

Tourists, especially those going to the third world, venture forth to survey the lands and peoples over which they reign: to catalogue it, exploit it, revel in its submission, and leave it, both in body and mind.

Tourism, contrary to popular belief, generally benefits the tourist far more than it does the residents of the country they visit. The often vast government subsidies poured into enabling tourism in many countries come at the expense of those funds being used to directly help the majority of the country's usually destitute residents. While such funds do help many residents to some extent, usually in the form of creating mostly low-paying, unskilled jobs, the resources are essentially being shared with, if not outright given to, tourists.

Additionally, the funds spent by tourists while on their sojourns rarely help the average resident. The spending, if it stays in the country, largely benefits the owners of the tourist structure in the country. In South Africa's case, this constitutes the often already wealthy, disproportionately white upper-class. However, much, and in some cases nearly all, of the money spent by tourists does not stay in the country at all. This is primarily due to a large portion of tourist infrastructure being foreign owned. Examples of this ownership include tour services, hotels, travel agencies, and many of the stores placed in tourist centers. Furthermore, these owners often employ expatriates or international workers instead of locals.

For instance, while on the return flight from South Africa I sat next to, and nearby, several groups who had spent the entirety of their stay in private game parks. Each group had a series of pictures of their loved ones proudly bestriding the various animals they had so bravely slain during the course of their so-called 'expeditions'.

Upon inquiry, I learned that by dealing exclusively with foreign-based outfitters, suppliers, agencies and owners, as apparently "all" of their friends did as well, these groups had managed to stay in South Africa for nearly a month without directly contributing a cent to the local economy. When I asked one group member, a portly man named Bill from Texas, why he had decided to only use foreign companies he, at first, seemed somewhat surprised by the question, giving me a quizzical look as if to say "surprised you'd need to ask". Then he answered "our outfitters are pros, they know what they're doin, the South Africans don't." In Kenya, Thailand, Fiji, and many other countries, this 'leakage', as it is commonly referred to, of tourist spending approaches, and often exceeds, 60%. (Brown 58), However, to lesser extents it is present in nearly every tourism integrated economy, including South Africa's.

As more tourists and wealthy first-world vacationers frequent a country, inflation and a rise in land prices begin to occur as a result of the strength of first-world currencies and by the disproportionate wealth of the foreigners. This hurts local residents by creating a barrier between their lives and the artificially created world of tourists. Tourist areas become far too expensive for locals to enjoy. Subsequently, the only use of the areas most local residents will have comes from working as the maids, cleaners, and other basic-service providing employees needed to run the sites.

In South Africa, we stayed in the "Waterfront" one area that demonstrates this point well. Of all the South African residents I spoke to not a single person frequented this area, the reason always being the, what one person at SABC called, "exorbitant" prices. This same effect has manifested itself in South African property, amusement parks, aquariums, museums, shopping centers, and even such national heritage sites as Table Mountain and Robben Island.

In my story for SABC I interviewed over 25 South African residents on the streets of Cape Town and not a single person had visited either Table Mountain or Robben Island. They unanimously cited, what one school teacher called, "insane" prices, while also stating that they would love to go if the pricing was not so high. Aside from this essentially financial separation, there are many instances where local residents have been physically removed from an area to make way for tourism. Often, this consists of the destitute who are perceived as a blight and/or crime threat, as in Times Square, and are forcibly removed in these instances are moved out of the areas as they are perceived to make the area less desirable for tourists.

For those remaining destitute residents in the Cape Town, Waterfront area, many of whom seem to subsist largely from soliciting money from tourists, life is made incredibly difficult by the harsh treatment doled out by nearly everyone they come into contact with. In one instance, while I was eating with our group in a café in the area, one ragged local man came to the door and, in plain view of all the patrons, the manager opened the door and yelled at the man "go away and don't ever come here again!". The man was most likely there to ask the patrons for money, and, as it could potentially disrupt business, I am not entirely surprised by the manager's reaction. It is the structural dynamic the example demonstrates that is most appalling: with most residents already priced out of the area, the most common remaining residents I encountered lived in various stages of destitution and had to resort to humiliating acts to get by. (Another cause of local resident displacement is the growing trend of ecotourism. Ecotourists want to see so-called 'unspoiled' nature. This, of course, does not include people. However, communities reside in many areas that might make excellent ecotourist havens. This conflict of interest is increasingly leading to confrontations between the developers who envision their own Kruger Park (which itself, as Herman mentioned, displaced former inhabitants in its development) and the people, often indigenous, who reside on the land. Not surprisingly, with the all-powerful tourist lobby in their corner, the developers are not encountering much trouble.

Earlier this year, in an effort to clear the area for an ecotourism venture, 250 residents of the Ambulong shore village in the Philippines were evicted from their homes. As they had refused to leave earlier, the eviction was violent: police attacked the village, wounding many inhabitants and demolishing 24 houses. While the people have pledged to continue the fight for their homes, the outlook is clearly not good. In Bangladesh over 1000 families of the Khasi and Garoare indigenous groups face eviction from their tribal land for development of a park. In Brazil two villages near the resort town of Fortaleza have gone to court to show that a real estate agency that forced them off their lands to build an "ecological resort" broke the law. In Africa, more recent examples than Kruger include the Masai in East Africa and the Bushmen of Botswana. (Mail & Guardian June, 2002). Even when the indigenous peoples themselves propose to start ecotourism, as the Botswana Bushmen did, governments, as occurred in the Botswana case, often refuse to relinquish their potential earnings to the residents. (Mail & Guardian June, 2002)

Tourism also plays a significant role in the continuing economic subordination and dependency of the third world upon the core nations. The first world has a long tradition of forcing first world ideology and concepts upon drastically different third world countries, often their former colonies. One example if the first world (WTO/IMF)'s forcing of globalization and neo-liberal policies upon the third world instead of encouraging more third world appropriate concepts like localization. Another example is that by forcing third world economies to be based upon precarious and unpredictable exports (i.e. coffee and bananas) the first world effectively inhibits autonomous growth in the third world countries. Tourism is a similarly unpredictable and fluctuating business and is entirely dependent on, essentially, entertaining visitors from outside the country. Thus, tourist based third-world economies become both dependent on, and subordinate to, tourists. This comes at the expense of fostering more organic, autonomous and lasting growth. The result is the perpetuation of a structure in which strong, industrialized countries are able to impose terms of trade to their advantage upon weaker states. Within this broader perspective of relationships, the first world tourist visiting a third world tourist based economy is akin to a colonizer both visiting, and perpetuating the domination of, a colony.

This dependency in a tourist economy manifests itself in the subordination of the people, culture and structures of the society to tourist interests. If a third world country wants and IMF loan, it must demonstrate its compliance with the IMF's interests. The tourist/service relationship is, in some ways, a microcosm of this exchange. If a third world tourist economy wants tourist money, it must be sensitive to tourist interests. In this sense, tourism is a form of domination and of the master/servant dynamic tracing its lineage to the colonial era. I could sense this dynamic in many instances on our trip. Nearly everyone staying at the Breakwater Inn were white tourists.

However, the staff, especially the cleaning and maintenance crew, was composed almost entirely of local blacks who had to serve us everyday, clean up after us, and ultimately treat us as if we were somehow above them. The people who would transport our luggage were like our servants, as well as the unseen maids at all the hotels we stayed at. The hundreds of vendors we encountered on the trip were entirely dependent on tourists, and many of them utilized, either by choice or desperation, that same master/servant dynamic. Often they would say things to me like "oh please sir, please buy something, I will never forget you, and my family will always remember you." I heard variations of that pitch throughout our trip from vendors of all kinds.

It seems that many tourists either consciously or unconsciously fulfill their 'master' role. I often encountered tourists treating vendors, staff and other employees with shocking rudeness and almost scornful disregard. Professor McCall drew my attention to one tourist becoming enraged at the black cooking staff for giving him what he called ¾ of an egg, as opposed to the whole egg he expected. On the return flight a member of the safari groups sitting near me verbally assaulted a stewardess when she said that she would need to take his suitcase to a storage compartment on the plane as the overhead bins were overflowing.

The tourist, after arguing with her about why she had no right to move his suitcase anywhere, on the plane or off, then yelled, as if to accuse the entire staff of being inept and corrupt, that "If anything and I mean anything is missing from that suitcase, there will be hell to pay!". These examples add to the countless instances I can recall throughout my experience of encountering stereotypically "angry tourists". They seem to consistently be appealing to a sense that they deserve better than everyone else, and are entitled to utter subservience. To this end, I have come to accept that I, like all tourists in a third world country, could, and probably often do, symbolize arrogance, oppression and the subservience of much of the country's people. In South Africa I often did feel people holding variations of this view of me, and I understand why they did. Several people said that they resented me, and people like me, who came to their country. Others mentioned my arrogance, which I am sure I do have to some extent, as well as the collective arrogance of the first world.

With the spread and intervention of capitalism into Third World societies, tourism has also had the effect of turning Third World places, landscapes and people into commodities. Essentially tourists consume elements of a vacation in the same way as we consume other objects or commodities. This is perhaps most obviously evident in the packaging of African culture, history and imagery into convenient souvenirs sold by vendors throughout the tourist enclaves. Another example is the play we saw, entitled "African Footsteps" which commoditized African history into a sanitized, tourist-pleasing, and overly simplistic package to be bought and consumed by tourists eager to move onto the next item. Trips to the country are sold as a package, but it is more importantly the country itself that is being transformed, along with its uniqueness, people, and cultural heritage, to be sold as a commodity to the golden hordes of tourists.

In the vein of commoditizing is the 'otherness' that is fostered by the separateness of tourism interactions with the local peoples and surroundings. Tourists, like the first world they come from, have come to view the core and periphery nations as a situation of 'us' and 'them', 'them' being the societies outside the first world which are variably defined by ideas of simplicity, disease, barbarism, instability, poverty and as generally problematic. Much tourism entrenches this sense of 'otherness.' For instance, the township tours (link to chapter on township tours) we went on consisted of driving through people's communities in buses, stopping occasionally to look around while guarded by police, perhaps asking a few questions (if the people are lucky) and then gathering to get back on the bus from whence we came, never to be seen again. We were, however, preceding, and will be followed by, a never-ending string of the same buses unloading the same people. Only the faces will really change, but even they won't change too drastically. Eventually it will just blend into a blur of otherness. Now I imagine if that was my community, if that backyard our bus pulled up in was my backyard.

If I had busses stopping in front of my house to momentarily let out peering faces and cameras who would peruse my driveway before getting back onto their bus. Then, a day later, another bus, and then another, and another. I would feel on display, like a commodity being captured in the visitors' cameras and taken away. Above all, I would feel like I was 'other'.

The yearning of first-world tourists to venture to third-world locales is a kind of postmodern reaction to a certain meaninglessness and dissatisfaction with modern life. One backlash against the post-industrial complex is the desire to return to the purity of pre-modern life and to experience the supposed authenticity of 'unspoiled' land, people and environments. As the continuing existence of any people or environment entirely unaffected by humans is nearly impossible, fabrications are necessary to satiate this yearning. Professor Wittenberg, in his introduction to Kruger Park, spoke at length about the desire of those who created the park to maintain a place where, in this case white men, could go to reconnect with pure nature and experience what their forefathers lived in, re-creating such lost rites of passage as "the first hunt".

Kruger, however, is not a real, natural habitat. It is an artificially maintained semblance of a time long past. This also holds true for the Zulu cultural village many of us went to see. It utilizes the desire to see pure indigenous cultures, but is in fact, no more than a reenactment of a lifestyle long since altered by the very societies of many who now come to gaze at the sights. These things are not real, they remain in a romanticized vision of "untouched" land and peoples that exists today only as a fantasy in the mind of tourists. It is a mentality that encourages the "disneyizing" of culture and of environments, creating some romanticized fantasy rather than grappling with the modern day reality and conflicts of the places.

The vision of "untouched" "virgin" land and peoples has a long history in the collective Western thought, tracing back to the mythologized colonial voyages and stories of explorers pushing to the frontier. For instance, as we drove through the Kruger terrain I wanted to imagine going to the area for the first time, I even remarked to Herman "imagine what it would have been like for the first voyagers coming to this area....how incredible and desperately hard it must have been". He then noted about the high death rate for them, but I was already drifting off into imaging how breathtaking it must have been to see these lands for the first time, yearning to have that experience as well. I had not realized it, but the efficacy of that idealized story had firmly enraptured my mind as well. This seems due, in large part, to the historical education I received. I was taught far more about the Indians of the 1700's in American high school than about the Indians of today. Additionally, I was bombarded with the supposedly heroic tales of explorers like Columbus and Magellan who first witnessed untouched people and lands. Few seem to care about, or have any desire to face, the complex, often difficult realities facing modern indigenous peoples or the crises facing many remaining tracts of actual wilderness. They would rather see a reenactment of a lifestyle long passed, or an artificially idyllic, maintained nature preserve, and leave with their preconceptions intact than have to deal with the often ugly and difficult reality. Tourists, after all, are not there to feel conflicted and are not paying to feel guilt; they want it to be simple, romantic, and easy to deal with.

In spite of all these problems, it must be noted that in many instances, utilization of third world tourism comes at a cost of less than many alternatives. For some areas, such as small islands, tourism is often the most viable means by which to develop the economy. Furthermore, given the desperate economic state of many third world countries, with unemployment often in double digits, it must be considered that there may be little choice other than tourism. While the jobs in the tourism market are mostly low-paying and unskilled, any job is better than none. Clearly, this does not excuse the multiplicity of problems endemic to third world tourism. Yet, it is often this lack of better economic alternative that leads countries to accept them. Thus, the goal must be to ensure that no country is in a position to need tourism to survive.

Tourism is, by many metrics, the world's largest industry. It has become a permanent part of the modern global economy and is only becoming more widespread. However, the third world tourism industry is obligated to address the multitude of aforesaid problems before it can become an equitable form of development. This will require the creation of alternate forms of tourism that truly benefit the majority of a country's residents as much, if not more, than the incoming tourists. Until then, third world tourism will continue to serve as a perpetuation of the colonial legacy, providing enjoyable exploration for tourists and festering exploitation for locals.

CHEAP SIGHTSEEING TOUR

A cheap and easy sightseeing tour idea, explore your own neighbourhood like it were a new exotic location, introduction and tips.

Sightseeing in Your Own Neighbourhood

Whether we pay attention to it or not, we all belong to a neighbourhood of one sort or another. Some of us live in city neighbourhoods, some in suburban ones, others in rural neighbourhoods, such as the mountains or the high plains. What is your neighbourhood? Is it a place, a group of buildings, or a collection of people? Before you get into knowing your neighbourhood, look at the Almanac's neighbourhood map, drawn up by one who lived there. As he spotted items onto the map—which he got from the local town hall—he took notes on each item and keyed these notes to the map. You can do the same for your own neighbourhood. Our sample neighbourhood is a suburb, about 1 1/2 hours from New York City. It contains 500 acres, about 200 houses, 275 apartments, and nearly 1,500 people. They are mostly young to middle-aged families with an average of slightly over 2 children per household. It can be described as a solidly middle-class neighbourhood. Listed below are its parts and a description of each:

1. *Shopping Center.* People from all over this town and surrounding towns come here to shop. The land was developed and owned by a national company and the stores are leased to large chains which are not oriented to the neighbourhood. Some smaller shops like the stationery and gift shops, however, are owned by neighbourhood people. They like the heavy traffic which the chains bring in. The neighbourhood on the whole, however, doesn't like it. Three years ago the shopping center was an orchard.

2. *Highway, U.S. Route* 1. Follows the old Boston Post Road. Four lanes of heavy traffic carry outsiders through this edge of the neighbourhood as well as neighbourhood residents to and from work and the many stores that line the highway strip. Two private companies have buses connecting the neighbourhood to the town and the nearest city. But the service is poor and is nonexistent on Sundays or in the evenings. The very young and the old who don't drive can't get out of the neighbourhood to do things. Take, for example, Mrs. Robin McKenna. You can meet her easily enough because, although she's 75 years old, you'll often find her hitchhiking along Shore Drive (4). Pick her up and she'll tell you that since the old trolley was abandoned 25 years ago, it's been harder and harder for oldsters like her to get into town. She doesn't drive, but all the large stores, doctors' offices, and meeting places are in the town or nearby city. She tells her friends to hitchhike but they're afraid. Mrs. McKenna admits that some strangers are weird, but most are friendly and all are interesting. Her regular rides get cookies from her at Christmas.
3. *Alps Road*. A feeder street for the neighbourhood it bounds. It is so narrow and winding over the small hills in the neighbourhood that the old farmers called it "Alps Road." Some of them live in older farmhouses along the road, but most have been squeezed out by single-family homes built over the last 10 years costing $30,000 to $40,000.
4. *Shore Drive*. Another feeder street and neighbourhood divider. It is also State Highway 142 and carries outsiders through the neighbourhood to the nearby shore and beaches which gave the road its name. Summer traffic is heavy and generally keeps people from crossing it to go to stores and schools in the next neighbourhood. The road has mostly older, single-family houses, lived in by older couples whose children have grown up.

5. *Echlin Company.* This factory makes automobile parts. It is owned by outsiders, employs a few people from the surrounding neighbourhood, and uses many inner-city blacks who commute by car from the nearby city because owning a house in the neighbourhood is expensive and nearby apartments are small and lived in only by whites. But according to realtors of the area, no discrimination takes place here. Bob Gillings thinks differently. He's black, lives in the nearby city, and hasn't found a place to live in this neighbourhood. "When the company moved from the city to this town, they promised the town fathers they'd bring good taxes but none of the workers. Too expensive for us to buy a house here. We can afford the rents here but we always get the 'no vacancy' sign when we ask. Heck, me and my wife are more comfortable in the city anyway."
6. *Old Colonial Farmhouse.* "For Sale." Although some of the town's famous families lived here, this home's place on the highway (2) makes its land more valuable for stores.
7. *Vacant Lot.* Owned by the owners of the shopping center next door (1), who want to build 152 apartments here. The neighbourhood opposes them because apartments would bring in more traffic, especially to Shore Drive (4), alter streams through the land (8), and possibly bring in low-income residents, such as the blacks who work nearby.
8. *Streams.* These collect water from the sloping land and carry it to the nearby river. These streams are relatively unpolluted since this part of the neighbourhood has been provided with sewer pipes beneath the streets to carry waste water to a plant which treats it before letting it flow out to the river. During rains, the streams here often flood the lot (7), which temporarily holds the water before it goes downstream. Buildings around these streams would make the water overflow faster and flood downstream houses. This kind of flooding already happens at the nearby apartments, where one building has been situated in the path of a stream.

9. *Apartments.* Seven buildings have 55 apartments. Developed and sold as condominiums, only about half are owner-occupied. Nonresidents own the rest as rental investments. They provide little in the way of maintenance or play facilities for those who rent from them. The renters tend to have lower incomes than the owners, are younger, and have young children. Because the owners tend not to have children living at home, they don't want to spend money on building a play lot. So the children play in the parking lots.
10. *More Apartments.* All 150 are rented to older couples or young families. The neighbourhood used to be all single-family or lots. But a major developer bought the land, made a large contribution to the local political party in power, and got permission to build apartments here. Because the earth is too rocky to absorb so much sewage, the developer 1st had to put in a sewer line. The chairman of the Sewer Authority, who doesn't live in the neighbourhood, is a land developer himself as well as the boss of the political party which received the contribution. So Mr. Chairman was happy to extend the sewer lines. This made the entire neighbourhood suitable for apartments, and developers are madly rushing to buy up the open space.
11. *Open Space.* The play area for the apartments (10) was supposed to be here. But the developer forgot to build it. Instead he quickly sold the land and buildings to outside investors such as Dr. Robert Kelley. Dr. Kelley is a dentist who has his offices in the local town center and lives in a wealthier part of town. Many of his patients live in our sample neighbourhood but they don't know that their dentist owns these apartments. Dr. Kelley doesn't want them to know.
12. *Vacant Lot.* But not for long! Another developer wants to fill in the pond with rock and dirt from the nearby hill, which he'll tear away to build 150 apartments. Mark Robbins, who lives in the apartments (9) with his mother and 2 sisters, has spotted a muskrat family

living in the pond. But the developer would rather have wealthier, childless families in condominium apartments living here instead of muskrats or little boys like Mark who befriend the local wildlife.

13. *Ballou Road.* A small, single-family housing tract owned and lived in by older, working-class families. Joe Ballou lives here. He built most of the houses and named the street that he put in for them. His youngest daughter, Lisa, is still in high school, but his other children are married and live in other suburbs. Joe doesn't build houses anymore. "The market isn't so good," he says. "And besides, my wife and I are getting old enough where we'd like to enjoy life." So he and his wife have spent the last 4 winters in Florida. During the rest of the year Joe occasionally remodels bathrooms and kitchens.
14. *Footpath.* Apartment dwellers shortcut to the shopping center or bus, rather than walk along the streets, which have no sidewalks in this part of the neighbourhood.
15. *Homes.* New, one-family houses worth $40,000 to $65,000. A typical owner is Bud Anderson. He is an accountant with a large firm in the city but he's planning to start his own firm soon. He and his wife Vicki send their 2 children to a private school on the other side of town rather than to the public one nearby (26) because "the quality of public schools here is poor." Streets in this section or tract have been named by the developer.
16. *Condominium Townhouses.* These townhouses have just been built on a lowland and marsh. The builder has installed a pond to collect the water that used to flow to the marsh, but this doesn't work and flooding now occurs. People who are buying the townhouses, according to the realtor, are very successful older couples. No one under the age of 18 is allowed to live here. "No burden on the schools," says the realtor. So far, families who have moved here all have 2 cars, which has added significantly to the traffic on Alps Road. The designer of these townhouses, an architect by the name of George

Boswell, has won an award for his scheme. He admits, however, that they should never have been built on this land: "It was really too wet for townhouses, but if it's going to be built it may as well be designed well." Whether the well-designed buildings survive on this soggy ground, only the future will tell.

17. *Streams.* Water on this side of the neighbourhood flows into a nearby tidal marsh and then into the bay.
18. *Farm.* This farmer presently raises corn for sale, vegetables for his family and friends. He also keeps some old horses and cows which graze on the fertile hillside. He has good, well-drained, upland soil which developers of nearby condominium townhouses covet. They've asked the farmer to sell, but he's holding out.
19. *Marsh.* Gradually being filled in by yet another developer, who plans 75 apartments here. His action has destroyed the marsh, forcing out ducks and other birdlife that once used the area. But, the developer argues, now that the area is filled in, how can the town deny me permission to build here? The neighbourhood wouldn't grant permission if it had its way, but it's the town's planning and zoning commission that will give permission. Its members don't live around here.
20. *Homes.* Large, newer homes on large lots. Mostly wealthy families live here with 2 to 4 children. Of course, they oppose the nearby apartments because they will reduce property values.
21. *Drain.* In this part of the neighbourhood, water flows directly into the bay either through a natural stream bed or storm drains beneath the built-up areas.
22. *Old Section.* Homes in this section of the neighbourhood were built on small lots and narrow streets over 50 years ago, as summer cottages for city people who wanted to be near the beach during the humid months. The houses are mostly wooden. Many have screen porches running around 3 sides. Since the soil here is quite rocky and there are no sewers, waste often

flows untreated and unabsorbed by the land, directly into the bay with its beaches. The area is no longer a desirable resort spot and over the years has become a year-round neighbourhood. Owners have winterized their cottages, closed in the porches, and either live here themselves or rent their places out to students during the winter.

23. *Baseball Diamond.* The only playground in the neighbourhood. Because the neighbourhood does not support the political party which has run the town for many years, the town doesn't build recreational facilities here. So Geno Pantani decided to take matters into his own hands. Geno moved here shortly after he married his wife Deborah. Ever since that time he's been a policeman for the local town. Now he's a sergeant. Having a lot of respect from his neighbours, he was able to get them to form a neighbourhood association. He was elected their 1st president and he took as his 1st task the building of a play lot. The association put up money for the land by taxing themselves. With their own hands they filled in the marsh, then bought benches and swings 2nd-hand from the city. Now they have a small play lot and baseball diamond, a facility that is well-used by kids and their parents alike.
24. *Vacant Land.* Held by a private local foundation that administers it for the benefit of town residents. Old evergreens line the pond on one side, steep cliffs line it on the other. Many hiking trails wind their way through the area, often alongside stone walls which mark the boundaries of old farms which were here in the last century. The pond is used by neighbours for swimming in summer and for ice skating in winter. It is called Altmansburger's Pond after the family who once owned and farmed the land. Their descendants live in houses at the end of the pond.
25. *Store.* At this corner is a local "mom-and-pop" grocery store owned by an older man and his wife who have lived next door for over 50 years. They know the

neighbourhood—its residents and its history. Their son was not interested in continuing the business, however, so mom and pop may close the store soon and the supermarket chain (1) will probably get their business.

26. *Public School.* Because it's on the edge of this neighbourhood, the school receives 1st through 4th graders from this neighbourhood and outside neighbourhoods. Older children attend the town-wide middle and high schools.
27. *Footpaths.* A narrow sidewalk along the road, trodden-down dirt paths through the woods. The town built the sidewalks so nearby children could walk safely to the school. The paths were made by children wearing down the shortest route home from school.
28. *Old Stone Wall.* An old property divider dating from the 18th century. Colonial farmers here cut the trees, and then dragged stones out of the fields and piled them along the edges. Crops no longer grow here and a 2nd generation of trees has sprung up—birch, pin oak, hickory, some maple and pine trees. According to the old-timers the elms were wiped out by the Dutch elm disease.

Now that you've examined the sample neighbourhood, you can start asking questions about your own neighbourhood: What makes it different? What makes it a neighbourhood? Is it part of a larger unit? You'll have to do a bit of legwork to answer some of these questions. But walking is the best way to get to know your neighbourhood. First, get an overview, maybe by car or bus. Whether you're new or old to your neighbourhood, you'll enjoy a special tour given by someone else. Many large cities offer such guided tours on foot or by bus. But if your area doesn't have one, be your own tour guide. Pretend you're a stranger and look around your neighbourhood through his eyes. Determine the shape and boundaries of the neighbourhood by looking for physical obstacles. Our sample neighbourhood is shaped by the major streets that cut off foot traffic. Would you ever think of walking across a 4-lane highway to borrow a cup of sugar? There are natural boundaries, too, such as rivers and hills. These characteristics often give names to the neighbourhoods, such as "Riverside," "Valley Acres," or "Hollywood Hills." Next, notice the street and road system. Generally they are the 1st things built. Houses and shops come after the roads or trolley lines have been built to link the neighbourhood to the city and other neighbourhoods. What are the links in your neighbourhood? Some streets are laid in regular, straight lines while others, like those in the older section of our sample, follow the crooked foot and cow paths of another century. Go to the town clerk and ask how the streets were named. Some street names follow an alphabetical pattern such as Ash, Bay, Church streets. Or they may be named for States, such as Michigan Avenue in Chicago. Or they may be named for historical events or personalities. Most cities have a Madison Avenue or Washington Street. The avenues may run in one direction, the streets in another.

Traffic arteries, heavily traveled streets, are often called boulevards or highways. What happens along such arteries is different from what happens along smaller residential streets. Arteries often form commercial strips. Because they draw more traffic, stores, apartments, and factories are often located along arteries and major intersections.

Not only the homes, stores, and factories of your neighbourhood feed traffic to local roads. So do outside neighbourhoods. Ask yourself where your neighbourhood's roads and streets begin and end. Are they carrying your neighbours' cars or outsiders'? What about buses and heavy trucks? They may be carrying goods or people to and from or through your area. Since streets, roads, and parking lots can consume as much as 50% of your neighbourhood's land area, it's good to question who uses so much of your area's resources. By comparison, look to see how much of your area's land is given over to sidewalks, bicycle trails, parks, or pure open space. In our sample neighbourhood, one apartment area (9, 10) provides parking for cars but no play area for children. You might also note the noise level of major streets and compare it with that of smaller ones. Walking or bicycling not only gives you more time to look closely at your neighbourhood, but also the occasional opportunity to talk to your neighbours. In addition, walking or bicycling will put your legs directly in touch with the land. In a car we tend to pay attention only to man-made features. On foot we know immediately if we're walking up the slightest hill. The lay of the land is often hidden from us. Most neighbourhoods do not have mountains or rivers in or around them. But they may have been there at one time. Unknown to most residents are the natural and artificial streams flowing under the neighbourhoods. Fresh water is often obtained from these sources. Dirty water is put back. Do you know where water drains from your neighbourhood? Does it settle into the ground? What if the ground is too rocky? Perhaps the waste water is carried off to a nearby river or sewage plant. These natural and man-made watercourses follow the land downhill and sometimes carve it out. Find the low points and gulleys of your neighbourhood and you will find the spots where water is collecting either below or above the ground. Follow the streams. Find their sources and outflow.

If you need help, get a topographic map of the area from a local library or the U.S. Geological Survey. The map will show elevations, streams, roads, buildings, and other prominent physical features. Agricultural maps go further and tell the types of soil and vegetation. But even without the maps you can examine the earth directly: Is it sandy or rocky? Light or dark? Wet or dry? The soils of your area will often tell you its history. What was your neighbourhood before it was built up? An Indian burial ground? A farm? The Back Bay neighbourhood of Boston and the Marina neighbourhood of San Francisco were built upon dirt hauled in to fill what was once part of a bay. Perhaps your neighbourhood stands upon a sliced-off hill or a filled-in valley. If you can't find any old-timers to tell you, go to the nearest library and ask for some old maps. A good place to go to find out about your neighbourhood's soils and vegetation is the nearby park. Look at the trees and shrubs that can be grown locally and talk with other strollers. The park caretaker can certainly tell you a lot about the trees and plantings. Ask him which trees were planted and which were standing before the park was built. Ask why certain kinds of trees are popular in the area. Perhaps the evergreens were planted in your neighbourhood to give privacy around the houses. Perhaps some trees have been planted to help retain sandy soil. Or still others, such as eucalyptus, might have been planted to shield crops from the wind when the neighbourhood was a farm. You may find that the land in your neighbourhood once bore a forest. Was it cut for timber to build the neighbourhood's buildings? Or was the forest cut to clear the land for farming? Find out which crops grew successfully in your soil and test your answer by growing them in your own backyard. Look also at the features of the park. Statues, monuments, markers, bandshells. They may reveal some local history. Find out what cultural events take place there. There are often important neighbourhood events such as parades or picnics. What was used to build the walkways or walls or fences in the park? These building materials will tell you a lot about the architecture and history of your neighbourhood. The same brick that was used to pave the walkway may have been used to build your house.

BIBLIOGRAPHY

Abram, Simone: *Tourists and Tourism: Identifying with People and Places*, New York, Berg, 1997.

Bennett, O.: *Financing for Tourism Projects in Developing Countries*, England, Wiley, 1994.

Chambers, Erve: *Tourism and Culture: An Applied Perspective*, Albany, State University of New York Press, 1997.

Davies, I.: *Competency Based Learning: Technology, Management, and Design*, New York, McGraw-Hill, 1973.

Fowler, Peter: *Heritage and Tourism*, New York, Routledge, 1993.

Howard Green: *Tourism and the Environment: A Sustainable Relationship*, New York, Routledge, 1995.

Knox, J.: *Tourism Research Priorities in Hawaii and the Pacific*, Honolulu, University of Hawaii, 1979.

Lickorish, Leonard J.: *An Introduction to Tourism*, New York, Butterworth-Heinemann, 1997.

Margaret Whitla: *Tourism Strategies for Rural Development*, Sackville, New Brunswick, 1993.

McCool, Stephen F.: *Linking Tourism, the Environment, and Sustainability*, Ogden, Utah, 1995.

Mieczkowski, Zbigniew: *Environmental Issues of Tourism and Recreation*, Lanham, University Press of America, 1995.

Purcell, Douglas C.: *Heritage Tourism is in the Future of Many Alabama Communities*, Auburn Univ., Auburn, 1991.

Sharpley, Richard: *Rural Tourism: An Introduction*, London, International Thomson Business Press, 1997.

Stabler, Michael J.: *Tourism and Sustainability: Principles to Practice*, New York, CAB International, 1997.

INDEX

□□□